FIVE KEY LESSONS
FROM TOP MONEY MANAGERS

SCOTT KAYS, CFP®

WILEY

JOHN WILEY & SONS, INC.

Published by John Wiley & Sons, Inc., Hoboken, New Jersey.
Published simultaneously in Canada.

For general information about our other products and services, please contact our Customer Care Department within the United States at 800-762-2974, outside the United States at 317-572-3993 or fax 317-572-4002.

Wiley also publishes its books in a variety of electronic formats. Some content that appears in print may not be available in electronic books. For more information about Wiley products, visit our web site at www.wiley.com.

Library of Congress Cataloging-in-Publication Data:
Kays, Scott, 1960–
  Five key lessons from top money managers / Scott Kays
    p. cm.
  Includes bibliographical references.
  ISBN-13 978-0-471-71183-4
  ISBN-10 0-471-71183-7 (cloth)
  1. Portfolio management.   2. Investment analysis.   3. Investment advisors.
  I. Title.
    HG4529.5.K39 2005
    332.6—dc22   2004029120

10 9 8 7 6 5 4 3 2 1

To Lisa. You are truly my best friend. I could never thank you enough for all your love, encouragement, and support.

CONTENTS

PREFACE

MY FIRM HAS MANAGED MUTUAL FUND PORTFOLIOS FOR A DECADE AND a half. Our selection process typically involves interviewing fund managers when possible before we invest clients' money in their portfolios. The point of the interviews is to learn all we can about the managers' strategies—why they buy a stock, why they sell, how they control risk, and so on. Over the years I have had the privilege of interviewing many of the top mutual fund managers in the country. I have also interviewed managers whose performances were less stellar—their funds may have performed well in certain environments, but they lagged their peers over longer periods of time.

I gradually came to realize that the truly outstanding managers who consistently outperform their peers share certain commonalities. I noticed they can better articulate their strategies—not that they are necessarily more formulaic in their approaches, but they have a clearer vision of the kinds of stocks they look for as well as the types of companies they want to avoid. The top managers have risk-control measures in place to limit losses while attempting to maximize their returns. They exercise extreme discipline in their approach and do not change their styles based on popular fads or to boost their short-term performances.

I decided to take a more formal approach to identifying the common practices of top equity managers and interviewed five of the country's best. I specifically chose managers with very different styles and philosophies because, of course, it would be no surprise to find commonalities among professional investors with similar strategies. As opposed to relegating our discussions to generalities about their strategies, I asked in-depth questions about each step of their processes. One manager actually gave me a copy of the worksheet he uses to value companies. I even delved into the managers' upbringings to see what early influences shaped their styles. Each manager was very generous with his time and reviewed and edited his chapter to make sure I accurately depicted the essence of his strategy. Chapters 2 through 6 capture the results of those interviews. I then pored over each manager's process to pinpoint common practices. While each manager had very definite and distinct ideas about investing, I discovered five common practices that they all shared, which I present in Chapter 7.

I strived to make this book different from other books that have featured celebrity money managers in two ways. First, I wanted to give as much detailed information about the actual investment processes of the selected managers as possible. I go beyond their general beliefs and give insight into how they apply their strategies to the actual selection of securities.

Second, as opposed to merely identifying and discussing the managers' common practices, I devote several chapters to developing an investment model that incorporates those practices. Understanding general investment principles is good, but I endeavor to give you specific tools to apply what you learn. In the final chapter, I examine three companies to illustrate how to use the model I develop.

As you read about our experts' strategies, it will be glaringly obvious that none of them invest in exactly the same way. There *is* no single correct way to invest! That is why you must decide what works for you and what doesn't.

Have fun implementing what you learn and experimenting with new techniques as you improve your skills and build your personal wealth. I hope you experience great rewards, both personally and financially, as you explore the *Five Key Lessons from Top Money Managers*.

ACKNOWLEDGMENTS

Without fail, each manager I interviewed for this book emphasized that his individual skills alone were not solely responsible for his success—it was a team effort. Writing a book is no different. Without the help of many others to whom I owe great thanks, this book would never have become a reality.

I want to thank each of our managers—John Calamos Sr., Chris Davis, Bill Fries, Bill Nygren, and Andy Stephens—for taking the time to talk with me and share their stories. Frankly, I was surprised at how down-to-earth and willing to help these men were, considering the level of success each has achieved.

Each manager had at least one representative assist me and coordinate their respective manager's activities for this project. These men and women worked diligently to keep the process moving forward and provided timely responses to my inquiries. Many thanks to David Miller, Dan Greifenkamp, Desiree Malanga, KimMarie Zamot, Russell Wiese, Michael Neary, Kelly Arnold, Jeff Kelley, and Klaris Tamazian.

Susan Golomb proved why she is one of the top literary agents in the business. She believed in this book early on and represented me as the true professional she is. I cannot overstate the value of her services.

My editor, Pamela Van Giessen, championed this book at John Wiley and Sons. She provided valuable advice that made this a better work, and she spent numerous hours explaining the book business to me.

My partner, Alan McKnight, was a patient sounding board and helped me think through many of the concepts I discuss in the book.

My daughter Elizabeth helped me greatly with the final edit. She let me know when I had communicated clearly and when I had missed the mark. How many writers have the benefit of a teenage daughter who is also a published author?

Many thanks to all my children—Elizabeth, Eric, Seth, Rachel, Peyton, and Carole—for putting up with Dad being busy all the time for several months. I'm ready to resume my fatherly duties—visiting colleges, changing diapers, jumping on the trampoline, reading bedtime stories and Bible studies.

Oliver Welch, PhD, JD, CPA, CFP, has been a mentor to me for twenty years. Both a business coach and a life coach, he has always believed I could do what I set my mind to, with God's help.

My dad, Ancil Kays, was a model of courage to me after losing his love of fifty-six years. He passed away as I was completing this book. I will miss him dearly.

Finally, I want to thank my wife, Lisa. She single-handedly ran the household and homeschooled our children while allowing me to seclude myself in the library and write, all while caring for a newborn. She encouraged me to pursue this idea from its inception, knowing all too well from my first book the sacrifices she would need to make. You're the best, Sweetheart!

SCOTT KAYS

Atlanta, Georgia
May 2005

More Praise for *Five Key Lessons from Top Money Managers*

Scott Kays has done a great job of extracting the golden nuggets of investment wisdom from five of the top investment managers. But the best part is the synthesis or "group genius" effect of the common threads they all share. This book is a "must-read" for serious long-term investors and their advisors.

CHRIS J. DARDAMAN, JR.
CPA, CFP®, CIMA®, PFS, and
CEO, Polstra & Dardaman, LLC

This book is an outstanding resource for those who either want to understand a bit about how the top money managers work or for those in the investment business to see how various money managers consistently apply their disciplines. Kays has given us a valuable resource which I recommend highly.

RON BLUE
President, Christian Financial Professionals Network (CFPN)

Kays's book has something for both experienced and less experienced investors so that they can start investing in stocks immediately. The five lessons give insight into what separates the best investors from everybody else. And, unlike many other investment books, you don't need a finance degree to understand the concepts discussed. It is one book you must read.

H. OLIVER WELCH
Chairman Emeritus,
Certified Financial Planner Board of Standards

CHAPTER 1

The Return of Common Sense

DURING THE LATTER HALF OF THE 1990S, INVESTORS CREATED ONE OF the greatest stock market bubbles in our nation's history. What began as a typical late-cycle push into aggressive growth stocks morphed into a self-perpetuating feeding frenzy of greed. Mesmerized by technology issues, market participants threw away common-sense investment principles and eventually propelled stock prices to incredible heights. "This time is different" became the mantra of investors.

As the technology bubble swelled, individuals staked their retirements on risky stock market bets. Like lemmings ignoring the cliff ahead, investors piled into grossly overvalued securities simply because they had been racing upward in value, hoping the party would last just long enough for them to make their fortune and leave. However, once they made their fortune, the seduction of still greater gains held them spellbound in a hypnotic clutch and kept them dancing into the wee hours.

A minority resisted the tide and sounded the alarm of a coming correction, but most investors ignored them as too old-fashioned to comprehend the potential of the new economy and the digital age we had entered. The forces of competition no longer applied. Earnings were a passé concept. The first companies to stake their claims in digital territories would rule for the foreseeable future.

Then common sense prevailed. Late in the cycle, many investors realized that entire classes of stocks were glaringly overvalued, and they decided to lock in the extraordinary profits they had garnered. Selling gained traction as stock prices tumbled. The market tried to rally back periodically as those desperate for further profits refused to concede defeat, but blind enthusiasm by investors who came to the

1

party late could not overcome the dreadful fundamentals of a classic bubble.

The prophets of technology did not give up easily. As prices fell, they made their voices heard. "We haven't seen a decline of 10 percent in tech stocks for years. This is a unique buying opportunity!" "A 20 percent discount in technology prices is unheard of. Buy now!" In the end, however, their efforts proved to be in vain as the turn in investor sentiment drowned their rally cries.

In addition to the valuation problems, other factors colluded to create a perfect economic storm. A contested presidential election that was eventually decided by just a few votes kept Americans glued to their television sets instead of spending at the malls. The impact of September 11, 2001, and the new specter of terrorism wreaked havoc with consumer sentiment. Spiking oil prices acted as a major drag on the economy. Finally, a parade of accounting scandals and corporate fraud destroyed investors' confidence in the equity markets as several major corporations publicly acknowledged faulty bookkeeping and high-profile CEOs being led away in handcuffs became an all too familiar sight. Before it was all over, the stock market collapsed in an emotional sell-off that spared few companies.

In the two and a half years that followed March 2000, investors lost trillions of dollars of wealth accumulated during the previous five years. Businesses once thought of as keys to unlocking the future potential of our economy were crushed in the worst stock market downturn since the Great Depression. Multitudes of Internet companies folded, and major technology and telecommunication firms struggled for survival. The stocks of many fundamentally sound, reasonably valued corporations plunged alongside those of speculative enterprises. Even businesses such as Home Depot and General Electric, which continued growing their earnings throughout this period, eventually lost over half their market values.

At its nadir, the Standard & Poor's (S&P) 500 dropped by half, while the tech-laden Nasdaq index lost 72 percent. The Dow Jones Internet index, the superstar of the stock market only a short while earlier, dived 93 percent.

As investors rummaged through the carnage that followed the bursting of the bubble, they asked themselves numerous questions:

"How did we let this happen?" "Why didn't we see this coming?" "How can we prevent something like this from happening again?"

WE'VE OVERCOME BEFORE

With all the problems since the turn of the millennium, many have concluded the stock market no longer represents a field of sound investing. However, the troubles we have faced in recent years, as bad as they seemed, were not too dissimilar from difficulties the financial markets have weathered in times past. Since the early 1960s, we have witnessed the assassination of a president, an unpopular multiyear war, two oil embargoes that eventually drove oil prices up twentyfold, double-digit inflation, the resignation of a disgraced president, the threat of nuclear war, and unceasing conflicts across the globe. Yet because our economy rests on the foundation of free enterprise principles and the ingenuity of hardworking Americans, we have endured all those past storms and emerged from them a stronger nation. We will do so this time as well.

KEY POINT

The stock market is essential to the smooth functioning of our economy. If we believe our economy will rebound from its travails and continue to grow, then we must believe that a portfolio of well-run American companies remains a sound and viable investment option. The appropriate question is not whether we should use stocks to accumulate wealth but, rather, how can we distinguish between quality investments and poor ones. Fortunately, there are those who can teach us.

THE INVESTMENT MASTERS

Any field of endeavor, such as sports, business, or music, is typically populated by three classes of participants. First there is the majority, whose members establish the average and defend the status quo. They enjoy the activity in which they are involved, but they never become fanatical about it. Those participants fail to master the finer points that separate the winners from the also-rans.

Then there are those that comprise the minority who consistently perform above the average. Hungry to succeed, those individuals understand there is always room to refine their abilities, so they study their fields and work hard at mastering those things that make a difference in what they can accomplish. They realize that above average performance does not come by luck, but it results from skills they can learn and improve upon. These are the men and women who turn their activity into an art.

But almost assuredly a few individuals go beyond even the attainments of the minority to achieve an elite status and ascend into a class all their own. Those individuals don't just push the envelope, they establish new envelopes. They are the true masters, the Bobby Fischers, the Wayne Gretzkys, and the Hank Aarons.

So it is in the investment world. A multitude plays the market and wants hot stock tips. Unwilling to learn the rudiments of investing, they invest in companies because "they've been going up." The thrill of the action is as important to them as the profits they make. Those individuals invest for a number of reasons other than maximizing their returns over time. They may be looking for status among their peers by obtaining bragging rights about one of their winners. Or the brokerage commissions may simply be less expensive than airfare to Vegas. Those individuals know little about investing, but because they constitute the majority, their collective opinion often carries sway.

A minority studies the art of investing in a constant effort to increase their knowledge and improve their skills. Those individuals take the time to learn what matters when buying the stocks of publicly traded companies. They don't gamble; they invest deliberately and purposefully, and they outperform the average investor as a result.

The true masters—legends such as Warren Buffett—set new standards and provide others with the vision for what can be achieved. Those individuals always seem to know what to do during troubling times when others are at a loss. They exercise tremendous discipline, holding religiously to a set of consistent beliefs they have developed over time. They focus on things and care about details others dismiss as unimportant. Most of all, they trust their judgment more than the opinions of others, regardless of how many people contradict them.

KEY POINT

What is often beguiling about the masters is the simplicity of their techniques. They often act puzzled when quizzed about the secrets of their outstanding success. "There are no secrets," they will say, "only an unwavering dedication to time-proven principles."

In the investment arena, many of the complex strategies only draw investors away from what really matters. What kind of pattern is the stock's price chart forming? What was the stock's relative strength last week? The masters classify these questions as irrelevant distractions. By staying focused on the important elements, the elite money managers have achieved tremendous success with their straightforward methodologies. Great investments sometimes demand gutsy moves, but more frequently they require executing the fundamentals with a single-minded passion.

The shame is that the straightforwardness of the money masters' techniques often causes others to overlook those strategies. Investors are frequently not impressed with the faithful execution of investing fundamentals. Instead, they often want something flashy, something unusual, to give them an edge. So they search for something new and different while the money masters keep executing the same techniques that have served them faithfully for years, willing to miss out on fads to stay focused on long-term objectives. The naive talk of what should do well over the next few weeks; the masters consider the long run.

INVESTORS' ATTITUDES ARE CHANGING

After experiencing the worst bear market in seventy years, like professional baseball players returning to spring training, investors are coming back to the fundamentals. As common sense returns to stock investing, so does the desire to learn what matters when selecting individual securities for accumulating wealth over the long term.

FOR THIS BOOK, I HAVE INTERVIEWED FIVE OF THE COUNTRY'S TOP money managers. All five are professionals who have consistently outperformed their peers over time.

In the pages that follow, I lay out the investment strategies and philosophies that have made these professionals among the best at what they do. Novice investors can absorb the fundamentals from what our experts graciously shared, while experienced investors can glean much from the masters' accumulated wisdom and experience. Readers can focus on learning the techniques of any of the professionals, or they can assimilate important points from all of them into their own unique strategy.

Investors often experience frustration because while they understand investment principles, they do not know how to implement what they know. Therefore, instead of just discussing general principles and philosophies, I spend the latter half of the book developing a step-by-step investment process that incorporates the common principles found in the strategies of all the masters. The process breaks down the principles into action steps that ensure each potential investment receives the same level of attention and is graded by the same objective criteria.

CHAPTER 2

Andy Stephens

Lead Portfolio Manager, Artisan Mid-Cap Fund

Andy Stephens has been the Lead Portfolio Manager of the Artisan Mid-Cap Fund since its inception in June 1997. In both 2000 and 2001, the annual Barron's/Value Line Fund Survey ranked Stephens the number one manager in its Growth Fund Category out of 213 managers.

A $10,000 investment in the Artisan Mid-Cap Fund made at its inauguration would have grown to $33,253 by the end of 2003; the same amount invested in the S&P 500 index would have grown to only $13,854.[1] Like many growth funds, Andy's fund performed exceptionally well during the bubble years of 1998 and 1999, generating a 110 percent return during that period and walloping the S&P 500 index by 54 percent and the Russell Mid-Cap Growth index by 32 percent. However, Stephens's careful attention to value helped him continue his exceptional relative performance during the next three bear years, besting the S&P by 31 percent and the Russell index by an astounding 42 percent![2]

STEPHENS'S CONSERVATIVE APPEARANCE AND CALM DEMEANOR ARE QUITE deceiving. Inside lies a competitive nature rivaling that of any top professional athlete. That competitive bent compelled Andy to overcome his austere upbringing and become one of the most successful money managers in the country. Relentless in his quest to create an investment process that would allow him to consistently outperform his competition, Stephens has dissected virtually every aspect of investment management to develop his winning style.

PERSONAL BACKGROUND

The Path to Money Management

Andy's unique approach to money management has its roots in his hometown of Wisconsin Rapids, a semirural town in central Wisconsin of about eighteen thousand people. Stephens's mother, a single parent from the time he was eight years old, struggled to support her family of five on the modest salary of a dental hygienist. Being raised in such humble circumstances instilled a respect for money in Andy and inspired him to declare at sixteen, "I will never be poor as an adult!" That pledge greatly influenced each of his career-related decisions, ultimately leading him to become a money manager.

"My resolution never to be poor isn't about being rich," Stephens explains. "It's more about a craving for financial security. I grew up being the kid who could never afford the things I wanted. I had to wear the same clothes two days in a row and was never able to go on school trips. My mom felt very bad about it, but that's the way life was."

No financial planners or money management firms operated in Wisconsin Rapids from whom Andy could learn about investing and wealth accumulation. While most families in Stephens's hometown were lower middle class, a few had achieved financial success. Andy noticed one dominant trait characterized those families that excelled financially—the breadwinners specialized in important areas of need. Becoming experts in their fields created demand for their services and made their time worth more than the average corporate employee's, allowing them to earn higher incomes. The lesson was obvious: if Stephens was to fulfill his vow, he had to become one of the best in a given area of expertise.

Stephens left home to attend the University of Wisconsin–Madison at eighteen. Unknown to Andy, the university offered one of the oldest and best-known applied securities programs in the country. Several top contemporary money managers graduated from this program, including Bill Nygren, manager of the Oakmark and Oakmark Select funds, and Rick Lane, manager of the FMI Focus Fund.

In addition to the applied securities curriculum, the university offered a real estate investment program headed by James Graskamp, a renowned real estate investor. The program, as well as the career opportunities it offered, impressed Stephens, so he opted to seek a Real Estate Finance degree under Graskamp's tutelage. Andy was convinced this was the field he should pursue as a livelihood—until he took a securities analysis class his senior year. That experience transformed his perspective on life and how he wanted to spend his future. Like Saul on the Damascus road, Stephens had discovered his calling.

Strong Corneliuson

Realizing his future lay in money management, Andy aggressively sought a career in that field. After graduation, he accepted a marketing position at Strong Corneliuson Capital Management, a mutual fund complex. "This was not an analyst's job," he says. "But it got my foot in the door at a reputable money management firm."

In time, Stephens transferred to trading and managed that area of the business before long. It was while running that department that Andy got his first big break.

Bill Corneliuson, one of the founders of the company, announced his retirement in late 1993. Corneliuson managed the conservative Strong Investment fund, a "widows-and-orphans" balanced fund that invested in both fixed-income securities and equities. Andrew Ziegler, Strong's president, began an immediate search for Corneliuson's replacement. Having worked with Stephens on several projects, Ziegler knew that Andy had been researching theories of investment management and was developing a securities selection process. Based on that knowledge and his positive experiences with Andy, Ziegler asked Stephens to manage the equity portion of the Investment fund.

Few money managers inherit a $110 million portfolio their first day on the job. Stephens fully understood his good fortune and for the next year and a half used his new position to test his investment theories and develop a successful, repeatable securities selection process.

Andy made his top priority achieving consistent performance in order to maximize the power of compounding for his investors. He also wanted to avoid taking much risk because he lacked experience in fundamental analysis. To accomplish both objectives most reliably, Stephens initially managed the portfolio in what he calls a *passive-active* manner. He employed a passive style of management for the bulk of the portfolio, largely mimicking the S&P 500 index, and used his own stock selections for only a minor portion of the fund.

The rub with this strategy was that Andy's performance largely shadowed the broader market. That may be sufficient for less ambitious money managers, but Stephens's competitive bent made such average returns unacceptable. He aspired to consistently outperform the market and kept asking, "How can I find more of the stocks that go up and fewer of those that go down?"

Dick Weiss's Influence

About that time, Dick Weiss joined the firm, moving over from Stein Roe. Weiss, a stock picker who thoroughly scours companies' financial statements in his search for quality investments, comanaged the Strong Special Fund with Carlene Murphy. Andy developed relationships with both managers and resolved to learn more about fundamental analysis from them. He was still pulling double duty, running the trading desk and managing the equity portion of the Investment fund.

Andy arranged to meet with Dick or Carlene almost every morning for about twenty minutes, showing them analysis he had worked on the night before and asking questions about it. After a year and a half of those meetings, Andy had acquired the analytical expertise he previously lacked and was sharing fresh investment ideas with Dick and Carlene on a regular basis. As his skills improved, Andy gradually increased the actively managed portion of his portfolio, giving greater weight to the securities his research generated.

A Fund of His Own

As time passed, Stephens began feeling constrained at Strong. He had worked hard refining his process and was eager to apply it in a greater way. Andy needed an outlet to express *his* convictions about investing and wanted a portfolio that allowed him to put his theories into practice. "As an artist, you want to paint your own art," he says. Stephens's frustration grew as circumstances prevented him from pursuing certain avenues his research indicated would be profitable. He became convinced he could fully develop his ideas only by managing his own fund.

Stephens also realized he needed a team to fully implement his strategy—one person was insufficient. He was missing opportunities in different pockets of the market solely because he lacked the time to pursue them. However, building a team required more resources than were available to him at Strong.

As Stephens considered possible solutions to his dilemma, he thought of his old friend Andrew Ziegler. Andrew, along with Carlene Murphy, had left Strong a couple of years earlier to start Artisan funds, of which he was now president. Andy decided to approach Ziegler with a proposal for a new mutual fund.

A former lawyer with a keen analytical mind, Ziegler understood that long-term success in the investment business required a well-defined process. Since Ziegler knew Stephens and had been impressed with his earlier work, he agreed to let Andy present his investment methodology to him and Carlene. Stephens reflects on that experience: "I'm still not convinced that Andrew really believed I had developed an adequately detailed process. However, a point-by-point three-hour presentation sold him." Ziegler offered Andy his own fund and committed the resources necessary to build a team.

STEPHENS'S INVESTMENT PROCESS

Andy confides that his desire for financial security influenced not only his decision to pursue a career in money management but also how he views risk and manages investments. Realizing the irony that you must take risks to achieve financial security, Stephens developed a style of money management he brands *daring prudence.* "You have to take some offensive moves," he says. "But at the same time you can't just leave your risk unlimited. I'm talking very calculated risk taking."

That fundamental belief clearly plays through in his investment strategy. "My process is all about handicapping risk," Andy states emphatically. "I evaluate the probability of failure and the potential payoff of any given situation. If I can get a handle on these things, then I can understand the risk I am taking to be involved and determine if the likely payoff justifies my investment." Andy first applies this concept to the selection of individual securities. Then he builds a mosaic of different risk levels and expected returns into a portfolio that protects investors on an overall basis.

KEY POINT

A performance benchmark serves as the foundation of Stephens's process—a process focused on generating consistent investment results. "I strive to perform at an above average level relative to the competition most of the time, and when I miss that mark, I try not to fall below the median. Then I can achieve the compounding offered by the capital markets and offer my clients superb performance."

Batting Average and Slugging Percentage

Andy divides his investment process into two parts: (1) security selection, which he talks about in terms of his batting average, and (2) portfolio management, which he thinks of as his slugging percentage. His batting average refers to the percentage of stocks he selects that are ultimately profitable, while his slugging percentage relates to the percentage of the fund's assets that gets invested in his best ideas. Since, like most money managers, Andy takes bigger positions in some securities than others, a high batting average does not necessarily translate into a high slugging percentage. For instance, if he invested the majority of the fund's cash in a minority of losing stocks, he would generate an inferior return. He must place the majority of the portfolio's funds in his most profitable stocks to beat the averages.

Andy understands that not every stock he buys will be a winner. As much as he respects Warren Buffett, this is one area where he disagrees with the Oracle of Omaha. Buffett has stated that on graduating from college every person should be given a punch card that permits them to make twenty investments during their lifetime. Their card gets punched each time they buy a stock, and they can make no more investments after twenty punches. Buffett makes the point that investors would research companies much more thoroughly before placing money in them if they were allowed to make only a few investments during their lives.

While Stephens understands the sentiment behind Buffett's statement, he also realizes that investors will make mistakes—indeed *must* make mistakes—to learn what investing is all about. "It may take two thousand punches before someone can boil everything down to what they really believe," Andy says. "It's a game of mistakes. It's how you control those mistakes and learn from them that is important."

A good batting average helps Stephens minimize losses and adds consistency to his investment results. It is, in a sense, the defensive side of money management. However, defense does not win games; it only prevents losing. Big offense wins games, which is why Stephens requires a healthy slugging percentage to beat the averages over time.

KEY POINT

"The art of portfolio management, at least the way I do it, is to be right more than I am wrong—at least to be right in a bigger way," Andy explains. "It's a trade-off between capitalizing on opportunities and protecting my downside if I make a mistake."

The Security Selection Process

Andy believes the stream of cash flow a business generates is what you ultimately acquire when you buy its stock. You capitalize that income—that is, place a current (net present) value on it—when valuing the corporation (see Chapter 10 for a detailed explanation of this concept). Other factors, such as the industry in which the firm competes and the country in which it operates, are generally unimportant except to the extent that they impact the company's cash flow. Not only is the level of the firm's earnings significant when valuing a business but the reliability of those earnings also matters. To maximize the reliability of a company's cash flow, a barrier must be in place to protect it from eroding due to competition.

Structural Competitive Advantages

Competition is a powerful force that makes it difficult for firms to earn above average returns for their shareholders. If a corporation generates excessive profits from engaging in a particular activity, whether it be producing a good or offering a service, the excess returns available will soon attract other businesses to that activity. The additional competition will then reduce the level of obtainable profits. Therefore, to secure a *protected* stream of cash flow, you must acquire a firm that possesses a *structural competitive advantage*. Money managers often describe such an advantage as a moat around a company that prevents other enterprises from entering its business and competing effectively with it. Andy looks for four types of structural advantages:

1. Dominant market share
2. Proprietary asset
3. Lowest cost structure
4. Defensible brand

Dominant Market Share.   Dominant means that when a firm makes a pricing or volume decision, the industry imitates it—that is, it drives industry actions instead of mimicking the leadership of others. For example, when AOL raised its monthly subscription fee from $19.95 to $21.95, virtually the entire Internet service provider (ISP) industry followed suit.

Proprietary Asset.   Most money managers define a proprietary asset as a patent or a technology that no one else possesses. Andy characterizes it in broader terms as something unique that a firm can leverage. It can be as simple as location—a retail shop resides on the corner of Main Street and Market Avenue, making the business visible to the heaviest traffic flow in town. Or for some financial services companies, this asset may be a twenty thousand–member sales force, the business equivalent of a huge army that would be almost impossible for a competitor to replicate.

Lowest Cost Structure.   This advantage especially benefits firms in cyclical industries at the low points of their business cycles. When all the companies in an industry are suffering, the low-cost producer often bankrupts it competitors or buys them out. Maintaining the lowest cost structure often correlates with possessing a proprietary asset. For example, a business might produce at a lower cost than its competition if it owns the only processing facility next to a particular coal mine.

Defensible Brand.   This structural advantage requires constant care and feeding, probably making it the most difficult to achieve and maintain. A business must continually spend on its brand to preserve its worth. The world is littered with leveraged buyouts where companies bought brands and then underspent on them, eroding their values and the competitive advantages for which the acquiring firms paid so dearly.

Andy looks for at least two of these four qualities in every company he buys. Finding suitable investments that possess all four characteristics is very unusual because such businesses are normally monopolies that operate in regulated industries. However, firms that possess two or more of these advantages will likely perform in the upper quartiles of their industries. Because their cash flow is safeguarded, investors can value these firms with a higher level of confidence.

The first step, therefore, in the security selection process is to find qualified companies—those earning above average returns with structural competitive advantages that protect their cash flows.

Valuing a Stream of Cash Flow

After finding a company that meets his criteria, Andy calculates an appropriate value for its projected stream of income. "Statistically, there is a correct price to pay for a company based on the amount of cash I expect it to generate," Andy says. "The factors involved in determining this price are the level and reliability of the company's cash flow and how rapidly I believe that cash flow will grow."

When investors capitalize a stream of income, they determine a present value for it by calculating what they would be willing to pay to own it. Owning a stream of income typically gives a person the right to control it. In the public capital markets, however, investors do not control a firm's cash flow. Company management, not the shareholders, decides how to allocate profits. Therefore, "I compensate for that lack of control by seeking to buy firms at discounts to their private market values," Stephens remarks. "In fact, I strive to pay no more than 60 percent of what a business is worth."

Andy advises investors to buy companies in a "window of cheapness." An investor gets a real bargain when acquiring a quality corporation at 60 percent of its private market value. If its price drops significantly below that, however, a private buyer will likely be able to finance the purchase of the corporation profitably, making it highly unlikely a business will become *too* cheap.

Andy sells a company once its price reaches its private market value, believing he is playing the "greater fool" game if he hangs on beyond that point. Investors may get lucky on occasion and profit by holding the stock longer, but that strategy generally increases the inconsistency of their returns without a commensurate reward.

Capitalizing on a Firm's Future Growth

Up to this point, everything in Andy's process has involved objective analysis—the *prudence* parts of his approach. First, make as certain as possible that a company possesses a reliable stream of recurring cash flow. Second, be sure you understand how to value its cash flow so that you do not overpay for the business. Now he introduces a subjective element to the process that affords investors who do their homework a possible advantage over other investors. In this third element of security selection, the *daring* part of his strategy, Andy attempts to capitalize on the growth potential of a company.

You must first understand the concept of profit cycles to grasp how this third area of security selection works. Andy has observed that most firms do not grow in a linear fashion—they do not increase revenues and earnings by the same percent every quarter. Rather, companies experience periods when profits advance at well above average rates followed by periods in which their earnings consolidate. Those cycles repeat over time.

KEY POINT

"Regarding business cycles, what I have come to understand is that when things go well for a company, they can't help but get better, and when things go bad, they can't help but get worse," Andy says. This belief is fundamental to Stephens's investment philosophy.

The power behind profit cycles lies in the notion of *incremental margin*. A high percentage of a company's operating costs is typically fixed, so any acceleration in the firm's revenues expands its margins and causes its net profits to grow disproportionately. An effective management team then reinvests some or all of the excess cash into perpetuating the company's sales growth, creating a positive profit cycle. To maximize a cycle's benefits and seize additional market share, an enterprise will pour money into such activities as hiring more sales professionals, increasing R&D expenditures, and beefing up advertising, all in an attempt to reach a higher profit level faster. The same process also works in reverse. When sales decelerate, margins wane and profits shrink disproportionately.

Andy endeavors to find businesses that are about to embark on positive profit cycles. Because the most powerful gains typically occur early on, you will often miss much of a stock's excess return if you buy it after the profit cycle has started. Stephens explains, "I want to buy a company when I have quality (structural competitive advantage) and value (price discounted to its private market value) on my side to protect me from downside risk, and a positive profit cycle lies in front of me. This gives me the ideal combination of limited downside with huge upside potential."

So try to buy a company a little early—just prior to the start of its profit cycle, giving you time to understand the business well enough to recognize when the positive cycle takes hold. If you buy a little early, your investment may tread water for a while after you purchase it. Be patient. As its cycle unfolds, you can increase your position in the stock.

Catalysts for Positive Profit Cycles

Positive profit cycles generally require a catalyst—a change of some sort that jump-starts them. Andy divides these changes into two categories: external and internal. External changes are secular events that cut across entire industries, whereas internal changes are company specific. Money managers commonly invest in change. However, Andy believes the change itself is not as important as the breakthrough that produced it.

Regarding external changes, Stephens looks for breakthroughs in two main areas: new technologies and regulatory events. For example, the shifting of our information infrastructure from an analog mode to a digital mode created tremendous excitement in the technology sector during the late 1990s. On the regulatory front, we witnessed the repeal of the Glass-Steagal Act and the passing of the Telecom Act in recent years. New technologies and regulatory events of those magnitudes drive tremendous changes that often create enormous investment opportunities.

Andy also looks for company-specific changes, such as a new management team, a big acquisition or divestiture, a major restructuring, or a new product launch. A positive internal change can turn an ailing company's fortunes and propel it forward, unlocking its inherent value. "My biggest gains have come from companies experiencing both types of changes," Andy explains. "External changes created secular tailwinds blowing through industries, and internal changes further amplified firms' performances. My biggest advantage in analyzing these businesses is that few people know how to predict the benefits of these changes. Everyone was taught in business school to calculate their impacts in a linear fashion."

The Risk of Companies Failing to Meet Your Expectations

Stephens considers the risks of companies falling short of the results he expects. "In valuing a firm, I think about the discount rate as the odds against an outcome," Andy says. "Just like in Vegas you handicap your odds, you must do the same in investing. The higher the risk of a business failing to meet your earnings expectations, the bigger the discount factor you apply to its projected cash flows to arrive at its private market value."

Uncovering Unexpected Growth

Stephens seeks to gain a competitive advantage by uncovering future growth potential in corporations that other money managers and analysts miss, so consistently growing enterprises do not interest him unless one of two conditions exists. First, a lack of consensus, or a shrinking consensus, regarding a firm's prospects can create opportunity. In this situation, the market misprices a company because investors underestimate the firm's growth potential, failing to recognize it is embarking on a new profit cycle. For instance, the market values a business based on 15 percent annual growth when in fact it is becoming a 20 percent grower. When this happens, investors often do not realize the extent of a change the company has experienced—a mistake on which Andy can capitalize.

The second condition occurs when a firm continues to grow earnings in line with historical trends, but investors discount its price because they fear a negative outcome to some issue on which the market lacks complete information. For example, a company is the subject of a lawsuit and investors differ in their opinions about the likely outcome. Another situation would be a lack of clarity on the extent of a recently discovered accounting irregularity. In recent years, because of the fear engendered by numerous scandals, quality companies that even hinted they may have accounted for revenues or expenses improperly were often punished well beyond any possible extent of their errors. Investors shot first and asked questions later, often resulting in undeservedly low prices.

Andy believes the market generally prices stocks efficiently except when investors differ markedly in their expectations for a firm's growth. If the projected earnings growth for a company is well defined, the stock price should accurately reflect those expectations. However, investors often price a stock based on a low-probability worst-case scenario when a lack of consensus is present.

YOU SHOULD IMPROVE YOUR BATTING AVERAGE AND UNCOVER SEVERAL winning situations by applying Andy's principles of security selection to your stock analysis. However, several questions remain: Should you buy the same amount of each investment in your portfolio, or should you weight them in some fashion? When should you sell a stock? How many stocks should you own? These and other questions lead us to Andy's philosophy on designing a portfolio.

CONSTRUCTING A WINNING PORTFOLIO

Having discovered some excellent candidates for investment, we must now combine these companies into a winning portfolio, leading us to Andy's capital allocation process. In other words, how do you get more money into the best-performing stocks and less into the ones that don't pan out as you expected?

Andy moves from baseball to farming to explain how he allocates money among his stock picks. He divides his portfolio into three categories: the garden, the crop, and the harvest (remember Chauncey Gardener?). "Everyone pokes fun at me for this analogy," he says. "But it's really the way I think about it." The object of this strategy is to limit the damage from being wrong about a company and to magnify the upside when you are right. Investing is a risk business, and how you manage that risk greatly influences your ultimate performance.

The Garden

In this segment of the portfolio, Andy takes risks on stocks that he believes meet his criteria but have not yet entered their profit cycles. It typically comprises between 20 and 40 percent of his fund. These companies carry a higher risk level because they have not yet proven their ability to fulfill their growth potential. Since he is not totally persuaded about these firms' prospects, he limits the size of each of these positions to about 1 percent of the portfolio.

Why would he invest in a corporation before he is convinced it will meet his growth expectations? First, Andy believes that unless he owns a company and puts some capital at risk with it, he cannot expend the effort necessary to analyze it thoroughly and develop confidence in his idea. Buying a firm and placing it in the garden commits him to following it. Second, in the public markets there is a trade-off between time to market and perfect knowledge. He will likely miss out on substantial appreciation in a stock's price if he waits to invest until the firm's positive earnings outlook is clear.

If a business begins to expand its earnings as he expects, he increases his allocation to it and moves it into his crop.

The Crop

In the crop, Andy takes big positions in companies that have entered their profit cycles and convinced him that they will meet his growth expectations. He generally makes the bulk of his profits from this part of the portfolio. However, he maintains he cannot produce a crop without a garden.

Stephens believes in the 80/20 rule, which states that 80 percent of most portfolio managers' returns come from 20 percent of their investments. His challenge is to place the majority of the portfolio's assets into the few companies that will generate the highest rewards. This approach means taking bigger positions in a smaller number of names.

The crop, therefore, typically comprises between 60 and 70 percent of the portfolio and consists of ten to twenty names. Andy generally invests 2 to 5 percent of the fund in each of these stocks, convinced he knows virtually everything there is to know about them. "I perform best," he explains, "when my top ten positions represent over 30 percent of the portfolio."

Even though the crop is more concentrated than the garden, he still diversifies this portion of his fund. Often, when one company experiences a profit cycle, other businesses in the same sector do likewise. Thus, Andy may own several similar firms in the crop at the same time. However, he avoids overconcentrating in any one sector of the market.

Andy varies the sizes of the crop and the garden based on how many companies he finds experiencing positive profit cycles. For example, gross domestic product (GDP) growth was decelerating sharply during the middle of 2001. Profit cycles were sparse, so the crop represented only 25 percent of his portfolio, while the garden comprised half of it. This allocation resulted in lots of 1 percent positions while Andy waited for the economy to rebound and generate more profit cycles. "In general, businesses rely on the overall level of economic activity. They're simply multiples of the total economy," he says. The crop constitutes a higher percentage of the portfolio when the economy spawns a greater number of profit cycles.

The Harvest

Andy uses the harvest to pocket gains and reduce, or eliminate, positions. He believes you should reduce your investment in a company for two main reasons: reaching your price target and decelerating earnings growth. The best reason to sell a stock is based on its price, largely because this basis removes emotion and subjectivity from the decision-making process. You establish a price you believe represents full value for the firm, the stock reaches that price, and you sell it. Simple enough, right? It is as long as you don't make the mother of all mistakes in this area—getting greedy! Too often investors try to squeeze every penny of profit from a stock and continue holding it after its price has reached full value, only to watch their hard-earned profits evaporate!

The full-value price for a company's stock is a moving target. As the firm's profit cycle begins and its earnings increase, its value grows as well. However, as its profit cycle accelerates, you cannot keep applying a faster growth rate to higher earnings numbers to determine its value. Otherwise, you eventually compound to a figure that is way above its actual private market value. (Author's note: Technology investors made this devastating mistake in the late 1990s, resulting in the infamous bubble.) Rather, you *normalize* the firm's growth rate to an average level that you believe it can sustain over the entire cycle and hold that figure constant. Credit the company for higher profit numbers as it reports them, but keep the growth rate static in your calculations.

Andy values a stock very conservatively at first, starting with a number based on his mid- to worst-case scenario. "I don't want to pay for the pro forma [the excess growth he projects above the consensus estimate of the market]," he says, "even if I think something good is going to happen. You should not have to pay for that. That is what you should get for assuming the risk of owning the stock."

As the corporation reports earnings each quarter and its profit cycle develops, he adjusts his calculations to reflect the higher income figures and boosts his valuation range. The company's price will likely ascend through the top of that range if its earnings move through the "hockey stick" as he expects. Selling the stock at that level leaves a little room for others to make money from purchasing it. Otherwise, no one will buy it from him. "It's hard for me to believe I will be able to sell $200 million to $300 million of a stock right at the top," Andy declares. "The purchaser must be able to make some money, or he will not buy it. However, in my mind it is overvalued at that point."

You should also sell a stock because the profit cycle for which you bought it decelerates. Remember a pillar of Andy's philosophy: "When things go well for a company, they can't help but get better, and when things go bad, they can't help but get worse." As a firm's earnings growth slows, the company's prospects will likely deteriorate more than most investors anticipate, so you should lock in your profits and reduce or eliminate your position at that point.

What about market timing? Does Andy increase his cash level in a slowing economy, when there are few positive profit cycles, as a defensive measure? While he finds it very seductive to think he can predict market trends, Stephens resists the temptation to time the market, convinced this is a mistake that ultimately costs investors. Studies show that about ten key days of trading during profit cycles materially impact the returns that investors capture. Experience has taught Andy that the market has a way of doing what nobody expects, and his timing could easily be off. Missing just a couple of those big days could significantly reduce his return and place his clients at a disadvantage—a risk he is not willing to take. Rather, he assumes shareholders want to be exposed to equities by investing in his fund.

GENERAL PORTFOLIO MANAGEMENT PRINCIPLES

Although Andy does not time the market, he does take one important step to lower the risk of investing in equities during an economic downturn. When a scarcity of positive profit cycles exists, he enlarges his garden and shrinks his crop—that is, he increases the number of stocks with small positions in his portfolio and reduces the number of his bigger bets. Statistically, that dampens his risk, since the damage from a losing garden stock is less than that of a bad crop investment. Stephens believes it is foolhardy to maintain concentrated positions in companies that are not experiencing positive profit cycles. Once earnings cycles develop, he winnows the garden and allocates more money to his top ideas.

KEY POINT

Andy's research suggests he maximizes his return during a normal profit cycle by holding forty-five to fifty names in the portfolio, with the crop constituting between 60 and 70 percent of the fund. This leaves him with several large (4 to 5 percent) positions that typically produce most of his gains.

When they see forty-five to fifty names in his portfolio, some investors wonder if such a diversified fund lacks the punching power of a more concentrated portfolio. Don't be fooled. Remember that Stephens invests most of the assets in only fifteen to twenty companies, giving his fund the potential to outperform its benchmark indices without focusing on especially high-risk businesses.

CREATING VALUE

How does Andy's strategy differ from that of traditional value investors? Andy tries to acquire a growing dollar instead of purchasing a static dollar for fifty cents and waiting for someone to buy it from him for seventy-five or eighty cents. He seeks companies that will create enormous *future* value by their actions—that is, he endeavors to pay a reasonable price for a current dollar that he hopes will grow to five dollars in a few years. He just doesn't want to pay for all that expected growth up front.

Since typical value managers do not take the same risk as Stephens in terms of banking on businesses creating future value, they can afford to take a rifle approach and concentrate their portfolios. Andy invests in growth companies that by their very nature carry a substantially higher failure rate—not failure as in going out of business but as in not meeting their profit cycle growth potential. He reduces the impact of this risk by taking only small positions in firms until he is confident they will meet his growth expectations.

As Andy explains it, "I *am* a value investor of sorts. But I don't determine what a company is worth today and buy it at a discount to that figure. Rather, I project what its actions will make it worth in three to five years and discount that number back to today to determine its current value. Ideally, I want to buy the business at about 40 percent below that amount. However, the firm must deliver on my growth expectations for my calculations to be correct. That's the extra risk I take for which I want to be rewarded."

A traditional value investor can justify buying stock in a corporation that fails to increase its earnings dramatically because she only pays fifty cents up front for a dollar's worth of value. To the contrary,

Stephens *requires* that a company grows its earnings to justify his purchase price. However, he hedges his bet by paying only sixty cents on the dollar for that expected growth. Stephens also increases the conservatism of his calculations by making sure he uses a prudent growth rate in his fair value computations. He arrives at that growth figure by starting with his best-case growth scenario and then backing it down to what he believes the firm can reasonably be expected to achieve under less than ideal circumstances.

WESTERN WIRELESS: A CASE ANALYSIS

Andy's initial analysis of Western Wireless typifies how he implements his strategy. "A traditional value investor would have appraised the company's assets and the worth of the licenses it had acquired to determine its present value. They would then have bought shares of the company only when it was selling for a large discount, maybe 50 percent, to that figure."

Andy viewed the situation differently. First, he considered the fact that Western Wireless had obtained licenses to function as one of only two wireless operators in numerous rural areas across the country, making them, in essence, a licensed duopoly.

Next, he estimated the potential customer base for Western's service. The number of users hinged on the penetration levels eventually reached in the areas where Western operated. In Europe, where they were about three to four years ahead of the United States in wireless operations, penetration rates for this type of service normally climbed quickly to about 50 percent once they passed the 20 percent threshold. Stephens saw no reason to assume results here would differ significantly. Since the United States was experiencing only 3 percent penetration at the time, Andy concluded that figure would mushroom over the next few years.

Western was in the process of building its wireless network, which required a huge initial capital investment. Once it completed this project, however, ongoing capital expenditures should be minimal, transforming the operation into a cash cow. When that occurred, what size margins would Western likely achieve? European wireless firms generated EBITDA (earnings before interest, taxes, depreciation, and amortization) margins averaging between 30 and 40 percent. Domestic cable companies operated at about 45 percent margins. Western's business was not so different from cable as to make its margin potential incomparable. Andy postulated Western could reasonably be expected to achieve 40 percent EBITDA margins.

Armed with that information, Stephens needed only a little detective work and simple mathematics to answer the following four questions and estimate Western's future cash flows: How many people reside in its areas of distribution? How many of those residents will likely become subscribers? What will each subscriber pay per month for wireless service? What margins will the company achieve in three years? Andy calculated Western's worth three years in the future using the resulting cash flow projections, and then discounted that figure back to the present to determine a fair market value for the firm. Those computations convinced Stephens that Western's price was discounted sufficiently to its value to justify investing in the company.

SUMMARY

The following summarizes the main points of Stephens's investment philosophy:

Security Selection

- Acquire companies with reliable cash flows. Look for firms that possess structural competitive advantages capable of protecting those cash flows from competition. A structural competitive advantage can be a dominant market share, a proprietary asset, low-cost producer status, or a defensible brand.
- Calculate the present value of a corporation's future cash flows to determine its fair market value. Try to buy the business at a sizable (ideally at least 40 percent) discount to its value.
- Buy companies just prior to the start of their profit cycles, looking for firms that are experiencing internal and/or external changes. Internal changes include such things as a new management team,

a big acquisition or divestiture, a major restructuring, or a new product launch. External changes include new technologies and regulatory events.

Portfolio Allocation

- Maintain a garden—a portion of the portfolio that includes small positions in stocks that meet your requirements but have not yet entered their profit cycles.
- Increase your positions in companies as they begin their profit cycles and move them to your crop—that part of the portfolio where you take bigger positions in firms that have proven their abilities to meet your growth expectations.
- When a stock reaches your target price or its profit cycle begins to decelerate, reduce or eliminate your position in it—harvest it.
- Do not time the market; always remain fully invested.
- Reduce the size of your crop and increase the size of your garden to lower your risk during economic downturns when profit cycles are sparse.
- Do not overconcentrate in a single sector of the market.

CHAPTER 3

Bill Nygren

Lead Portfolio Manager, Oakmark Select Fund, Oakmark Fund

Bill Nygren is the Lead Portfolio Manager of the Oakmark Select Fund. Morningstar named him Domestic Stock Fund Manager of the Year in 2001. A $10,000 investment in Oakmark Select at its inception in November 1996 would have grown to $42,177 by the end of December 2003, a period of time that included the worst bear market since the Great Depression. The same amount invested in the S&P 500 index would have appreciated to only $17,613. During the five-year period ending December 31, 2003, Nygren's fund posted average annual returns of 15.4 percent, trouncing the S&P 500 by an average of 16 percent per year.[1]

Bill has performed with a high level of consistency during his tenure as manager of Oakmark Select. According to Morningstar, in the seven years from the beginning of 1997 to the end of 2003, Nygren performed in the top 5 percent of managers in his category three times; he scored in the top third an additional two times; and he placed in the lower half of his category only once.[2] During the bull market years of 1997–1999, Select came within 1.3 percent of matching the S&P 500's performance. During the following bear market years of 2000–2002, Select beat the popular index by over 76 percent.[3]

BILL NYGREN LEARNED EVERYTHING HE KNOWS ABOUT INVESTING FROM his mother. Well, maybe not *everything*. But the lessons she taught him as a child about value certainly helped shape his investment personality.

Nygren's investment genius lies in the simplicity of his style. He does little that investors would consider exotic or esoteric. In fact, his lack of complexity frustrates those wanting to learn the "secrets" that have made him one of the top money managers in the country. If he has a secret, it is that he relentlessly performs the basics better than almost anybody else. Focused on what is important and refusing to be distracted by what isn't, he religiously executes a time-tested strategy that has propelled him to best-in-class status.

PERSONAL BACKGROUND

Growing Up with the Cleavers

Bill grew up in St. Paul, Minnesota, in a traditional middle-class family that his older brother nicknamed the Cleavers. His father managed the credit department for the 3M Company. His mother stayed home to raise three boys, of which Bill is the middle child, and to handle the daily affairs of the household.

Mrs. Nygren kept the family on a strict budget. A true value shopper, she visited three supermarkets each week, checking out the specials they were each running. From the time he was in kindergarten, Bill observed that his mother bought more of items when they went on sale. If an item was fully priced, she bought less of it or passed on it completely.

An Early Lesson about Risk

When Bill was ten, his family took off to Disneyland for a vacation. They spent a night in Las Vegas to have dinner with a relative who was stationed there with the Air Force. Bill's dad took advantage of the opportunity to teach his two older sons a lesson about the evils of gambling.

A slot machine sat in the entry way of the grocery store across the street from their motel. Mr. Nygren hauled the boys over there, pulled out a handful of nickels, and announced to his sons, "I don't gamble because I don't think it's smart. I want to show you why it's not smart. I'm going to put these nickels in this slot, and we'll lose them, because that's what happens when you gamble. You lose your money."

The responsible father confidently popped the first nickel into the machine, pulled the handle, and seven nickels fell out! Bill stared wide-eyed at the money-making machine. Trying to salvage the object lesson gone awry, his dad stuck another nickel in the machine, and five came out in its place! The eldest Nygren started getting angry. Ten-year-old Bill, obviously missing the point of the example, said, "Dad, why don't you stop? You're so far ahead!" The exasperated father played the slot machine for another half hour, trying desperately to get rid of the nickels and prove to his sons that gambling was stupid.

That experience taught young Bill a lesson, but not the one his father intended. Instead, it started for Bill what has become a lifelong fascination with risk and return. "My dad was a smart, successful businessman. His job was all about assessing risk," Bill says. "He was telling me gambling was stupid, but I saw all that free money coming out of the machine. I needed to square that, so later on I started researching what kinds of returns you get when you take risk."

The World of Investing Beckons

Bill was first bitten by the investment bug about the time he entered high school. At fifteen, he started reading whatever was available on the topic at the local library, which unfortunately wasn't much. All the investment books fit in a three-foot-wide section on one shelf, indicating how few people were interested in stocks at the time. Bill devoured the entire collection book by book.

Bill was naturally drawn to those books that focused on buying companies when they were out of favor and undervalued—books written by and about such investing legends as Benjamin Graham and Warren Buffett. That investment philosophy made sense to him because it paralleled the consumer behavior he had learned. To the contrary, technically oriented momentum philosophies seemed foreign.

NYGREN ON RISK

Bill's interest in risk and return led him to explore various types of financial risk taking and the average payoffs each offered. He discovered, for instance, that if you put a dollar in a state lottery, the state typically keeps fifty cents. Almost everybody comes away empty-handed, and someone hits a huge home run. If you bought all the tickets, you would get back only half your money. Not good odds.

In horse racing, the track keeps between 15 and 20 percent of your money—better than the lottery, but still a net loss.

At the very positive end of the gambling spectrum, casinos keep about 1 percent of what you bet at the craps table.

Further up the return/risk scale, you move into the field of investing, where expected returns are positive. Put money into high-quality bonds and you will typically earn just a tad above inflation. It's a low-risk/low-return venture, but at least the result is positive, which beats any of the gambling options. Stocks on average outperform bonds by several percentage points, and the longer you hold them, the more certain you can be that your returns will beat other asset classes of investments.

So Bill learned early on that just because a venture is risky doesn't mean you should avoid it. Some risks make sense to take, and investing in stocks is one of them.

He never understood the logic behind the notion that something going up in price in itself indicates the price might go higher.

By the time Bill went to the University of Minnesota, not only was investing his primary hobby, but he knew he wanted to make it his vocation as well. He believed that if he was going to have a career studying and valuing companies, he needed to thoroughly understand the language, so he majored in accounting.

Nygren interviewed for some low-level investment jobs after graduation. He quickly realized that to be seriously considered for almost any investment industry position, he needed to get an MBA in finance from a highly respected business school such as Harvard, Wharton,

THE TRIP THAT CHANGED HIS LIFE

Bill's number one passion from kindergarten through early high school was baseball (in fact, Nygren still participates in softball, playing for his company team, the Mighty Oaks). It didn't matter whether he was playing the game, watching the Twins on television, or listening to a game on the radio—he just loved being around the sport. He was also infatuated with numbers, which led him to excel in math. The two interests came together in an obsession for baseball statistics. Young Nygren often whiled away the time analyzing box scores, searching for significance in the numbers beyond the obvious on which the sportscasters focused.

In the business section of the local paper, the *St. Paul Pioneer Press*, a page of stock quotes was conveniently located just behind the sports section. This meant the baseball statistics often filled the left-hand side of the paper, and a mysterious table full of unintelligible figures filled the right. Bill's fascination with numbers eventually attracted him to the stock page.

One day Nygren asked his dad what the mysterious numbers meant. His father explained they represented stock prices. As Bill studied the figures, the magnitude of their changes grabbed his attention. While he was earning 5 percent a *year* on the allowance money in his savings account, many stocks moved more than that on any given *day*. The obvious question came to his mind: "Is there a way to predict which ones will go up?" The elder Nygren suggested a trip to the library. Bill took his dad's advice. That trip opened up a new world to the teenager and ultimately changed the course of his life.

Stanford, or Chicago. So Bill applied to all these schools. Then an unexpected event led him down a different path.

Nygren worked as an intern his senior year of college in General Mills's accounting department. During his exit interviews, a manager told him of an incident he had just experienced while visiting his daughter at the University of Wisconsin–Madison. The applied securities analysis class owned General Mills stock and insisted on interviewing him regarding a problem with the women's apparel division. He was surprised at the quality of the students questions and their knowledge level. The manager knew Nygren's goals and was friends with Steve Hawk, the professor who ran the program. He encouraged Bill to check it out.

Bill was amenable, so the manager helped him arrange an interview with Hawk. After talking with Hawk and learning about the curricula, Nygren knew the University of Wisconsin program was for him. In addition to being a professor of finance, Professor Hawk was also a partner in a money management firm. This gave him a unique ability to explain theory to students and then demonstrate how the theory applied in the real world. As a result, Hawk had designed the course work to be practically focused instead of academically focused, which Bill found especially appealing.

The practical focus extended beyond the classroom. The students in the applied securities analysis program split into two groups, each of which was given $50,000 of real money to invest. So each team essentially formed an investment firm that managed its allotted funds over the course of the year. The teams had to develop investment philosophies and formal asset allocations. Members had to convince their group of the merits of equities they thought should be included in the portfolio. Professor Hawk played the client's role and asked the tough questions that real clients might ask.

Northwestern Mutual Life

Upon obtaining his MBA, Nygren took a job at Northwestern Mutual Life (NML) in Milwaukee, where he worked just short of two years as a generalist equity analyst. Bill learned the importance of working with others who share his investment philosophy. At that time, NML portfolio managers combined fundamental analysis with technical analysis in an effort to identify fundamentally above average companies whose technical signs suggested they were ready to outperform. That approach ran counter to the way Nygren thought. To him, a stock became more attractive as it got cheaper. In contrast, his colleagues needed to see a security get more expensive before it

attracted them. By the time they became interested in a company recommended by Nygren, the valuation that initially attracted Bill was no
longer there.

Nygren realized that he needed to leave NML and join a firm that
practiced his value-oriented philosophy. He had asked a few people
to let him know if they came across anything interesting. Steve Hawk,
his old finance professor, was among that group.

One day Steve called and said, "You are going to get a call in a
few minutes from someone you don't know named Clyde McGregor.
He works for a firm you've never heard of, Harris Associates. You
should take the job. I told him to call you now, so I have to hang up!"
Before Bill could say anything, Steve was gone. Nygren hung up the
phone and it rang immediately. Clyde McGregor was on the other end,
calling to invite Bill to interview in Chicago for a position that was becoming available.

The group interview at Harris was a breath of fresh air for Nygren.
At one point, the interviewers asked him to discuss some of the names
that interested him. So he talked about Hasbro and other companies
that sold for between four and six times earnings (interest rates were
much higher then, so PE ratios were significantly lower than today—
close to ten on average). Harris either owned or was looking at almost
every company Nygren mentioned. Bill was convinced he wanted that
job. Apparently the feeling was mutual. Two months later, the position
was his.

The Harris people were very successful investors with the value
approach. Not only could they use Nygren's ideas, but he felt he could
learn a lot from them. "I certainly have not been disappointed," he
says. "Twenty years later, I still like the people I work with and I feel
that I still learn from them. Working with these people makes me a
better investor than if I worked somewhere else."

Bill started at Harris as a generalist analyst, which was something
else that appealed to Nygren about the firm. Because all the analysts
have a common investment philosophy, Harris gives them more lat-
itude than most firms in terms of the areas they cover. Harris analysts
are able to look for ideas that match their criteria wherever they can
find them. If one day that leads to studying a transactions processing
company and another day it leads to a food company, then so be it.

Bill appreciates that freedom to explore lots of different investment ideas and not be confined to a particular sector.

Nygren has thrived at Harris. In 1990, the firm promoted him to Director of Research.

Launching the Oakmark Select Fund

Harris required a $2.5 million minimum account size to manage money for individuals. The firm launched the Oakmark Fund in 1991 as a way to provide lower-dollar clients with an introduction to Harris Associates, having no idea of the potential the mutual fund business offered. The idea was to get those people comfortable with the firm's management style so that when they had enough money to qualify for separate account management, Harris would be the natural place for them.

The Oakmark Fund turned in an exceptional performance its first year. Capitalizing on its success, other funds soon followed. Within three years, mutual funds had grown into Harris Associates' primary business.

The firm launched the Oakmark Select Fund in November 1996 and tapped Nygren to manage it. Bill's goal was to establish a superior investment record over a five-year period. He also wanted to utilize a more concentrated approach than the other funds, so the product was registered as a nondiversified fund. Bottom line—he would manage the fund in the manner he wanted his own money managed.

NYGREN'S INVESTMENT PROCESS

Peter Foreman, one of the firm's partners, told Bill when he started at Harris, "Two things happen when you buy a company. You acquire a balance sheet and you partner with the people who manage it." Based on that philosophy, Nygren requires any business he buys to possess these three characteristics:

1. Discounted price
2. Growing per share value
3. Shareholder-oriented management

Bill is quick to point out that these requirements are not peculiar to his management style. Rather, they reflect a firm-wide philosophy. All the managers and analysts at Harris Associates employ the same value strategy and adhere to the same three criteria. As a result, a lot of idea sharing goes on, and many of the names in the portfolio come to Bill from the research of the firm-wide group of analysts.

Buy Firms at a 40 Percent Discount to Their Intrinsic Value

Nygren defines a company's intrinsic value or worth as "the maximum amount an intelligent, knowledgeable buyer could pay to own the whole business and still earn an adequate return on his investment." When determining a firm's worth, Bill does not focus on one magic statistic that he believes works for all companies, such as its price-to-earnings (PE) ratio, PE-to-growth (PEG) ratio, or price-to-cash flow. He believes different statistics do a better job of estimating values for different industries.

To estimate a firm's intrinsic value, Bill first examines prior purchase transactions for other businesses in the same sector to identify the key variables analyzed by buyers. He prefers to look at cash transactions because he does not want to be influenced by companies that were anxious to issue overvalued equity to buy stock. To facilitate this process, Harris Associates maintains an extensive database of transactions where entire businesses have been purchased.

Having scrutinized the numbers for a multitude of acquisitions, Nygren has identified common valuation factors for numerous industries. For instance, the PE ratio roams all over the map in the auto parts business, but the price-to-sales ratio correlates strongly with purchase prices. The price-to-subscriber and price-to-cash flow figures remain consistent for cable TV acquisitions. R&D expenditures as a percentage of revenues vary greatly between companies within the pharmaceutical sector. However, when you remove that figure, the price-to-cash flow before R&D spending stays fairly constant.

Nygren then develops benchmarks for the relevant metrics within each industry as indicators of value. For instance, an auto parts business may be worth 60 percent of its annual sales, whereas a cable TV company might be valued at $3,000 per subscriber.

Bill compares qualitative characteristics of businesses he examines to those that were purchased to determine if he should tweak numbers up or down. For example, is a firm he is analyzing growing faster or slower than the average acquired firm? Does it have a higher or lower cost of capital? Has it achieved superior economies of scale or other structural competitive advantages?

A few company-specific adjustments must still be made. For example, debt holders have to be paid before the owners realize any value, so Nygren deducts lenders' claims that have priority over equity holders. Non-cash-generating assets and excess cash (above working capital needs) get added to the business value. Bill uses the resulting number to determine a firm's worth to a cash buyer. He then divides that final figure by the number of shares outstanding to determine a per share value for the firm.

Discounting Cash Flows

Nygren's approach differs from that of most fundamental investors, who typically value businesses by discounting their projected cash flows. Bill does not ignore this tool, but he calculates discounted cash flow numbers only to understand the economics behind his valuation metrics. Why is a cable TV subscriber worth $3,000? Why is an auto parts company worth 60 percent of its sales? He wants to thoroughly understand the cash flow returns buyers achieved on their investments before he uses a valuation measure he has developed for an industry. However, once he understands why a cable TV subscriber can be worth $3,000, for instance, he does not perform a separate discounted cash flow valuation for every cable company he looks at.

Expected Returns Reflect Market Interest Rates

Bill believes the price you should be willing to pay for a stock depends not only on the company's growth rate, but also on the interest rates available on competing investments—that is, the return you should aim for changes based on the available alternatives. So when Bill looks at what buyers paid for businesses in the past, he adjusts those prices for the change in market interest rates since that time. When Treasury bonds paid 13 percent in the late 1970s, you would not have wanted to buy a business at a 10 percent return. In early 2004, however, a 10 percent return would have been almost heroic relative to the 4 percent you could get on government bonds.

Bill wants to always outperform what he could earn from another investment class. If he can make 13 percent on a government bond, then he wants to generate at least 17 percent from a stock. If bonds offer only a 4 percent return, then he'd like to earn a minimum of 8 percent on stocks.

Once Bill has determined that a business sells for less than 60 percent of what he believes it is worth, he moves to the second criterion.

Buy Companies Whose Values Are Growing

By scrounging for the cheapest companies, value investors often fall into the ditch of buying structurally disadvantaged businesses that need a catalyst to release their potential value. Among other things, that catalyst could include being acquired by another company, a management change, or a legal victory. Without the benefit of such a change, the company's value might continue to languish or even shrink for an extended period of time. Businesses decline in value for a number of reasons, such as losing market share, or they require capital expenditures above the cash flows they generate just to maintain their current levels of operations.

Bill tries to avoid that error with his second criterion. He requires that companies' expected per share value growth *plus dividends* at least matches the growth in value he expects from the market (note that he focuses on the market's *value growth*, not price changes).

Nygren defines the market as the S&P 500 index. Companies that comprise that index will likely grow their earnings by 5 to 6 percent a year over the long term. They also currently sport about a 2 percent dividend yield. In a steady-state environment, therefore, you would expect to make 7 to 8 percent a year if you owned the whole marketplace (assuming you bought it at fair value). So Nygren wants to buy firms whose growth in value plus dividend yields equal at least 7 to 8 percent a year.

Bill is agnostic between no value growth and an 8 percent dividend, or 8 percent value growth and no dividend. Nygren looks at the combination of the two because in his mind dividends and expected value growth are equivalent. Based on either academic research or historical results, he knows of no reason why an investor should prefer dividends over value growth, or vice versa.

Benefits of Free Cash Flow

Nygren believes the market does a good job of forecasting companies' top-line growth. However, he believes he gains an advantage over others by drilling deeper and examining the impact a firm's sales growth should have on the cash it will generate. He asks three key questions in this regard: (1) Will the business produce free cash flow over the next five years? (2) If so, how will it likely use that cash? (3) If its growth will require financing, how much dilution will that bring to equity holders? The answers he develops help him forecast a company's cash flow down to the per share level, including its financing needs or excess cash generation.

"A lot of my companies achieve my growth estimates through relatively modest top-line growth," Bill says. "A business can use excess cash to improve its balance sheet, buy back shares and shrink its share base, or acquire firms. Any of those can incrementally boost the firm's growth rate. On a per share basis, this can make a relatively mundane business look pretty good."

Shareholder-Oriented Management

Nygren demands that a company's management treat its shareholders like partners before he'll invest. You'll frequently hear Harris analysts ask: "If I wasn't able to sell this stock for the next five years, would I be comfortable investing in it—that is, do I trust management enough to commit cash to the business if bailing out were not an option?"

To the investment world, great management is motherhood and apple pie. Of course, everybody wants it. But what constitutes great management? Most professionals characterize an outstanding leadership team by a history of success. Nygren wants an accomplished history, of course, but more importantly, he requires that management's economic incentives be well aligned with shareholders' goals. Thus, the leaders should get rich only if the shareholders prosper.

As a prudent investor, you must assume that corporate executives will act in their own best interests. Therefore, you want their personal goals to line up with shareholders' well-being, so if the leaders do what benefits them personally, the shareholders also profit.

The present values of executives' salaries often exceed their incentives to grow their firms' values and generate higher stock prices. This problem creates a conflict of interest, causing some management teams to focus on simply making their companies bigger. A bigger company does not automatically produce a higher per share value. Therefore, Bill tries to avoid those situations where the job of managing the firm becomes more important and more lucrative than maximizing the company's value.

Many key decisions faced by executives impact them differently as managers than as shareholders. For example, assume a potential buyer offers a great price for a division of a company. Whereas the shareholders might vote unanimously to sell the division, the manager may view a sell as shrinking her job. The value of the income stream she controls attenuates if she does the right thing. Nygren wants to make sure that managers are properly incentivized to do the right thing in such situations by having a high percentage of their compensation be equity based.

Stock Options

Analysts and business leaders debate the role stock options play in encouraging management to act on shareholders' behalf. Bill believes options are a good but imperfect motivator. Good because leaders benefit more the higher the stock price goes. Imperfect because a stock's price can rise for lots of reasons unrelated to the company's performance, thereby rewarding executives for circumstances beyond their control. Also, an option holder does not carry nearly as much downside risk as an equity holder.

So would Bill rather that upper management own shares of stock as opposed to options? Not necessarily. Is it necessary for company leaders to tie up a high percentage of their net worth in their firm's stock? No. What matters is when managers face important business decisions and you consider executives' *total compensation packages*—their various pay incentives, option plans, and the amounts of stock they own—the economics of the shareholder grabs their attention more than their own economics.

Frank Communication

Bill wants to partner with managers who believe they have an obligation to communicate openly with shareholders regarding the state of the business in addition to having proper economic incentives. Corporate leaders have to be accountable to shareholders, the owners of the company. Too many top executives have acted as though their relationships with shareholders were adversarial in nature. Bill must believe he is getting a candid assessment of how the company is doing, why it has performed as it has, and what might affect it going forward. Nygren will examine the situation closely and consider selling a stock if he loses confidence in management's honesty. Discovering that a company's leaders are trying to hide something triggers an automatic sell.

Increasing Returns While Decreasing Risk

Bill looks for all three criteria—a discounted price, expanding per share value, and shareholder-oriented management—in every investment he makes. Each requirement is designed to help him do what academics say is impossible: simultaneously decrease the risk and increase the expected return of an investment. This notion directly contradicts what almost every finance student learns in college: that you must accept a lower return in order to decrease risk.

Consider just the first criterion: Only buy a stock when it sells at a substantial discount to its intrinsic value. If a company experiences problems and things go worse than you project, its stock will likely tumble. However, the level from which its price falls is lower than if you bought the business at full value. This should provide downside protection and reduce your risk.

In contrast, if things go as expected, the market should eventually close the gap between the firm's price and its value. This provides a slingshot effect on the upside, increasing your expected return.

In similar fashion, the latter two criteria cushion the downside if unforeseen adversities knock a company off its original course or if you miscalculated something. If you pay too much for a business, the fallout should be minimal as long as it continues to grow in value. If unexpected competition arises, the country suffers from recession, or new government regulations threaten a firm's growth prospects, a competent, shareholder-oriented management team should make the best decisions possible on behalf of the owners for dealing with the negative developments.

On the upside, a growing value and management decisions aligned with shareholders' interests increase the odds of an under-valued stock outperforming the market.

Long-Term Investment Horizon

As we have seen, possessing any one of the three criteria should en-hance a stock's performance. However, combining them gives Bill what he considers his greatest luxury: a very long time horizon. Wall Street analysts who pass through Harris's offices frequently comment that the firm is one of their very few clients who care about a com-pany's three- to five-year outlook. Most investors try to outguess each other about next quarter's earnings. Those considered long-term thinkers normally look out a year instead of a quarter. Rarely do you find a money manager who focuses on how a business will change over five years—Nygren's time horizon. "I start with an undervalued company that's growing at least as fast as the market. Management is taking incremental steps that benefit shareholders," Nygren says. "I don't have to worry about things like catalysts or how the stock is likely to perform in the next quarter. The longer it takes for the mar-ket to realize the potential of one of our companies, the greater my return is."

To illustrate, suppose Bill thinks a firm is currently worth $100. He buys it for $60 and would sell it today at $90. If things go as expected, in a year he's looking at a business he believes is worth $110 that he would sell at $99. Two years from now, the business should be worth $121, and Bill would sell it at $109. His price target keeps ratcheting up as the time frame lengthens.

So how does Bill respond when he buys a stock and the company performs as he expects, but its price goes nowhere? Does he ever throw in the towel because the market fails to recognize the value of a firm? To the contrary. According to Nygren, "That scenario is one where I frequently add to my position." Because he has a very long time horizon, he is willing to accept the risk of underperforming in any individual year.

The Sell Criteria

Buying quality undervalued companies gets you only halfway to a successful investment experience. Knowing when to sell a security is just as important. Fortunes have been lost because investors have tried to squeeze every penny out of winning situations and held on to positions long after they should have gotten rid of them. Bill sells portfolio holdings for three reasons:

1. Valuation
2. Poor fundamental performance
3. Dealing with mistakes

Valuation.   Ideally Bill liquidates a security because his analysis was right and the market comes to recognize the value of his investment. In that situation, he unloads a stock when its price reaches 90 percent of its fair value.

Why sell a stock at 90 percent instead of waiting for it to reach full value? Several reasons.

First, a company is often worth less as a stand-alone entity than as an acquisition target. This is especially true for small- and mid-cap firms. Remember that Bill develops his valuation estimate from prices buyers actually paid for similar businesses. Acquiring firms often obtain synergies and achieve greater economies of scale when they purchase other businesses. Those synergies may include such things as eliminating duplicate job functions, consolidating facilities, reducing combined R&D budgets, and standardizing information technology systems. That ability to gain efficiencies and cut costs increases the acquired firm's worth to a buyer. Bill adjusts for this by selling a stock before its price reaches his full-value estimate.

Second, Bill recognizes that valuation is not a precise exercise—he simply tries to get in the right ballpark. A company's true worth likely falls within at least a 10 percent range on either side of his single point estimate. If he is going to err, Nygren would rather sell early than wait for the stock to reach what may be an overvalued level.

Third, Bill needs someone to sell his shares to. If everybody had similar ideas about a firm's worth and waited for its price to reach fair value before they sold it, finding a purchaser would prove difficult.

Finally, if you buy into the logic of Bill's philosophy, you have to believe that *buying* a stock at 60 percent of its value will generate a higher return than *holding* one selling for 90 percent of its worth. The latter stock might climb to 100 percent of its fair value if you wait, but hopefully the first stock will ascend to 75 percent of its worth during the same time frame, generating a higher return.

Bill has a problem with value managers who become momentum investors on the sell side. "To me," he says, "to believe that your stocks selling for 90 percent of their value will perform as well or better than those priced at 60 percent says you really don't believe in your process. It only makes sense to me to sell the 90 percenters and buy the 60 percenters."

Nygren makes one exception to this sell discipline: He will hold on to a stock longer than normal for tax purposes. Taxes are an underappreciated cost to investors in the mutual fund business. Thus, Bill may retain a position beyond 90 percent of its fair value while he waits for the gains to become long term. However, there comes a point where the risk of losing capital exceeds the potential tax savings from waiting. He sells at that point regardless of the tax consequences.

As much as Nygren sticks to his discipline, he realizes that mechanically adhering to a set of rules could result in poor decisions during unusual periods. He modifies his 60/90 range during such times to take advantage of uncommon opportunities. For example, stock prices plunged sharply several times during the vicious bear market that began in early 2000. As a result, quality businesses sometimes traded for significantly less than 60 percent of their fair values. When Bill had the opportunity to purchase a stock for 50 percent of its worth instead of 60 percent, he would let go of another company early, say at 80 percent, to buy it. He simply adjusted the entire range down. What he won't do, however, is adjust the range up. He draws the selling line at 90 percent.

If purchasing firms at 60 percent of their intrinsic values is good, why not go a step further and only buy stocks selling at less than 50 percent of their fair values? Or 40 percent? Remember, the more stringent your buy criteria, the narrower your universe. Bill needs twenty stocks that meet his criteria at all times to execute his strategy. (This applies to the Oakmark Select Fund. The Oakmark Fund invests in about fifty stocks.) Experience has convinced him that the 60/90 rule lets him stay fully invested in most market environments. Stricter buy criteria would have forced him to keep money in cash at times.

Poor Fundamental Performance.   Nygren considers exiting a position when the business does not perform fundamentally like he thought it would. He considers two primary factors in this regard: management's actions and earnings progress.

As discussed earlier, Bill only invests in firms that he believes possess shareholder-oriented management. However, just because leadership is acting on behalf of the company's owners today does not mean they will continue doing so in the future. Management personnel can change. Executives' attitudes can veer off track. Compensation structures can be modified. Losing confidence that company leaders are continuing to act in the shareholders' best interests elicits a sell.

Nygren will also liquidate a security if he no longer believes the company can grow its profits at the market rate or if its earnings fall substantially below his original projections. "It's one thing if it earns 95 percent of what I thought it would. That's within a reasonable range of error," he explains. "However, if a couple of years go by and it has not grown, that is a serious error in my forecasting. Unless I can get comfortable with the reasons that caused the disappointment and am convinced they are not recurring issues with the business, I'll sell and replace it with another undervalued situation."

Just because a business generates results below Nygren's expectations does not necessarily mean it is faltering. He must also take into account how well it is performing relative to its peers. Perhaps a slumping economy or another external situation has caused every firm in its industry to deliver sub-par results. In such cases, the business may be executing just fine. However, if competitors are doing well and his company is not performing as expected—for example, it is losing instead of gaining market share—he will gladly sell it for 50 to 60 percent of what he hoped it was worth to move into something new.

Dealing with Mistakes.   Finally, Bill will sell a security because he realizes he made a mistake and the time has come to deal with it. Every serious investor will make numerous errors, even our masters. In Bill's words, "A big part of any investor's success or failure in this business is how they manage mistakes. Generally, the sooner you can admit them, the more likely you minimize their impact on your performance."

Hopefully his strict buy criteria keep his mistakes from costing as much as they might for most managers. With his knowledge and the research staff and technology he has at his disposal, you would think only a small percentage of Bill's investments turn out to be mistakes, right? Surprisingly, in hindsight, Nygren thinks he erred on as many as 40 percent of his stock picks! On the positive side, however, getting it right 60 percent of the time let him outperform the market by a wide margin.

Avoid Losses

When compounding money, a negative return one year can seriously damage your overall average returns, which explains why Bill focuses on minimizing the percentage of investments in which he makes mistakes and reducing the magnitude of those errors. He keeps the downside risk of an idea foremost in his mind before he looks at its upside potential.

When considering an investment, most investors focus on the question: "If everything works wonderfully, how great will it be?"

Instead, Nygren firsts asks: "If I am wrong, how bad can it be?" In that vein, he often repeats a Buffett quote: "There are two rules of investing. Rule number one is don't lose money. Rule number two is don't forget rule number one."

"If you focus on the not losing part," he says, "the upside usually takes care of itself."

Concentrated Portfolios

Bill believes a concentrated portfolio best utilizes his stock-picking ability and maximizes his performance potential. Although this belief goes against the grain of conventional wisdom, academic research supports it. In fact, studies have indicated that as few as twelve stocks spread across several industries can achieve adequate diversification. "The average mutual fund that holds 150 names goes that far out on the spectrum more for business reasons than for performance reasons," Nygren says. "This is a profession where managers focus a lot on the question: 'What mistake would it take to get me fired?' The answer usually centers around underperforming by a certain amount, so they develop a strategy to minimize the probability of that outcome."

Harris Associates takes the opposite approach and asks, "What maximizes the firm's chance of adding value relative to an index fund?" Index funds are worthy competitors and their fees are cheap relative to actively managed funds. Therefore, Harris believes that each of its portfolios must outperform its appropriate index to justify its existence. To help accomplish this, the firm concentrates all its funds more than the comparison benchmarks.

The Oakmark Select Fund takes that philosophy to the next level. The fund will always consist of approximately twenty stocks, and the top five positions will at times constitute 50 percent of its assets.

Money managers frequently mimic index funds with the majority of their portfolios and actively manage only a minor portion of them. However, investors pay active management fees based on the total portfolio value. Harris believes investors can accomplish this same goal much cheaper by putting 80 percent of their assets in index funds and giving 20 percent to real stock pickers who do not broadly diversify.

The Myth of Growth Versus Value Investing

Although Nygren considers himself a value investor, he believes the financial world has created an artificial distinction between the growth and value investment styles. When they use the terms *growth* versus *value*, investors are usually referring to *fundamental* versus *momentum* investing. A fundamental investor, whether growth or value, always prefers a cheaper stock price. To the contrary, a momentum investor views a lower stock price as a negative.

In practice, a lot of growth investors behave like momentum investors, and a lot of value investors act like antimomentum investors, which Bill believes makes for the confusion. This false distinction leads to the point of view that a stock should be tagged as growth or value based on the company's characteristics as opposed to the stock price. Bill bases that distinction entirely on a stock's price.

For example, when Bill bought Sun Microsystems, he received lots of e-mails from shareholders complaining that he had abandoned his value style and suddenly morphed into a growth investor. "It wasn't me that changed," he says. "It was the price on Sun. It used to sell at ten times sales. I bought it when it sold for a fraction of sales." Prices change, and a stock becomes under- or overvalued based on those changes.

KEY POINT
Bill's style does not limit the types of companies he'll buy. It just limits what he will pay for them.

The value universe constantly changes. In late 1999 and early 2000, the value arena contained almost no large-cap or technology stocks.

Instead, it was filled with mundane businesses that you had to stretch a little bit just to say they were average companies. But they sold at a third of the market multiple. Those stocks went up during the crash while large-cap and growth names plunged. As a result, by early 2003, an abundance of large-cap names and rapidly growing companies met Bill's value criteria.

Nygren's value bent does not cause him to shy away from buying shares of high-growth businesses. That stands in direct opposition to the idea that when a stock reaches a certain level of growth, those who carry the value investor card can no longer look there. Actually, the faster a firm is growing, the more it is worth. Because it possesses a higher intrinsic value, Bill is willing to pay a higher multiple for it. However, this is where his value orientation sets him apart from typical growth investors: the higher multiple he pays must still qualify as a 40 percent discount to the company's fair value PE.

Even so, Bill gets queasy with above market PE multiples. His experience has shown that a very small percentage of businesses grow at significantly above average rates long enough to justify high PEs. Therefore, he tends to look at entry prices that equal market multiples at most.

What characteristics would convince Bill to pay close to a market PE for a company? Anheuser-Busch (BUD) provides a good example.

At the time he bought it, BUD sported one of the highest entry multiples Bill has paid for a business (although it was still below the S&P 500's PE). "BUD's earnings growth history was very stable. I believe it had as much visibility as I could have gotten at the time for a five-year outlook of above average growth," Bill says. "It deserved a substantial premium multiple because of that. Even so, I'd still be unlikely to pay thirty times earnings for a stock I felt was worth forty-five times earnings. There are some growth investors who are good at that. I'm not, so I don't do it."

This belief goes back to Warren Buffett's circle of competence philosophy. Whether you are a professional or an individual investor, Bill says you must figure out what you are not good at. Then do not waste time developing a process for that style. If you stick with what you know, your areas of incompetence do not matter. For example, Bill believes he is not good at forecasting interest rates, predicting the future direction of the stock market, and identifying hypergrowth companies, so he uses a process that doesn't require him to do those things.

HOME DEPOT: A CLASSIC NYGREN BUY

Over a one-and-a-half–year period, Home Depot (HD) stock dropped from around $70 a share into the low twenties. Then in January 2003, Robert Nardelli, the retail giant's chief, announced that earnings growth would permanently slow from 18 to 20 percent a year to about 14 percent. The morning after the announcement, several analysts issued sell recommendations on the company. The stock plunged anew, hitting bottom at about $20 a share. Predictably, Nygren was buying throughout this tumultuous period. Within six months, the stock's price had climbed to $34. What did the master investor see that other analysts completely overlooked?

Background

Known for more than two decades for its consistently rapid growth, Home Depot once sold at close to *sixty times* its annual earnings. The board brought Robert Nardelli in from GE in 2000 to run the company when Arthur Blank, one of the cofounders, retired as CEO. The company's growth was slowing at the time, and the stock price fell sharply in response. When it reached the low twenties, the company was priced at a significant PE discount relative to both the market and to where other successful retailers had been purchased.

Nygren's Analysis

Home Depot was like many of Bill's finds—a fallen angel growth stock. The market had taken it from one pricing extreme to another. At the peak, the company needed to grow at an above average rate almost forever to justify its price. In the low twenties, investors had priced it for near-disastrous performance.

In analyzing the situation, others focused on gaining clarity as to which quarter the firm's growth would accelerate. Instead, Bill tried to determine what the company would look like in three to five years, taking into account the likelihood that the business would continue growing at an above average rate. He considered several factors in drawing his conclusions.

Bill thought the modifications Nardelli was making to the retailer would greatly benefit the business over time. The new CEO was taking advantage of the economies of scale that Home Depot had developed in its purchasing. He implemented six-sigma management principles. The organization structure was altered. Nardelli also instituted numerous other changes that tightened the company's operations.

Nygren also considered the stepped-up competition from Lowe's, which had seized the investment world's attention. Lowe's was outperforming Home Depot businesswise and in the stock market. In a classic case of David versus Goliath, the smaller competitor had come to dominate its larger adversary in same-store sales increases and income growth. Lowe's also appeared to be gobbling market share from the bigger retailer.

While Lowe's would likely impact Home Depot's sales over time, the home improvement market appeared big enough to support both concepts. It was clear that Lowe's was not going to put the orange-box stores out of business. Which was the better company, Home Depot or Lowe's, was not the issue for Bill. Home Depot did not have to perform as well as Lowe's for Bill to own its stock.

Nygren concluded that investors had overreacted and were pricing a great business experiencing temporary problems like it was headed for catastrophe. Bill completely disagreed with the market's interpretation of Home Depot's situation. "I could not imagine going out there and trying to argue this was a below average company. For the price to have been right when it was in the lower twenties, that was what you would have had to believe."

If Nygren was correct and the home improvement leader worked its way through its problems, investors were being set up to profit two ways: the company's PE would likely increase to reflect its still superior growth and at the same time its earnings were projected to grow faster than the market. This combination presented an opportunity that offered low downside risk with lots of upside potential.

SUMMARY

The following summarizes the main points of Nygren's investment philosophy:

Buy Criteria

- Buy stocks only when they sell for at least a 40 percent discount from their fair market values. If things do not go as well as you expect with an investment, this provides downside protection. If things go well, this gives a slingshot effect on the upside as the market closes the gap between a firm's price and its value.
- Avoid purchasing structurally disadvantaged businesses by requiring that companies' per share value growth plus dividends at least match the market's value growth.
- Demand that a firm's management treat its shareholders like partners. Make sure leaders' economic incentives are well aligned with shareholders' goals. Look for management that communicates openly with owners regarding the state of the business.
- Maintain a very long-term investment horizon. Focus on what a business will look like in five years.

Sell Criteria

- Sell a company when its price reaches 90 percent of its fair market value because (1) a firm is often worth less as a stand-alone entity than as an acquisition target; (2) valuing a business is not a precise exercise, and it is better to sell early than wait for a stock to reach what may be an overvalued level; (3) finding a buyer could prove difficult if all the shareholders hold on to a company until it reaches its full value before they sell it; and (4) buying a stock at 60 percent of its fair value should generate a higher return than holding one selling for 90 percent of its worth.
- Liquidate a position when a company fails to perform fundamentally as you expected.
- If you realize you made a mistake, the sooner you admit it and deal with it, the more likely you will minimize its impact on your performance.

Miscellaneous

- When you look at an investment, thoroughly explore its downside risk before you consider its upside potential.
- Running a concentrated portfolio maximizes your opportunity to outperform index funds.

CHAPTER 4

Christopher C. Davis

Portfolio Manager, Selected American Shares

Davis Advisors has accumulated a very impressive performance record since its founding over three decades ago. As of year-end 2003, the firm's Davis New York Venture Fund had outperformed the S&P 500 index in every rolling ten-year period since the fund's inception in 1969.[1] Managed almost identically to Davis New York Venture, Selected American Shares had bested the S&P 500, S&P/Barra Value, and S&P/Barra Growth indices since Davis began managing the portfolio in May 1993.

Davis's style of management has led him to consistently strong performance in both up and down markets. Selected American Shares nearly matched the performance of the S&P 500 during the heady years of 1996 to 1999—a time period that greatly favored growth funds, underperforming the index by only 4.1 percent. However, during the subsequent three bear market years of 2000 to 2002, Selected beat that index by over 18 percent.[2]

Christopher's performance has also shone relative to other managers in his category. As of December 31, 2003, Morningstar ranked Selected American Shares in the top 7 percent of its peer group over a five-year period and in the top 3 percent for the previous ten years.[3] During the eight years from 1996 to 2003, Selected performed in the top 12 percent of its category five times and underperformed its category average only once.[4]

CHRISTOPHER DAVIS COMES BY HIS INVESTMENT SKILLS HONESTLY. BORN into a family with deep roots on Wall Street, he is the grandson of legendary investor Shelby Cullom Davis and the son of Shelby M. C. Davis, founder of Davis Advisors.

PERSONAL BACKGROUND

Shelby Cullom Davis

Shelby Cullom Davis became a Wall Street legend by compounding $100,000 into over $800 million over a forty-five-year period. However, he did not start his career with the intention of becoming fabulously wealthy. Rather, he wanted to become an expert in public policy and earned a Ph.D. in international relations. He eventually wrote a book called *America Faces the Forties* that attracted the attention of Thomas Dewey, then governor of New York. Dewey hired Davis as an advisor and speechwriter in his failed presidential campaign against Harry S. Truman. After the election, Dewey retained his position as governor and appointed Davis as Deputy Superintendent of Insurance. "I often wonder how bad those speeches must have been to get an appointment like that," Christopher jokes. "It just doesn't sound like a plum job."

Spotting the Opportunity of a Lifetime

While serving in that office, Davis came to realize the enormous opportunity that the stock market and insurance companies in particular presented. Security prices remained depressed as the pain of the 1929 crash and the fear of another meltdown lingered in investors' minds. As a result, common stocks offered dividend yields higher than bond yields. Insurance companies, especially life insurance firms, were growing rapidly, but complex accounting masked their true values.

Life insurance businesses generally lost money the first year on new policies because they paid selling agents up-front commissions that typically exceeded the annual premiums. Yet companies obviously created value with each policy sold when considering the life expectancies of those insured and the fact that policies usually stayed in force for a number of years. On an accounting basis, however, it looked like a loss. Therefore, the fastest-growing firms often reported the biggest losses.

As a result, when Wall Street looked at insurance companies, it saw terrible businesses. Davis saw just the opposite. He recognized that if you modified insurance companies' accounting earnings to better reflect their true economic situations, many of those businesses traded for two or three times their adjusted earnings.

Inspired by this revelation and the opportunity at hand, Davis moved to New York and started a brokerage firm that specialized in insurance stocks. While his business sold research on those firms to institutional clients, the company served primarily as a vehicle for Shelby Cullom to invest his own capital in those businesses. He borrowed $100,000 to launch the firm. At his death his personal holdings had compounded to approximately $800 million.

Shelby M. C. Davis

Christopher's father began working for the Bank of New York in 1959. His claim to fame is that he became the bank's youngest vice president since Alexander Hamilton. He left in 1966 to start his own fee-based money management and financial counseling firm, Davis, Palmer, and Biggs. The company served a number of very high-quality institutions including the Smithsonian. In 1969, the firm expanded its offerings to attract noninstitutional clients by launching the Davis New York Venture Fund.

Shelby M. C. sold the institutional part of his business to Fiduciary Trust Company (FTC) in 1977. However, securities regulations prevented FTC from acquiring the mutual fund as part of the deal. So the mutual fund management company remained a separate entity, and managing the mutual fund became Shelby's primary focus.

A LEGACY OF FINANCIAL STOCKS

Christopher's grandfather taught him the many benefits of financial companies. As a result, those types of businesses comprise about 50 percent of Selected American Shares' assets. Although that represents a slightly higher level than normal, Christopher believes that financial firms currently offer the best opportunity to find expanding businesses at value prices. His grandfather called them growth stocks in disguise. The elder Davis saw several advantages to financial stocks: companies in that sector can often grow rapidly for many years and still own very low market shares, their products do not grow obsolete, and they operate in an industry where management makes a tremendous difference in a firm's performance.

Shelby Cullom Davis faced his share of critics who cast those same characteristics in a negative light to argue financial firms deserved to sell at a discount. They asserted that while insurance products may not grow obsolete, they were commodities. Davis contended that meant everybody was a potential customer, which explained why companies could expand at above average rates for long periods of time and still possess only a small share of the market.

Detractors also complained the industry was managed in a mediocre fashion. Davis countered that a field riddled with poor management allowed exceptional leadership to add tremendous value. In industries where the bar was high, a strong management team would not significantly enhance a firm's worth.

Finally, Davis liked that these companies generated a high level of cash. Because they did not have to reinvest much of their earnings in capital equipment, usually more than half of their profits were distributed to shareholders through either share repurchases or dividends.

Many of the qualities that first attracted Shelby Cullom Davis to financial stocks endure. Because of the expertise Christopher has developed in that area, those businesses offer him a wide circle of competence.

Christopher's Background

Christopher was born in New York. As you might expect, his father made a high priority of teaching his children about investing. Shelby M. C. had a gift to make investing not just comprehensible for the Davis children but genuinely interesting as well. As a result, he taught them about stocks much like any other father might teach his kids about basic home repair or changing a tire. His concern was not that they managed money for a living one day, but he felt they needed to understand investing as part of their necessary preparation for life.

Shelby believed that the technical concepts, such as accounting and PE ratios, would come with time. The children needed to understand only the basics—that a stock represents an ownership interest in a business and that a company's value is determined by its leaders' fundamental decisions that either create value or destroy it, not the price of its stock.

Beginning when the children were very young, he talked to them about Nike, Apple, and other businesses that were exciting to kids. As an added incentive to learn, he paid them $50 to write research papers on individual companies. Each paper had to describe the nature of the business and what competitive advantages it possessed. The children also had to call the company's Investor Relations Department, a daunting task for a young teenager. And, of course, they had to read the annual report.

Through the years, the research end of the business remained interesting to Christopher. When he started working full-time in the profession, he learned to dig deep into the numbers. But at that point he was only adding tools. His dad's tutelage had taught him the big picture years earlier.

The Beginning of a New Life

Christopher intended to start college when he had just turned eighteen, originally thinking he would attend Cornell University. However, an admissions officer recommended he delay his plans a year because he was younger than the other upcoming freshmen. The idea of taking off from school didn't fly at home, but a compromise solution opened up. Chris learned from his college counselor that St. Andrews in Scotland had begun accepting direct enrollment from American students for the first time ever. He could go there for a year and then come back to attend Cornell. His dad agreed with the plan, so Christopher was off to Scotland at summer's end.

Since he would attend St. Andrews for only a year, it made sense to take subjects he'd never be able to study again, so he picked philosophy, theology, and medieval history. The young Davis had never experienced anything like Scotland and St. Andrews, and he quickly came to relish several aspects of his life there. In particular, he cherished his newfound independence. He lived in a small cottage on a sheep farm with three other friends 3,000 miles away from home. For the first time, he was totally in charge of his life. It didn't take long for Christopher to fall in love with his surroundings and abandon his plans to attend Cornell.

A Left Turn

The time Christopher spent in Scotland encompassed the infamous coal miners strike, a very painful conflict that devastated many families and communities. Living in the middle of this grueling period in Scotland's history influenced Christopher to develop a strong left-wing political stance, which caused a lot of interesting discussion at home.

His grandfather was a staunch conservative and strong Reagan supporter who once chaired the Heritage Foundation, a conservative think tank. His father had adopted similar political and social views. Nevertheless, the two older Davises wisely tolerated Christopher's ideological differences and never let his beliefs become a major issue in their relationships.

In fact, their political differences became a source of some good-natured ribbing. His grandfather used to tell him, "If you're young and conservative, you lack a heart. If you're old and liberal, you lack a mind."

Christopher once took advantage of a business trip visiting Japanese insurance companies to enjoy a ten-day vacation in Thailand. While there he sent his dad what has become a well-publicized telegram telling him "the Revolution has begun here, and I have joined it."

"The subcontext of my degree was in moral philosophy and practical theology, so it was very much about ethics. I was really trying to understand the ethics of the capitalist system and the ethics of the socialist system," Christopher states. "I just don't think you can have a heart and look at the situation of the coal miners and their families and not think something ought to have been done."

While he still wishes a picture of Nixon did not adorn one of the walls in the Davis Advisors offices, life and working in the investment profession have tempered the extremism of Christopher's views. "There is a balance between helping others and the realities of our economic system. As you go through life, you see the benefits of free enterprise and the importance of the unfettered movement of capital."

An American in Paris

Chris spent his entire college career in Scotland. He completed the master's program at St. Andrews and received a dual degree in philosophy and theology, the first joint degree given by St. Andrews in those two subjects in five hundred years. A priest who Davis had known since childhood subsequently offered him a seminarian job at the American Cathedral in Paris. Chris accepted and left for France.

Moving to Paris after living in rural Scotland for several years was akin to arriving in Oz—everything turned to color. Davis was amazed at the city's beauty and culture.

The parish at which Christopher worked consisted largely of English-speaking young adults who attended college in Paris. From interacting with them, Chris discerned they had a common question: "What am I going to do when I graduate?" To help them answer that question, he put together a program on vocational opportunities.

As part of the weekly agenda, Davis invited members of the parish who were successful and happy with their career to speak to the group about their professions. Guests included a European editor from *Newsweek*, a priest, a diplomat, and an IBM executive among others.

The program greatly impacted Chris. He recognized that his strong desire to help people did not mean he wanted to become a priest. He also realized he had ignored a longstanding, excited interest in the research part of the investment profession.

Chris told his grandmother he had rediscovered an interest in business and was considering a career change. She gave him sage advice: "You're in your twenties. What you should do in your twenties is try as many lives as possible—different people, different jobs, and different geographies. If you're interested in business, try it! But don't dabble. Immerse yourself in it!"

Returning to His Investment Roots

Christopher was convinced. He moved to Boston and landed a job at State Street Bank as an entry-level fund accountant. State Street offered a terrific training program, paying for employees to take as many courses as they wanted. Christopher took full advantage of this program and attended several classes, accounting courses in particular. "That job," he says, "gave me the numerical grounding I did not have."

Davis left State Street during his second year to work for a New York money management firm, Tanaka Capital Management. Tanaka was small, but Chris felt he could play a big role there in terms of research processes. He specialized in financial companies, partly because of the tutoring he had growing up and partly because so many businesses in that space sold at ridiculously low prices due to the savings and loan crisis.

"I kept thinking about the movie *It's a Wonderful Life*," Chris says. "I realized that many ailing building and loan companies were all being tarred with the same brush as the corrupt S&Ls—you just had to separate them out. A lot of them were trading at low, single-digit multiples."

While at Tanaka, a watershed event occurred for Christopher. As he walked into a Chubb analyst meeting one afternoon, he looked around the room and saw his dad seated at the conference table taking notes on his signature yellow pad. Christopher sat down and noticed the older Davis gesturing. He looked in the designated direction and found his grandfather sitting across the table! Chris contemplated the fact that all three of them were studying Chubb and for the first time thought maybe there was a way they could work together.

Shortly after that incident, Shelby Cullom asked his grandson to come into his office on weekends and look over his books. The grandfather owned a number of small businesses and wanted to make sure their accounting was in order. The elder Davis gradually began discussing his concerns about the administration of his fortune after he died. It would first be used to support Christopher's grandmother for as long as she lived, then it would be transferred into a charitable foundation requiring ongoing supervision. He expressed apprehension about how those funds would be managed once he passed away.

Chris talked with his father and they worked out a plan by which the grandfather would gradually shift his portfolio to Davis-managed funds, where his assets would be overseen by an independent board of directors. Christopher left Tanaka in 1990 to work with his father and help coordinate this transition. He started by analyzing savings and loans during the S&L crisis, then expanded into banks and insurance companies. He continued to branch out from there.

When Chris came to work at Davis Advisors, his dad insisted they start a new mutual fund for Chris to manage. He argued that Chris needed his own report card, especially if the son was ever to approach the board to pursue a larger role in managing the funds. So they started the Davis Financial Fund in 1991. Christopher ran that fund until 1996, and it outperformed all the other Davis-advised funds during his tenure. Having his own successful performance record, the board felt comfortable with Christopher taking over as co-portfolio manager of Selected American Shares in 1994 and as the sole manager in 1997. Kenneth Feinberg joined Davis Advisors in 1994 and now equally shares responsibilities with Christopher in managing Selected American Shares and the Davis New York Venture Fund.

Fund Governance

Because of recent scandals and investigations, governance has become a hot topic in the mutual fund industry. Chris has always held strong views on how funds should be governed. Very importantly, he believes boards should consist of a supermajority—greater than 75 percent—of independent directors. That works well for Davis Advisors because Selected American's board is fiercely independent. In fact, it holds the distinction of being the only fund of significant size that has fired its manager proactively and voluntarily.

In addition to being independent, Davis and Selected funds board members have millions of dollars of their own family money invested in the funds. Chris thinks that constitutes the perfect governing structure because they don't care what the last name of the manager is— they only care about performance and fees.

DAVIS'S INVESTMENT PROCESS

Over a half century ago, Shelby Cullom Davis articulated the investment discipline that Davis Advisors still employs today: buy high-quality well-managed businesses at bargain prices and hold them for a long time. The process is designed to produce consistently strong performance over long periods of time. Christopher understands that placing among the very best over time does not require him to be number one every year. A popular saying among the Davis Advisors investment team is "Boring is beautiful."

Davis attempts to reduce risk and boost his returns through the two elements of his investment process: portfolio construction and security selection.

Portfolio Construction

Christopher groups his portfolio holdings into three major categories:

1. *Market leaders*: These companies represent the largest proportion of the fund. They are well-capitalized brand-name corporations that maintain strong balance sheets.
2. *Out-of-the-spotlight businesses*: These firms possess strong business fundamentals and capable managements but are typically under-followed or overlooked by investors. They make up a smaller percentage of the portfolio.
3. *Controversial names*: These businesses comprise the smallest segment of the fund. Their *headline risk* has caused investors to discount their prices relative to their fair values. Davis thinks the market has overcompensated for the actual risk associated with these names and believes they may appreciate significantly once

the controversy is resolved. Importantly, many companies now considered market leaders experienced periods of controversy when investors could buy them cheaply, such as American Express and Citicorp (now Citigroup).

Dividing the portfolio into these three categories allows Davis to invest in some higher-risk names that offer the potential for greater returns without jeopardizing the overall risk characteristics of the portfolio. However, even the higher-risk companies meet the same rigorous standards as all the other businesses in the fund.

Security Selection

The security selection process begins with the foundational principle that stocks are not pieces of paper like lottery tickets, but they represent ownership interests in real businesses. Once you accept that, there are only two questions you need to answer: (1) What kind of businesses do you want to own? and (2) How much should you pay for them?

What Kind of Businesses Make Good Investments?

Davis believes businesses that grow their values at above average rates for long periods of time make the best investments. To find those companies, you must first define what business characteristics foster the creation of value. Too often investors try to select securities without knowing specifically what qualities they are looking for. This makes the return they get more a matter of luck than of purposeful investing. Davis groups the criteria that describe superior businesses into three categories: financial strength, competitive advantages, and shareholder-oriented management.

Financial Strength.   Christopher looks for companies with two key financial characteristics: a strong balance sheet and high returns on invested capital.

Strong Balance Sheet.   "Because we hold investments for long periods, I want to feel confident the businesses we buy can endure an economic downturn," Davis says. Good liquidity and low debt levels help corporations survive lean times and even take advantage of opportunities that sometimes arise when industry conditions get tough.

Return on Invested Capital.   Beyond a clean balance sheet, Chris looks for companies that can reinvest capital at high rates of return. A firm's worth is determined by its earnings and the rate at which they grow. The return a business generates on its invested capital plays a key role in determining how fast its earnings will increase and therefore how quickly and consistently the firm's value will rise.

To better understand a company's return on capital, let's review some concepts. A business makes money by investing in profitable ventures, such as building a manufacturing plant or opening a new store. The capital it invests comes from selling shares of stock to the public, borrowing, issuing stock for acquisitions, and retained earnings. Dividing the firm's annual income by its invested capital gives its return on capital—the return management has earned on shareholders' money.

To measure the company's income, Chris calculates a figure he refers to as owner earnings. (Please refer to the section on "Valuing a Company" later in this chapter for a discussion on how to compute owner earnings.) This figure is similar to a firm's net income but with a few adjustments to reflect a business's true cash earnings.

Theoretically, most corporations only grow because they reinvest some or all of their earnings back into their operations or raise additional capital. The profit they make on the new capital they invest each year is known as their *return on incremental capital*, or their *reinvestment rate*. Rather than looking at the company's total return on its entire capital base, this figure reveals the returns a business gets on new money it invests and lets you see current trends in the firm's earnings ability—that is: Is it generating higher or lower returns than in the past?

KEY POINT

Firms with high returns on incremental capital can compound their earnings and grow their values very rapidly.

Think of a company's management team as money managers. When you invest in a corporation, its leaders invest your capital and generate a return on it. Each year they reinvest some or all of the gains on your behalf. Evaluating their past performance helps you determine how skillfully they have reinvested capital and gives you an idea of the future return they will generate. To facilitate this analysis, Chris manipulates a company's financial statements to make them resemble a money manager's performance report. This is illustrated in the appendix at the end of the chapter.

Determining a firm's reinvestment rate serves several purposes: First, it gives you insight into a key aspect of the company's financial strength. Second, it answers the question: How effectively has management allocated shareholders' capital? Finally, it plays an important role in determining a corporation's fair market value, as I will discuss shortly.

Competitive Advantages.   Good businesses generate high returns on invested capital. Bad businesses generate very low returns. In a capitalist society such as the United States, money flows where returns are high. So if a corporation earns above average returns, Christopher wants to know why. He then tries to determine if those superior returns are sustainable or if competition is likely to eat away at them. To make this determination, he asks: Does the business possess competitive advantages that will protect its earnings from being eroded by others? Or, as Warren Buffett would ask: What are the moats around the business?

Competitive advantages can take many forms. Companies can develop strong brand names that inspire tremendous customer loyalty. Firms might possess legal advantages that prevent competitors from entering their fields, such as licenses, patents, or copyrights. Perhaps their lean cost structures allow them to sell their products at the lowest prices. Maybe they have achieved enormous economies of scale. These are but a few of the competitive advantages firms may possess.

Shareholder-Oriented Management.   Apart from external factors, it is the decisions of management that determine whether a business grows in the future. Therefore, Chris wants to learn everything he can about the quality of the partner who will run the business. He meets directly with management as an essential part of his process.

Davis determines whether the leaders have a history of allocating capital efficiently on behalf of shareholders. The work he has done to understand their return on incremental capital goes a long way in this regard. However, he goes deeper—he strives to understand the thought process and logic behind their capital allocation decisions. Before he invests in a company, he ensures that managers have a strong understanding of their cost of capital and the return they expect to achieve on investments. It is surprising how many managers do not understand these basic concepts or their roles as stewards of shareholders' capital.

Furthermore, management must have a strategic vision for the company and a realistic plan to achieve it. A business can go no further than its managers see. A vision helps focus a business's energies and resources into the most productive areas. Without that focus, a firm will tend to be easily distracted from its main mission and become vulnerable to losing market share.

Finally, management's interests must be aligned with shareholders. Davis looks for owner-operators who deal honestly and forthrightly with stockholders.

Dealing with Subjective Information

When evaluating a business and its management, you will sift through a lot of objective, quantitative information. You can easily calculate and measure data such as PE ratios, debt-to-equity ratios, and profit growth. However, some qualitative aspects of your analysis will require you to make subjective judgments. Unfortunately, you cannot compute an honesty ratio that ensures management will always be truthful with shareholders.

So how do you grade companies and management teams on subjective issues? Christopher completes a table on every business he analyzes, as illustrated in Table 4.1. He divides the table into two categories: a business analysis and a management analysis. The far left column lists several relevant topics of consideration under each category. Davis assigns one of five grades—above average, average, below

TABLE 4.1

Subjective Information

	Above Avg	Avg	Below Avg	N/A	Not Known	Notes
Business Analysis						
Return on Invested Capital		X				Return on equity 12.6%; Reinvestment Rate 9.8%
Pricing Power		X				Increasing competition pressuring margins
Brand Power			X			2nd-tier products
Low Cost Structure		X				Some economies of scale
Enduring Products		X				Wide product range; a few lines nonobsoletable
Management Analysis						
Honesty	X					Straightforward and truthful; openly shares negatives
Reflect Shareholders' Interest			X			No incentive programs for employees to buy stock
Compensation Policies			X			Too many options issued
Nonpromotional		X				View of industry too optimistic

average, not applicable, and not known—to each topic based on his analysis. He makes notes to the side of each grade to substantiate his score.

Chris includes the following topics, among others, in his table:

Business Analysis

- *Return on invested capital*: Davis uses several measures to determine the return a business earns on its capital. The easiest figure to obtain is the return on equity. The return on invested capital, return on adjusted invested capital, and reinvestment rate figures also go here.
- *Pricing power*: The nature of a company's products and/or a lack of competition may give a business the ability to raise prices or

keep prices high. However, competition forces the prices of some commodity-like products, such as computers, to remain low.

- *Brand power*: Is the brand well known and dominant in its field, or is it a second-tier product?
- *Low cost structure*: This quality may result in higher margins and/or give a business the ability to sell its products at lower prices than its competitors.
- *Enduring products*: Trendy goods—for example, most fashion apparel—force management to continually forecast popular styles correctly in order to generate consistent revenue growth. Other goods such as many technology products become obsolete quickly. Both score low because there is more margin for error. Enduring products that score high include such varied items as paper towels, laundry detergent, savings accounts, and mortgages.

Management Analysis:

- *Honesty*: Compare past statements to what later became public knowledge to determine how honest management has been.
- *Reflect shareholders' interests*: Does the business repurchase shares? Do management and employees own a high percentage of the company's stock?
- *Compensation policies*: A high use of stock options dilutes ownership for shareholders. High-scoring companies encourage employees to purchase shares of the business through various types of stock purchase plans.
- *Nonpromotional*: You want management to openly discuss the good, the bad, and the ugly regarding the state of the business and not to constantly put a positive spin on all the issues.

Valuing a Company

Once Christopher's analysis has convinced him that a business generates high returns on capital and is capable of sustaining those returns, he determines a fair value price for the company.

Wall Street frequently uses the PE ratio to value stocks. However, fundamental problems with both the price and the earnings figures limit the ratio's usefulness. Accordingly, Chris adjusts both numbers to come up with what he believes is a much more accurate measure.

True Price.   A stock's market price does not convey the total cost you pay to buy a business. It ignores the company's debt, cash, and other adjustments needed to determine a company's real price, as shown in Table 4.2.

Let me illustrate this concept with an example. Assume you are evaluating two rental houses for possible purchase. One sells free of debt, but you must assume a $50,000 mortgage liability to buy the second. Otherwise, the houses are identical in every respect. Obviously the debt on the second house reduces its value. Its *purchase price* reflects only what you would pay for its equity, but your *total cost* would include the debt as well. The first house is worth $50,000 more than the second one.

In the same way, a stock's price shows what you would pay to buy only the company's equity. That price times the number of common shares outstanding equals a firm's market capitalization, or market cap—the total value the market has placed on the corporation's equity. However, the company's creditors have senior claims on the

---

TABLE 4.2

Enterprise Value

   Price
X Number Shares Outstanding
   Market Capitalization

+ Long-Term Debt
− Cash
   Net Debt

− Other Assets Marked to Market
+ Other Liabilities Marked to Market
   Enterprise Value

÷ Number Shares Outstanding
   Enterprise Value Per Share (Adjusted Price Per Share)

firm's assets, and the business must service its debt before it can pay a dividend. Thus, shareholders can't get their hands on the corporation's money until its obligations to the creditors have been met. So you must add the company's debt to its market cap in calculating your total cost. Chris includes underfunded pension and health care liabilities as part of the debt.

On the positive side, not only do you acquire a firm's debt when you buy the company, but you get its cash as well. The business can pay down debt or make a distribution to shareholders with this money. Therefore, you should subtract a company's cash from your cost of purchasing its stock.

Chris makes other changes as well to reflect the true value of various assets and liabilities on a firm's balance sheet.

Davis calls the total cost you pay for a business after all the modifications its *adjusted enterprise value*. He divides the adjusted enterprise value of the firm by the average number of shares outstanding to obtain its adjusted enterprise value per share, or adjusted price per share. This figure represents your true cost to buy the business.

Owner Earnings

Just as a company's price does not reflect the total cost to buy the firm, a corporation's reported earnings do not necessarily mirror its true cash profits. Accounting rules give businesses a lot of flexibility in handling numerous issues. Depending on their objectives, managers can accelerate or defer the recognition of many revenue and expense items, giving them room to manipulate their annual performance. Keep in mind that the market strongly incentivizes corporate managers to adopt those accounting policies that will optimize their firm's current results.

For example, assume management wants to minimize its company's taxable income. Managers would expense purchases immediately that could be written off over a period of years, use the shortest available depreciation schedules, defer revenue, and put up reserves to increase current expenses. Conversely, if managers want to maximize their firm's current income, they would take just the opposite actions.

To arrive at a firm's true profits, Chris calculates a cash-based figure he calls *owner earnings*. Owner earnings reflect the excess profits a company generates after reinvesting enough earnings to maintain its current level of operations before it reinvests for growth. This is the real cash corporations can use to pay dividends, acquire other businesses, buy back shares, or reinvest for growth, as opposed to a derived accounting figure. To calculate its owner earnings, Davis adjusts a company's accounting profits for depreciation, capital expenditures, and other miscellaneous items.

Depreciation.   A company that buys an asset with a useful life of several years does not generally *expense* the asset—that is, it does not write the item's entire cost off the first year. Rather, the firm *allocates* part of its cost to each year of the asset's operation. So even though the business may pay the entire purchase price of the asset up front, it shows only part of that cost each year as *depreciation* expense. (A similar concept known as *amortization* applies to certain types of assets. I will use depreciation to include both concepts.) Because depreciation is an allocated cost, or paper expense, it does not reflect the actual cash the company spends on equipment and other long-lived assets in any given year.

Maintenance Spending.   Investors refer to the money corporations must spend each year on capital assets, such as equipment and facilities, as capital expenditures, or capex (pronounced kap-ex) for short. Some of that money goes to replace assets that wear out and are no longer useful. Chris refers to the expenditures necessary just to sustain the firm's current level of operations as *maintenance spending*. Management invests the remaining funds in new assets used to grow the business.

A company's financial statements do not capture the difference between depreciation, the costs *allocated* for capital expenditures, and maintenance spending, the *actual cash spent* to maintain the firm's production level. Most corporations' maintenance spending exceeds their depreciation because of inflation, although this is not always true. Some capital-intensive businesses must spend well above their depreciation every year to replace worn-out assets. These companies tend to operate at lower profit margins and either grow slowly or carry high debt levels to support their growth. Other firms can maintain their current level of production with only minor capital expenditures, thereby boosting margins and often leaving management with lots of excess cash to reinvest or distribute to shareholders.

Computing Owner Earnings.   Table 4.3 illustrates Davis's owner earnings calculations. He first multiplies a firm's pretax operating income by its reported tax rate to arrive at its after-tax operating income. He then adds the difference between depreciation and maintenance spending to that figure. This adjustment substitutes true cash expenditures for paper expenses and results in the corporation's *cash after-tax operating income*. Chris will adjust this number further for the cost of options granted, inflated pension assumptions, and other miscellaneous items to arrive at the firm's owner earnings.

Company Coupon

Now that Christopher knows a business's cash earnings and the total cost to buy the firm, he can compute its POE (price-to-owner earnings ratio), or adjusted PE. For example, assume you pay an adjusted price of $130 per share for a company that generates $10 in owner earnings the first year. The firm's POE, or *multiple*, equals 13.

TABLE 4.3

Owner Earnings

	Operating Income
−	Taxes at Reported Rate
	After-Tax Operating Income
+	Depreciation and Amortization
−	Maintenance Spending
	Cash After-Tax Operating Income
−	Stock Option Cost
+/−	Pension Adjustments
+/−	Miscellaneous Items
	Owner Earnings

Although a company's POE is useful, it is really only a step toward a more important number. Chris inverts this figure to develop a firm's owner earnings yield, or coupon rate, analogous to a bond's interest rate and a key tool in his valuation process. Since a business's earnings correspond to a bond's interest, it makes sense that a firm's coupon equals its owner earnings per share divided by its adjusted price. *A company's coupon is the initial return Davis expects an investment in the business to produce.* In our example, it equals about 7.7 percent.

KEY POINT

Note that Davis does not try to predict a stock's future price to determine a business's potential return. *Rather, he focuses on issues related to the company's fundamental performance and the earnings the firm generates on its invested capital* to evaluate the firm's investment potential. He assumes a stock's price will follow the corporation's value over time.

The higher a stock's price, the lower its owner earnings yield. To make sure he doesn't pay too much for a stock, Christopher compares the owner earnings yield of a company to that of other potential investments as well as the risk-free rate (he uses the yield on the thirty-year Treasury bond as a proxy for the risk-free rate).

KEY POINT

Davis views a compelling value investment as a business with a high reinvestment rate that can be purchased at an owner earnings yield above the risk-free rate. His ideal investment is analogous to a bond that offers an attractive current yield and a growing stream of future coupons.

A company that reinvests retained earnings at a higher rate than its earnings yield is like a bond that pays 7 percent initially but reinvests interest payments at 15 percent. As your principal grows and the bond continues returning the higher rate on reinvested funds, your effective yield eventually approaches 15 percent.

Developing a Fair Value Range

Every financial asset is worth the same thing—the discounted present value of its future cash flows. Davis's analysis up to this point offers a realistic picture of those cash flows for a company—its owner earnings this year plus the future incremental returns on retained earnings—and the price you'll pay to capture them.

Starting from this "most likely" case, you can plug in a variety of optimistic and pessimistic growth-rate assumptions to compute a range of possible future cash flows. Discounting those cash flows back to present values yields a range of fair values for the stock. Since the projections contain a number of uncertainties and many figures are involved in the calculations, there is obviously some room for error. Therefore, you should develop a rather wide valuation range.

According to Christopher, "That's how I deal with risk. I don't change the discount rate I use. Instead, I just broaden the possible outcomes, which means widening the range of fair values."

Davis's fair value range for a business establishes the basis for his buy/hold/sell decisions. He buys a stock only when it sells below the lowest price in his range. He holds a company when it sells within the range, and he sells it when its price pops out of the top of the range.

A company's fair value range should move up over time as its earnings grow. If the range is $30 to $60 per share this year, it might be $33 to $66 next year, and so on, depending on how the business performs fundamentally.

With all his calculations, Davis understands that valuation is not a precise science. His partner, comanager Ken Feinberg, jokes, "We'd rather be approximately right than precisely wrong." Fortunately, making good investment choices does not typically require a high degree of precision. Generally, the numbers will clearly show that company

A would make a substantially better investment than company B. Rather than try to calculate precise values for both businesses, Chris just wants to make sure he owns A instead of B and that he does not overpay for A. Buying a stock below its fair value range gives him a wide margin of safety so that a company does not have to perform perfectly for his investment to do well.

Davis stresses the importance of the durability of a company's earnings growth. "Buffett said that 20 percent of the companies in the S&P 500 will earn substantially less five years from now than they earn today because of changes in the competitive landscape," Christopher says. "Another 5 to 10 percent may be earning less because of litigation or some fundamental flaws in their businesses. So one out of four companies that comprise the S&P 500 might be earning less in five years than today. With those odds, picking the right businesses is far more important than whether or not you are precisely right about their future cash flows."

How does Davis determine a discount rate for computing the present value of a firm's future cash flows? He begins by asking, "What return do I need to own a business?" Each investor needs to answer this critical question. Christopher strives to earn a minimum of 10 percent on every investment. Once he has projected a company's cash flows, simple math yields the maximum price he can pay to generate that return. However, since his process stresses valuing firms relative to each other, he believes the specific discount rate he chooses is not critical as long as he uses the same rate for every company.

A TALE OF TWO COMPANIES

Christopher's owner earnings analysis reveals a lot about the quality of businesses he examines. Some companies with low returns on incremental capital are forced to reinvest money at low returns. Others suffer from self-inflicted wounds. Davis uses a specialty retailer and a railroad to illustrate how two firms can generate low returns on capital for completely different reasons.

In the case of the retailer, the core business generated very predictable earnings and required little capital to maintain its operations—two key ingredients in the formula for a successful investment. Management, however, did a poor job reinvesting the company's retained earnings. For example, it spent huge sums on new concepts that eventually failed and built a very expensive headquarters facility.

If the company's leaders had simply returned its excess cash to shareholders, investors would have obtained a 10 percent return based on the stock's price at the time Davis examined it. Fortunately, management eventually realized its mistakes and started returning more of the firm's earnings to shareholders by aggressively repurchasing shares.

For a different scenario, consider a railroad company that Davis once analyzed. Although well managed, it also reinvested earnings at low returns. Assume it sold at a 10 percent owner earnings yield. Like the electronics store, it would be tempting to think that it could have generated an adequate return for investors by simply distributing its excess cash instead of reinvesting it. Unfortunately, that wasn't the case. Unlike the electronics retailer, the railroad had to reinvest a large part of its earnings just to maintain its operations, and it got very poor incremental returns on that reinvested capital.

Both situations involved cheap stocks that generated low returns on incremental money. However, in the first case, the electronics store's managers created the problem. Therefore, they could correct the problem. In the second case, low returns on reinvested capital were a *structural* problem caused by the nature of the business. Nothing was going to fix that.

Although not his ideal investment, Davis will sometimes buy businesses such as the specialty retailer if they get cheap enough, figuring that sooner or later management will come to its senses and correct its mistakes. Shareholders will likely get their hands on the excess cash at some point. However, it would be hard to justify buying the railroad. Its need to reinvest incremental earnings at low returns makes it unlikely that the shareholders will ever receive substantial cash from their investment.

The country's largest retailer illustrates the benefits of profitably reinvesting cash flow. "What has made Wal-Mart so powerful," Chris says, "has been their ability to reinvest massive amounts of capital at very high returns."

COMMON MISTAKES THAT GROWTH AND VALUE INVESTORS MAKE

By ignoring any of the steps in evaluating companies, growth and value investors tend to repeat certain mistakes. When a typical value investor buys a stock with a 15 percent earnings yield, he believes he will average at least that return on his investment. However, if management reinvests that yield in building factories that generate only 5 percent, his return over time will likely fall well short of that 15 percent.

Conversely, if an investor focuses solely on a firm's growth and overpays for its stock, she too will likely earn a sub-par return over time. Suppose she buys a business at a 2 percent earnings yield and it doubles its income over the next five years. At that point she is earning only 4 percent on her original investment, which is still below the current risk-free rate.

Both sides often miss the balance that exists between the two extremes. Growth investors would do well to pay attention to the prices they pay for businesses, and value investors should pay heed to companies' returns on incremental capital.

KEY POINT

Once you understand the roles that price and reinvestment rate play in determining the quality of an investment, you realize why the growth versus value argument makes no sense. Growth is a component of valuation. Companies that grow profitably are worth more than those that don't.

Rapidly growing businesses can sell at undervalued and overvalued prices, just like slow-growing firms. Their over- or undervaluation is unrelated to the fact that they are growing rapidly.

SELL DISCIPLINE

Christopher bases his sell discipline on the same criteria as his buy discipline: financial strength, competitive advantages, quality of management, and value. Therefore, he will sell positions partially or in their entirety for any of three reasons: (1) The business's fundamentals deteriorate in financial strength or competitive advantages. (2) He loses confidence that management is acting in the shareholders' best interests or believes management is not being honest and forthright. (3) A stock becomes overvalued.

RISK MANAGEMENT

In order to manage risk, you must first define it: What exactly are you trying to manage? Academic literature often characterizes risk as stock price volatility. Davis disagrees with this view. In a given year, the share price of any publicly traded company can fluctuate significantly for a number of reasons. Most of these reasons reflect short-term changes in investor psychology about the business, not changes in the quality of the business.

Christopher prefers Benjamin Graham's definition of risk: "a loss of value which . . . is caused by a significant deterioration in the company's position—or, more frequently perhaps, is the result of the payment of an excessive price in relation to the intrinsic worth of the security."[5] Thus, Graham viewed risk as a permanent loss of capital, which he distinguished from what he called quotational loss—the likelihood that a stock will trade *temporarily* below an investor's cost.[6] Price fluctuations have no bearing on an asset's intrinsic value, which is based on its long-term earning power and therefore should not be confused with risk.

Davis believes that trying to manage short-term price fluctuations is a loser's game and misses the point of risk control. Instead, he focuses his attention on the long-term drivers of business value and avoiding a permanent loss of capital.

Most investors think of risk management in terms of dealing with problems as they arise in a portfolio. Davis believes that risk manage-

CONTRASTING MANAGEMENT STYLES

Christopher shares a similar investment philosophy with his grandfather and father. Any style differences relate more to nuances than to different approaches.

Christopher's grandfather rarely sold anything. Upon his death, he owned almost every stock he had ever bought. The eldest Davis heavily concentrated his portfolio in just a few companies. In fact, ten firms accounted for about 70 percent of his assets. Almost all of those were focused in two subsectors of the financial services sector: property and casualty firms and life insurance businesses. Internationally he held big positions in Japanese insurance companies.

Christopher's father was much more of a generalist, so he normally stayed more diversified and held less concentrated positions than the elder Davis. His largest holdings generally represented no more than 5 percent of his portfolio, and about forty stocks comprised 70 percent of his funds. Shelby M. C. Davis bought and sold stocks more frequently as well, with turnover ranging from 20 to 60 percent annually. He held virtually no foreign securities.

Christopher comes down between the two of them in virtually every category. His annual turnover ranges between 15 and 30 percent. Forty stocks typically comprise 85 percent of his portfolios, with the top ten companies making up 40 percent. His largest positions will take up between 4 and 8 percent of his funds' assets.

ment starts before he makes an investment. Experience has taught him that a long-term track record of success is built as much by avoiding big mistakes as by picking big winners. Therefore, he designed his buy criteria to help him steer clear of future problems. He conducts extensive research to convince himself that a company's long-term earnings power is sustainable, reducing the odds of declining performance. Christopher hopes to further lessen his chances of losing capital by purchasing businesses at discounts to their fair values.

Christopher's sell discipline attempts to manage the risk of existing holdings by liquidating a security when a loss of capital becomes more probable. As Graham pointed out, this could be due to declining fundamentals or the price having become excessive relative to the company's value.

Finally, Davis understands that his batting average is what matters as a money manager. Not every stock pick will develop as he anticipates. Therefore, he will always hold a meaningful number of securities in the portfolio, many of them uncorrelated, to limit the potential negative impact of any single stock. He weights each stock according to his view of its valuation and business risk.

THEMATIC INVESTING

As I discussed earlier, Davis invests mostly in companies with competitive advantages that are leaders in their industries. Christopher hunts mostly in the fields of large corporations to find firms with these traits. Additionally, he wants businesses that can consistently grow their values over long periods of time. To unearth these companies, Davis tries to identify themes or long-term trends that will benefit certain types of businesses disproportionately. While well-managed firms sometimes prosper in industries that are not doing well, having an industry-wide tailwind can only benefit a business and help propel it to above average performance.

Thematic investing differs from sector investing, with which most investors are familiar. When investors focus on a sector, they concentrate on a particular area of the stock market, such as retail or managed health care. In contrast, themes can be very specific and impact individual companies or industries, or they can affect broad areas of the economy and encompass many sectors. Davis offers two themes as examples of the kinds of trends he looks for: America's changing age demographics and the expansion of the Internet.

The graying of America represents one of the most obvious current trends. As the huge baby-boom generation reaches senior status, Davis believes the long-term demand for certain financial services and health care products will soar.

For example, the leading edge of the baby boomers will start exiting the workforce around 2008, increasing the demand for retirement services. Also, as members of the World War II generation pass on, they will transfer trillions of dollars to their children, who will need help investing those funds. Finally, older people consume a disproportionately high percentage of prescription medicines. While not all financial service firms and pharmaceutical companies will benefit, trends like these provide a logical starting point for researching individual companies.

Regarding Internet usage, online commerce will likely grow, both absolutely and as a percentage of total commerce, for many years into the future. You can play this theme two ways:

1. Invest directly in dot-com companies, many of which have not yet become profitable.
2. Buy firms that provide infrastructure for online commerce, such as overnight delivery companies and protective packaging businesses. Financial companies with large credit-card operations should also benefit since Internet firms do not accept cash.

Davis gravitates toward businesses in the second category as a safer way to take advantage of the trend. Many of those firms are well-established, highly profitable leaders in their fields.

Thematic investing not only helps Davis identify opportunities, but it also helps him avoid future problems. The same forces that will propel some companies forward will create a strong headwind against others. For instance, as the aging of baby boomers ignites the demand for health care products, health care costs will likely rise. This situation threatens to undermine the profits of firms with large underfunded health care liabilities. Retiring boomers will likewise strain the economics of corporations with sizable underfunded pension liabilities.

Investors need to consider both the opportunities and the dangers brought about by major trends. Big secular changes can create enormous opportunities to accumulate wealth by compounding money at above average rates for very long periods of time. However, thematic investing should not substitute for rigorous company-by-company research. Davis combines thematic top-down investing with thorough fundamental analysis to find those businesses he believes can reinvest capital at high rates of return for many years.

THE MISTAKE WALL

Christopher insists that dealing with mistakes is an important part of his, as well as any investor's, success. So he devised a unique way for the Davis Advisors investment team members to learn from their errors: the Mistake Wall. They hang framed stock certificates of their biggest mistakes every year on a wall in the research department. Those certificates, which remain on the wall permanently, have plaques attached at the bottom that detail the lessons learned by team members.

"We look for lessons that can transfer to other situations," Davis says. "Sometimes mistakes in judgment, like misjudging an individual or misevaluating a business strategy, are hard to transfer to other situations because they are so specific. However, we want to make sure we never make the quantifiable mistakes again. Rubbing our noses in mistakes is very important because it helps keep the process rational and keeps us learning from them."

Chris comments on how the Mistake Wall helped team members sidestep one disaster: "What we learned from our mistakes in Lucent saved us a fortune by helping us avoid the Enron fiasco. It was the same situation: Where's the cash? We couldn't get over the fact they were generating accounting earnings but no cash."

THE UNRECOGNIZED SCANDAL

Christopher has one final piece of advice for stock market investors—stay invested!

Jack Bogel, former chairman of the Vanguard Group, conducted a study that revealed stock mutual fund investors compounded their money over a long period of time at a significantly lower rate than the funds in which they invested. Why did this happen? Because of constantly switching funds at the wrong times—the result of chasing performance.

"Our team focuses on adding value above the S&P 500 over time. I could look myself in the mirror at the end of my career if I felt like we achieved that goal," Chris says. "But it's important to make sure that as many of our investors as possible participate in that performance. I feel very strongly about that in terms of the whole culture of the organization. I think it's an enormous unrecognized scandal in the industry."

Several factors, many of which are embedded in the very nature of the mutual fund industry, contribute to the problem. Fund salespeople push hot recent performance. Investment firms often incentivize money managers and analysts based on short-term results. Magazine ads focus on trailing three-year performance (which always seems to be high). "Desiring good short-term results is human nature; it's what people want. But investors have to discipline themselves to focus on the long term and avoid overreacting to the short term," Davis concludes.

SUMMARY

The following summarizes the main points of Davis's investment philosophy:

Portfolio Construction

- The highest percentage of the portfolio over time should consist of market leaders, large brand-name corporations, with strong balance sheets.
- Also look for potential investments in out-of-the-spotlight companies—that is, underfollowed firms with strong business fundamentals.
- Controversy often creates great buying opportunities, but these names should comprise a relatively small segment of your

portfolio at any given time. These firms offer substantial appreciation potential because their headline risks have caused investors to discount their values significantly below their fair values.

Security Selection

- Proper investing begins with the foundational principle that stocks are not pieces of paper, but they represent ownership positions in real businesses. Once you understand this, only two questions must be answered: (1) What kind of businesses do you want to own? (2) How much should you pay for them?
- Corporations that grow their values at above average rates for long periods of time make the best investments if they are purchased at fair prices. The criteria that describe superior businesses fall into three categories: (1) financial strength, including a clean balance sheet and the ability to reinvest capital at high rates of return; (2) durable competitive advantages; and (3) shareholder-oriented management.
- To value a company, first determine how much you must really pay to own it by calculating its enterprise value, or adjusted price, per share. Next, compute its owner earnings to arrive at its true cash profits. Dividing its adjusted price by its owner earnings gives its POE ratio, a more accurate version of the standard PE.
- Inverting a firm's POE ratio produces its owner earnings yield, also known as its bond equivalent yield, or coupon. An ideal investment has a high reinvestment rate and can be purchased at a coupon above the risk-free rate.
- A company's future cash flows equal its owner earnings this year plus its future incremental returns on retained earnings. From this "most likely" scenario, you can plug in several optimistic and pessimistic assumptions to develop a range of possible cash flows. Discounting these future cash flows to a present value generates a range of fair values for the firm.
- Buy a stock only when it is priced below the fair value range, hold it when it sells within the range, and liquidate a security when its price pops out of the top of the range.

APPENDIX:
COMPUTING THE REINVESTMENT RATE

To compute a company's reinvestment rate, Christopher first calculates the return the business earned on its invested capital every year for the past ten years, as illustrated in Table 4.4. This shows not only the company's total return on capital, but it allows him to calculate the annual return on incremental capital as well. The key to these computations is determining exactly how much capital shareholders had invested with the company each year.

The standard formula for calculating a firm's invested capital is straightforward:

> Total Assets
> − Cash
> − Non-Interest-Bearing Current Liabilities
> _____
> Invested Capital

Dividing the owner earnings by the average invested capital for any year gives the company's total return on capital for that year. As you can see, the firm in our illustration generated returns of about 7.5 percent in 1995 and 1996. Those returns grew to 10.6 percent by 2001, then slipped back to 9.9 percent by 2003.

Think of this company as a bond. It appears that shareholders received an average 8.8 percent return over ten years. However, management generated a 10 percent return on the incremental capital it invested. Not bad!

However, to analyze the situation correctly, Davis wants to make sure he properly charges managers for all the money invested with them. So, Chris makes a couple of adjustments. First, he adds back charge-offs. A charge-off, which represents an evaporation of capital, occurs when a company writes off a bad investment. Money managers can't write off investments that go sour, so corporate managers should be held accountable for charge-offs when evaluating their performance.

TABLE 4.4

Reinvestment Rate

	1994	1995	1996	1997	1998	1999	2000	2001	2002	2003	Cum	Change	Wtd Avg[1]
Owner Earnings	200.0	230.0	264.5	312.0	378.0	469.0	565.0	674.0	712.0	804.0		604.0	
Incremental O/E		30.0	34.5	47.5	66.0	91.0	96.0	109.0	38.0	92.0			
Invested Capital													
Total Assets	3,287.0	3,714.3	4,197.2	4,742.8	5,359.4	6,056.1	6,843.4	7,733.0	8,738.3	9,874.3		6,587.3	
− Cash	25.0	28.0	31.4	35.1	39.3	44.1	49.3	55.3	61.9	69.3		44.3	
− Noninterest Bearing CL	362.0	412.7	470.5	536.3	611.4	697.0	794.6	905.8	1,032.6	1,177.2		815.2	
Invested Capital	2,900	3,273.6	3,695.4	4,174.4	4,708.6	5,315.0	5,999.4	6,771.9	7,643.8	8,627.8	53,106.9	5,727.8	
Incremental Invested Capital		373.6	421.7	476.0	537.3	606.4	684.4	772.5	871.8	984.0			
OE/Avg Invested Capital[2]		7.5%	7.6%	7.9%	8.5%	9.4%	10.0%	10.6%	9.9%	9.9%			8.8%
Return on Incremental Capital		8.0%	8.2%	10.0%	12.3%	15.0%	14.0%	14.1%	4.4%	9.3%			10.0%

+ Charge-offs	98.0					1,000		532.0	12.0	662.0	2,628.0
+ Poolings		297.0	422.0	147.0		762.0		3,212.0			4,418.0
+ Amortization of Goodwill		32.0	14.0	24.0	8.0	16.0	22.0	37.0	49.0	0.0	300.0
Adjusted Invested Capital	2,998.0	3,700.6	4,558.4	5,205.4	6,750.6	8,135.0	9,373.4	13,394.9	14,327.8	84,417.9	12,975.8
Incremental Adjusted Invested Capital		*702.6*	*857.7*	*647.0*	*1,543.3*	*1,384.4*	*1,238.4*	*4,021.5*	*932.8*	*1,646.0*	
OE/Avg Adjusted Invested Capital		6.9%	6.4%	6.4%	6.3%	6.3%	6.5%	5.9%	5.1%	5.3%	5.7%
Return on Adjusted Incremental Capital		*4.3%*	*4.0%*	*7.3%*	*4.3%*	*6.6%*	*7.8%*	*2.7%*	*4.1%*	*5.6%*	*4.9%*

[1] These figures weight each year's numbers by dividing the capital invested for the year by the cum capital invested.

[2] This figure is calculated based on the average capital invested during the period, calculated as the sum of the current year's ending capital and the prior year's ending capital. divided by 2.

A second adjustment needs to be made for poolings, a complicated way of accounting for an acquisition. Think of it like this: Any time one business buys another business for stock, adjust the accounting as if the company takes two steps. First, corporation A sells stock to the general public for cash. Second, it takes that cash and buys corporation B. In reality, companies eliminate the middle step and simply issue stock to the shareholders of the acquired business. Pooling accounting, however, allowed the acquiring firm to simply merge the balance sheets of the two businesses and never record the true amount it paid. So when Christopher looks at ten years of past performance, he adds back to the capital base the amount of stock issued for acquisitions.

Finally, he increases capital by any amortization of goodwill.

The adjusted invested capital figures give a more accurate picture of how well management has invested capital over the years. Based on those numbers, instead of producing an 8.8 percent average annual return over the previous ten years, management really averaged only 5.7 percent. Furthermore, it earned even less—only 4.9 percent—on every incremental dollar it invested. Shareholders would have been better off if the company had paid out the excess earnings as dividends instead of reinvesting them. Christopher generally avoids businesses with low reinvestment rates. Experience has taught him that companies with bad managements are capable of destroying capital in bigger and bigger increments.

If a bond paid 5.7 percent initially but forced you to reinvest the dividends at 4.9 percent, your return would drop to 4.9 percent over time. You would obviously pay less for that bond than one that continually reinvested dividends at the initial 5.7 percent rate or higher.

CHAPTER 5

Bill Fries, CFA

Portfolio Manager, Thornburg Value Fund, Thornburg International Value Fund

Bill Fries has managed the Thornburg Value fund since its inception in October 1995 and the Thornburg International Value fund since it started operations in May 1998. Morningstar selected him as International Fund Manager of the Year for 2003. That same year, he was chosen as one of nine Standard & Poor's/Business Week's best fund managers of the year.

According to Morningstar, during the seven annual periods from 1997 to 2003, the Thornburg Value Fund (A shares) performed in the top 16 percent of its category five times.[1] The fund landed in the top 5 percent of its category for the five-year period ended December 31, 2003, outperforming the S&P 500 index by an annual average of almost 6.5 percent.[2]

ASK SIXTY-FIVE-YEAR-OLD BILL FRIES IF HE'S THINKING ABOUT RETIRING and he'll chuckle. He's one of those rare individuals who doesn't work for a living—he spends every day doing what he truly enjoys. Like many of the great managers, Fries exhibited an affinity for investing early in life. When his eighth-grade teacher, Mrs. Shelley, unlocked the mystery of compound interest and explained how savings accounts work, young Bill was fascinated by the concept that he could make money grow without physical effort. That fascination eventually blossomed into a successful career that has spanned almost four decades.

PERSONAL BACKGROUND

Growing Up

Bill was raised in Sussex, New Jersey, a rural town northwest of New York City nestled in a little valley between the first two ridges of the Appalachians. The agricultural industry, dairy farming in particular, sustained the local economy. With its population of about fifteen hundred, Sussex provided support services to the surrounding communities.

Fries's dad worked as an educator in the same school system for over thirty-five years, first as a teacher, then as principal. An energetic person, he also built houses on the side. Bill's mom stayed home to raise her son and two daughters—one older than Bill and one younger—until he entered the fifth grade. Then she too joined the school system, teaching kids who were identified as "educables." The work was challenging, but she enjoyed helping the less-abled children.

Fries's childhood encompassed the tumultuous years of World War II. Some of his earliest recollections are of blackout drills, where entire communities would practice turning out all their lights in case German warplanes conducted bombing raids in the United States.

Bill developed a love for sports as a young man and remains an avid sports fan to this day. The community in which he grew up did not offer organized youth athletic leagues, so the town boys just gathered on their own almost every day in the summer to play baseball on the high school field. He also learned to fish, swim, and boat at the local lake, and at age seven he took up snow skiing, an avocation he still enjoys today.

Because of his agricultural surroundings, Bill also spent time on dairy farms. When he was a teenager, he would help friends bring in hay and he assisted with other chores. Perhaps this firsthand experience with John Deere equipment led him to buy the company's stock forty years later!

Early Influences

No singular incident initially attracted Fries to investing. Rather, a number of influences drew out a natural interest over time that pulled him in that direction.

Fries's dad, who worked as a pattern maker for Ingersoll-Rand before he started teaching, initially kindled Bill's awareness of business. As the family traveled throughout New England on summer vacations, he would often point out the industrial plants they passed and talk about what they manufactured. "I was a curious person, so I'd ask him a lot of questions," Bill says. "Something about seeing factories and mills intrigued me."

Bill had his first brush with money management in grammar school. "My school participated in a program with the local bank where we kids were given a passbook and made deposits into a savings account. That experience always stuck with me," Bill explains. But it was the explanation of compound interest by his eighth-grade teacher, Mrs. Shelley, that really sparked Bill's interest in saving and earning money on his money. Through that junior high school class, Bill learned his first lessons about compound interest—more is better than less, and if you put money into an account that offers a return, it grows. That process appealed to him.

Penn State and His First Taste of Wall Street

As a teenager, Bill considered following in his dad's footsteps and building homes as well. In fact, Pennsylvania State University initially accepted him in its School of Architecture. However, that dream came to an abrupt end when he took an aptitude test and realized architects need to be able to draw. His mother was an artist, but he did not inherit any of those genes. "I wound up not even taking one class in architecture," he says. "They told me I was much better suited for the military or business. I gained exposure to the military through the

Reserve Officer Training Corp (ROTC), which was involuntary at that time for students of land grant universities. I also switched my major to finance."

At some point during his studies, Fries graduated from bank savings accounts and developed an interest in stocks, motivated in part by the faculty at the university. Two people in particular influenced Bill's thinking about investments. One, a guest professor from the University of Michigan by the name of Sussman, taught Investment Analysis. The visiting professor challenged Fries with the high standards of the course while capturing his interest. The other, Frank Smeal, after whom Penn State has named its College of Business, was an executive at Morgan Guaranty Trust. Smeal eventually left his post there as Executive Vice President and Treasurer and moved to Goldman Sachs and Co., where he became Partner and Managing Director of the Fixed-Income Department.

While he was at Morgan, Smeal invited the Penn State finance majors to visit his place of work. Bill experienced Wall Street for the first time and saw what a major financial institution was actually like. "I had no real exposure to Wall Street before then. I think that influenced me, too, to think in terms of both bonds and stocks," Bill explains. "I didn't really have a preference between the two at that time. They were both securities and ways to invest."

After that experience, Bill knew he wanted to work in the investment field. He planned to initially pursue a position as a stockbroker or an investment analyst. "I don't think I really understood what an analyst did," he notes. "I understood you had to research companies, and I had a pretty good notion of what that might involve. However, at that time the analyst's job had not evolved on Wall Street to what it is today in terms of definition."

Uncle Sam, however, had different plans for Fries.

Military Tour

After graduating from Penn State, Bill found out he was not exempt from the draft as he had previously thought and would have to serve in the military. He enlisted in the Marine Corps, in part because he could get a faster commission there. Officer Candidates School (OCS) started on October 2, and he received his commission on December 15, 1961. Bill spent most of the next year at the Marine Corps Schools learning about communications.

Fries's time in the military would prove to be of value later in his career by opening his eyes to the investment potential offered by overseas markets. After spending some time in California, Bill was transferred to Japan. His position required him to travel extensively, resulting in a familiarity with that part of the world. Frequent journeys piqued his awareness of different cultures and primed his interest in foreign companies. Bill jokes about the very expensive stereo system he bought in Japan in the early sixties. "I spent about $1,000 on hi-fi equipment instead of buying Sony stock. That $1,000 system was a big opportunity loss compared with the value that could have accrued from buying $1,000 in Sony stock. It was evident the Japanese were working very hard to stimulate their economy, and they were growing at a fast rate."

Gaining Experience and Developing His Investment Philosophy

Once he completed his military duty, Bill resumed his pursuit of an investment career. He quickly landed a job as an equity analyst at Girard Trust Bank in Philadelphia. In a sign of how the investment field was evolving, the firm had just changed the title of its research function from statistician to analyst. "I think I got the job because I went in and told them what I wanted to do, but I didn't really know what the job was," Bill recounts. "Because I had been in the military, I was a couple of years older than some of the other people there. I think they probably thought I knew what I was doing, but I frankly didn't."

Fries was trained by Bill Davis, a very capable analyst who headed Girard's research department. Fries's training consisted mostly of sitting next to Davis for three weeks and watching everything he did. During his time at Girard, Fries also learned the bond business, virtually by osmosis, from sitting in front of the bank's principal bond analyst, Al Hanger, and interacting with him.

Fries spent three years at Girard, then moved on to Fidelity Bank, where he worked for two years as a bond fund manager. He then left Fidelity and spent five years as an equity analyst at a small regional firm, DeHaven and Townsend, Crouter and Bodine. Bill's investment skills flourished at DeHaven. The firm employed only three analysts, so Fries had the freedom to hone his process and focus on money-making ideas in whatever sectors he found solid investment opportunities. He also attended night school during his time there and earned his MBA in finance from Temple University.

A DECADE IN THE CITY OF BROTHERLY LOVE

Working ten years in Philadelphia provided Fries with an excellent setting to develop a relatively conservative investment philosophy. John Neff, whom Bill had the pleasure of meeting on a few occasions, was one of the most influential members of the local financial analysts society. A key characteristic Bill observed in the master investor was a strict adherence to his discipline regardless of market conditions. "You have to be true to your convictions," Bill says. "It's challenging to be contrarian. That aspect of Neff influenced me in terms of my philosophy."

Moving to USAA

In 1974, the same year Fries received his Chartered Financial Analyst designation, Bill decided he had endured the East Coast's high pollen count long enough. Allergies were causing him major discomfort, so he determined a move west would significantly enhance his quality of life. It so happened that USAA in San Antonio, a financial services firm that specialized in offering insurance and investment products to military officers, was looking for analysts. The company was in the process of bringing its investment management in-house and launching some mutual funds, requiring it to upgrade its research capabilities. Bill knew the firm well from his experience as a Marine officer and decided to talk with its managers.

USAA's managed investments consisted of the insurance company's assets of approximately $200 million in equities; the USAA Capital Growth Fund, with about $60 million; and a small income fund that was roughly $1 million. The firm had just a few analysts, most of whom had been recently hired.

Fries accepted the company's offer and worked as an analyst for five years. During that time, the Capital Growth Fund struggled with its performance under several different portfolio managers. Then management asked Bill to assume the fund's helm in 1979.

Along with his team of analysts, Fries turned the fund's performance around. Assets grew as a result. The success enabled the investment operation to expand and introduce additional mutual funds, helping the entire business to grow. "My experience at USAA was invaluable, and I appreciate the opportunities they gave me," Bill says. "Over the twenty years I spent there, we developed an investment shop that went from essentially two funds and equities in the insurance company's portfolio to a business with about $15 billion in total assets under management." Fries left to join Thornburg in 1995.

USAA started a number of funds while Bill worked there, several of which he helped establish and even managed for some time. At various times during his tenure at the firm, Fries managed yield-oriented portfolios, growth portfolios, value portfolios, and an international portfolio for the Cornerstone Fund. That experience of managing numerous different strategies sets the veteran investor apart from most of his contemporaries.

A New Life in Santa Fe

In early 1995, Bill responded to a *Wall Street Journal* ad for a portfolio manager position run by Thornburg Investment Management. He was familiar with Santa Fe, where Thornburg was headquartered, because he frequently skied in Taos, just 70 miles north of the city.

The New Mexico–based company managed several bond mutual funds at the time and wanted to establish an equity fund. The partners had invested in stocks successfully since 1990 with a strategy that focused on building a concentrated portfolio of value-oriented securities. To create a mutual fund and take its strategy public, the company decided to hire somebody with credible experience. After meeting Bill, everyone agreed Fries was that person. He left his employer of twenty years and moved to the Land of Enchantment.

Thornburg's philosophy did not differ much from Bill's. While the partners had a fairly firm idea of what they wanted to do, they were open to Fries's thoughts. However, he did not come to the firm with a preconceived notion of exactly what the value fund should look like. Rather, he and the partners hammered out those details throughout the summer as they prepared the prospectus, which the Securities and Exchange Commission (SEC) approved for the public in October 1995.

FRIES'S INVESTMENT PROCESS

Fries differs from the typical money manager, who only ever runs one style of fund. The broad experience he has gained from managing a variety of styles has taught him that value surfaces at different places in different markets. As a result, he is less formulaic than most of his peers.

Since Thornburg planned to offer only one equity fund at the time, Fries wanted to make sure it could compete effectively in all environments. So understanding that no single style works 100 percent of the time, he and Thornburg's partners developed an all-weather strategy that utilized a signature "comprehensive" approach to value investing. They believed this strategy could serve investors well as a core portfolio. "When you're just starting something, you want to be able to offer a value-added product that serves the needs of potential investors," Bill explains. "The value-added we could provide was to identify promising companies priced at a discount to intrinsic value."

Three Categories of Stocks

Fries divides his portfolio into three types of stocks: *basic value*, *consistent earners*, and *emerging franchises*. Combining these various elements helps Bill and his hand-picked team take advantage of values created by volatility in different market segments, which should give him the opportunity to achieve competitive returns over time. He also strives to buy companies in all three categories when they are out of favor to help control risk.

Basic-Value Companies.   These are primarily well-established companies in leading cyclical industries. These companies must demonstrate that they can survive tough times and remain viable for the long term. Although these businesses tend to have low *average* growth rates, their earnings can increase rapidly as they emerge from cyclical downturns. This potential for explosive earnings growth when the stock prices of these firms are depressed creates the investment opportunity. Basic-value companies such as Deere and Co. and Union Pacific are examples of companies whose fortunes depend on economic cycles. In contrast, the fortunes of banks and insurance companies depend on interest rate cycles.

Basic-value businesses tend to sell at low valuations relative to their net assets or their potential future earnings. This normally happens near troughs of their business cycles. Ironically, these companies often sell at high PEs at those times because their current or trailing earnings are very low. Fries is not afraid to buy a good company that is selling at a high multiple of current earnings if he believes today's stock price is only a low multiple of next year's earnings.

Consistent Earners.   These companies are characterized by consistent revenue and earnings streams from products and services that enjoy steady demand. Most of these well-known companies are thought of as blue chip. They generally maintain high returns on equity and are normally found in industries such as food and beverage, health care, retail, and household goods. Pfizer, Lowe's Companies, and Colgate-Palmolive typify the stocks that populate this category.

The consistency of these firms' earnings might lead you to believe they are always attractive investments, but they are not usually available at compelling prices. Investors are willing to pay premiums for these businesses because they tend to be highly profitable and less responsive to macro factors that create volatility in most companies' performance. Their steady performance and growth normally makes them an investor favorite during market downturns.

"The decision to buy these stocks is easy if they're cheap enough, which is not a frequent occurrence," says Bill.

Emerging Franchises.   These businesses are growing rapidly and are in the process of establishing a leading position in a significant product, service, or market. Their performances are typically not tied to any particular cycle. Their prices tend to fluctuate a good deal because they can carry above average valuations, but their future prospects are subject to wide variability. They tend to have smaller market capitalizations, although they're not necessarily all small. Fries notes, "They have a greater capacity to disappoint." Fries limits his exposure to emerging franchises to maintain favorable risk characteristics for the portfolio as a whole.

Equity Diversification

By combining these three types of stocks in his portfolio, Fries believes he can go where value gets created in order to produce competitive returns over time and still keep risk under control.

His fund varies around a nominal 40–40–20 distribution respectively among the three categories. Bill normally allots 2.5 to 3.5 percent of the fund to each new stock he purchases, except for emerging franchises. Positions in emerging franchise stock are typically less than 2 percent on initial purchase, but through appreciation a position can rise to become a more meaningful portion of the portfolio. However, if any individual position becomes too large, regardless of category, Fries will trim to manage the overall risk exposure of the portfolio and not be too heavily concentrated in any one name. How big will he allow a position to grow? "I don't have a pedantic cutoff for any category, but in the case of an emerging franchise stock, I get heartburn over 4 percent," he says. "We've had cases in the past where appreciation is dramatic, so we may be working pretty hard to keep it under 5 percent. I love to have that problem."

The Value Proposition

Fundamental research drives Bill's investment process. He and his team look for stocks that offer both promise and discount. Together these elements comprise a firm's *value proposition*.

To determine if a company is currently priced at a discount, Fries takes several approaches to equity valuation. Using one such approach, he compares a company's current stock price relative to its earnings or its cash flow, for instance, to that of its peers, as well as to the company's own historical ratios. He also tries to value the cash flows in today's dollars that he expects the company to generate in the future. Additionally, he asks himself what a private buyer might pay for the whole company.

Value is typically created when negative issues cloud investors' opinions about the affected company's future. "To invest in a company, we have to believe the depressing negative issues are temporary. This necessarily requires a view of the future involving a time period beyond the next quarter," states Fries.

An inexpensive stock price, however, is not enough to compel Bill to buy a company. Experience has taught him that without an identifiable path to future success, a cheap stock can remain cheap indefinitely. Bill must have good reason to believe the company has the potential for business improvement, which Fries refers to as its promise. That improvement can stem from management fixing a problem or ongoing good business execution. Since a firm's earning power drives its worth, Bill expects the anticipated change in earnings to produce a higher stock value—and hopefully price—in the next year or two.

According to Fries, identifying cheap stocks is the easy part—he does this by screening on standard valuation measures as described below. Finding companies that can achieve a healthier than generally expected future poses a much greater challenge. Bill spends time contemplating the potential of out-of-favor and underappreciated businesses, trying to determine if they have a path to future success.

Since a firm's value is ultimately based on its cash flows, earnings, and revenue-generating capability, Bill attempts to develop a thorough

A CLASSIC VALUE PROPOSITION

Banks in 1990 offer a classic example of a value proposition that worked well for the Thornburg partners before Bill joined the firm. Many of those stocks sank to book value or lower when investors lost confidence in the banking system. Temporary problems looked as though they would become permanent and eventually affect every bank. As a result, fearful investors tarred many resilient companies with the same brush as weak ones, creating some tremendous buying opportunities. As the banking system worked through its problems, many of those investments turned in exceptional returns.

understanding of what drives these elements in each company that he analyzes. He primarily takes into account company-specific factors, but he does not ignore the macroenvironment in which the business operates. By looking at the total picture, he either identifies a path to future success for the company or moves on.

Cheap by What Definition?

It is tempting to reduce Bill's investment approach to simply buying stocks at bargain prices that will grow in value. That is akin to saying Wal-Mart achieved its dominance by selling products cheaper than its competitors. There's more to it than that.

Examining a variety of classic value screens for numeric advantages is only the first step. Fries believes it is simplistic to think you can merely run some valuation metrics on a business, such as its PE, price-to-cash-flow, and so forth, and determine its stock is undervalued. Those figures are useful, but they identify value only in the context of a firm's previous operations. Investing, however, is all about the future. Past metrics work well only if you are very confident that a company's future will mirror its past.

A low PE stock, for instance, can actually be a value trap. Auto stocks typically sell at low PEs and at a significant discount to the average equity. Yet acquiring these stocks at low PEs (based on trailing earnings) may prove to be unproductive because low multiples occur at the peak of this industry's business cycle.

The home-building industry, however, illustrates a situation where buying low PE stocks has worked. In the late 1990s, investors could have reasonably concluded that these companies offered no special value. True, they looked inexpensive relative to other businesses, but that was not unusual. Many investors concluded that with interest rates and inflation at historically low levels, the cycle would likely turn and those stocks would take a beating.

Then the world changed as several circumstances converged to make housing more affordable. Lower-rate variable mortgages grew in popularity. A bout with deflation extended the interest rate cycle both in direction and duration, producing abnormally low rates for an extended period of time. Those events brought a new crop of young buyers who could not have previously afforded a house and encouraged existing homeowners to "trade up." As a result, demand for housing boomed and remained strong for much longer than most people expected. Home-building stocks in turn performed exceptionally well.

"Individual companies are just not that simple," Bill says. "It would be really easy if you could merely buy every cheap stock based on some measure that's below its historic mean and produce results. I don't think it really happens that way."

In summary, a combination of valuation and promise drives the investment decisions of Bill and his team. "It's pretty easy to be right about the valuation in a historic context, but to invest successfully you have to be right about the promise of a company as well as being disciplined about valuation," says Fries.

The Quest for Value

The search for new investments starts by looking for cheap stocks. To do this, Bill runs a number of classic value screens. He first looks for businesses with low PE ratios. Since investors' expectations of *future* earnings drive stock prices, Bill uses the forward PE ratio. "I look at trailing twelve months earnings for other aspects of my analysis," he says, "because you certainly want to know where a company has been to understand where it is and where it might be going. But in terms of valuation, I'm forward-looking when I run my screens." Bill also reviews his database for stocks with high dividend yields or low price-to-trailing twelve-month cash flow.

A separate screen focuses on the promise. Fries calls it a fundamental improvement screen. This screen spotlights businesses that have experienced a positive earnings surprise—either quarterly net income above expectations or upward revision of earnings estimates. These filters yield a relatively small universe of stocks.

Fries puts the stocks in this small universe through a rejection process. One element of this process applies to classic low-valuation stocks. Fries rejects those that have no path to future success that he and his team can identify. Stocks from the universe of companies experiencing fundamental improvement—those for which he has identified a path to future success—go through a rejection process focused on valuation measures.

Ultimately Fries winnows the list down to just a few stocks. Because these businesses appear to offer compelling value propositions, Bill moves on to the challenging task of gaining a deeper understanding of these companies' business models. This involves communicating with both street analysts and firms' managements as well as using valuable tools such as the Internet (i.e., company web site). Company visits are also an integral part of the process, and visits are made when appropriate and possible prior to or shortly after an initial investment. This process culminates in the documentation of a company's positives, negatives, and Fries's overall investment thesis.

KEY POINT

The thesis focuses on drivers of earnings more than the actual earnings.

The Last Hurdle

Bill doesn't always buy all the stocks that make it through this process. Typically a new stock is only added to the portfolio when one of his current positions hits its target price, its fundamentals deteriorate in a way that was not anticipated, or the risk/reward profile of the new company is superior to that of a current holding. If none of these things happen, the candidate stock could remain on the bench.

AON

Aon, an insurance broker, serves as an example of a stock that made it through the process. Management had lacked focus and pursued a number of disappointing business ideas. As a result, the company failed to generate significant earnings improvement over a number of years, causing its price to fall—too far according to Bill's calculus.

As he studied the firm, Fries learned that its corporate heads were narrowing the focus of the business and cutting costs. At the same time, insurance premiums were rising industry wide, providing an opportunity to further increase the firm's revenues. Bill believed a macro environment that promoted growth combined with cutting costs and getting out of unprofitable businesses would drive the company's earnings higher and elevate the stock's value.

Qualitative Issues Involved in Valuing a Firm

A comprehensive value proposition must consider qualitative as well as quantitative issues. For example, virtually every company will face unforeseen obstacles in achieving its goals. Experienced leadership can make the difference between gaining market share and giving up ground to competitors during such times. The value of outstanding management is not quantifiable, but other things being equal, businesses that possess it are worth more than those that lack it.

While Bill considers a number of subjective factors, he zeroes in on three such dynamics: business model, competitive position in the marketplace, and management and corporate culture.

Business Model. A business model describes how a company is designed and operates. Among other things, it addresses how the firm generates and books revenue, sustains its profit margins, and funds its growth, which are crucial to the company maintaining its operations and growing its profitability. These things also influence the return a business generates on its equity—a key determinant of the firm's value. Stated simply, a company that compounds retained earnings at 25 percent annually is worth more than one that compounds at 10 percent.

The third item listed—how a corporation funds its ongoing capital requirements for growth—dovetails into the firm's financial needs. A business that self-funds its capital needs is more valuable than an otherwise identical company that needs equity or credit financing. Therefore, when evaluating a firm's value proposition, its debt level and trend must be considered as well as how that compares to other businesses in similar industries.

Competitive Position in the Marketplace.

Market leadership means having developed a recognizable brand name (e.g., Coke, Pampers, and Dell) or manufacturing dominant best-of-breed products within a specific industry. For example, if you're about to sneeze, do you reach for a tissue or a Kleenex?

Market leadership can give a company pricing power, which further increases the firm's value. Conversely, lack of pricing power reduces a company's worth. For instance, the market tends to assign lower multiples to original equipment manufacturers because they often make parts for powerful customers who can squeeze their suppliers' margins. As an example, a smaller company selling a computer component to Dell has scant ability to raise its prices on a regular basis. The computer behemoth can demand the lowest possible prices from most of its vendors because it controls such a huge segment of the PC market.

Compare the situation of the component supplier to a biotechnology company that manufactures the only approved treatment for a rare but fatal genetic disorder. This virtual monopoly would give the biotech firm tremendous pricing power for its critical product.

Management and Corporate Culture.

As part of a company's value proposition, Bill pays a good deal of attention to its management and the ethos it has created at the firm. Bill explains, "Corporate culture provides the context within which business decisions are made. The nature of this culture starts at the top. The drive and discipline of employees to succeed will probably not exist if it is not embedded in corporate leadership."

Bill especially likes environments that encourage rational decision making and discourage wasting money. He also values managements that exhibit integrity and the willingness to communicate forthrightly—he does not like mystery firms. If he can't get an understanding of the business, it is best not to invest.

EARNINGS' IMPACT ON VALUE

Many factors—quantitative and qualitative—influence a company's value. However, their influence reaches only as far as their impact on the firm's earnings. In fact, Bill believes the idea of value outside the context of profits and earnings growth is a hollow concept. Improving a company's earnings picture virtually always equates to increasing its worth. "As a value investor, growth is not something that I ignore. Rather, it is *part of* a stock's value," Bill says. "To me, this bifurcation of growth and value into separate and distinct categories, while convenient for style box evaluation, is a notion one must be careful with. I believe Warren Buffet said the two are connected at the hip. The differentiation should have been between value and momentum. Unfortunately, it wasn't."

Developing a Fair Market Value

Before he buys a stock, Bill synthesizes everything he has learned and believes about a company and its future and establishes a price at which he believes it would be fairly valued. That figure becomes the target price Fries expects the stock to achieve within the next twelve to eighteen months. As a rule of thumb, Bill uses 25 percent as his minimum total return target. "You should certainly look for that kind of return if you are dealing in equities," Fries says.

No single valuation metric captures the whole story for any company. Bill bases his target price on a number of factors, among which are the firm's historical valuation measures, the company's valuation relative to similar businesses, its earnings, and the present value of its expected cash flows.

Bill cautions, however, that while a discounted cash flow model can be a powerful valuation tool, its usefulness hinges on the accuracy of projections, which are more uncertain the further out you try to project.

When a stock has performed well and approaches his target price, it is tempting to maintain the position even though its valuation no longer justifies doing so. At that point, a disconnect often exists between the firm's *likely* growth and how fast it *needs* to grow for the investment to produce an above average return. An earnings discount model reveals this disconnect by allowing him to test the reasonableness of his assumptions. That has saved him some real pain over the years by keeping his process rational and helping him avoid holding emotionally appealing issues that should be sold based on valuation fundamentals.

KEY POINT

Not every tool suits every business. Some companies' earnings are straightforward and easy to understand. Other firms, especially those that are capital intensive, have more complex earnings situations that require extra effort to fully comprehend. Experience determines the appropriate tools to value each type of company.

The Sell Strategy

Bill sells a company for any of three reasons: the stock approaches his target price, fundamentals do not develop according to the investment thesis, or the perception of a better opportunity surfaces.

Target Price Achievement.   As discussed earlier, Fries establishes a target price for each investment at the time of purchase. He reevaluates the stock as it approaches that price to reaffirm the value proposition and target price validity.

"The target price is not something a company has to hit, but I look at selling a holding as it approaches that price," Bill explains. "Let's say you have a $20 stock with a target of $40. Target valuations are estimates not set in concrete. It makes sense to reconsider them before they are reached and begin selling if appropriate."

When a basic value company achieves Fries's price target, it is usually sold. This represents Bill's perfect scenario and normally occurs when a cyclical stock works out just like he thought it would. Fries treats consistent earners the same way. However, he exercises a little more leniency with an emerging franchise stock and may trim positions rather than eliminating them entirely. Given the exceptional long-run potential of emerging franchise stocks, this fosters participation in exceptional gains while keeping risk under control.

Let's say Fries gets the story right about an emerging franchise stock. He buys it at a significant discount to its intrinsic value, its earnings rise considerably over the next year, and its price reaches his target. Instead of automatically liquidating the holding, he considers the fact that its higher earnings may have increased its fair value. If that is the case, he might adjust his price target upward and trim the position but hold a portion for its further potential. This enables participation in what can be exceptional long-term capital appreciation in excess of the typical investor's twelve- to eighteen-month investment time horizon while keeping risk in check.

Fundamentals Don't Meet Bill's Investment Thesis.   Once Bill has developed his thesis for a company and purchased its stock, he pays close attention to the firm's business progress. If the information flow indicates the thesis is not unfolding as he expected, even shortly after buying the stock, experience has taught him the investment thesis was likely flawed to begin with. "If that occurs, you're better off taking your losses at that point instead of holding on," Fries states. "There have been some cases where I've let things go on too long. Things hadn't turned out the way I thought they would. I thought they'd get better.

They didn't, and I paid a price for being too patient. So I'm more inclined to take my losses sooner than later."

What does Bill mean by information flow? A report that a company's quarterly income fell short of analysts' estimates? No. While an earnings miss might be an element of information flow, the real issue is why and how that relates to the investment thesis. *Why* the firm fell short of its projected net income concerns him much more than the simple fact that the business failed to achieve a specific expected number, such as earnings per share.

Even meeting projections does not necessarily assure the investment thesis is developing as expected. What's behind the numbers is just as important. This is why investors must look at the details to gain understanding.

A Better Opportunity Surfaces.   The third reason for selling a position relates back to what shows up on recent screens and newly researched issues. Let's say a company makes it through the research process and appears to offer a value proposition. It can only make it into the portfolio if it is judged to offer a better risk/reward trade-off than a current holding. Chances are it won't make it into the fund. This principle of portfolio construction supports Fries's continuous improvement philosophy.

Managing Risk

In Bill's mind, investing is as much about managing risks as it is striving for returns. Returns will take care of themselves over time if you manage the downside well. Most professionals will tell you that you must broadly diversify your investments to cut risk. Bill believes security selection—the methodology for choosing each investment that goes into a portfolio—represents the ultimate form of risk control. He attempts to make each new name improve the fund's risk/reward characteristics. Indeed, while Bill seeks capital appreciation as his primary goal, his process considers the potential downside.

Fries understands and accepts the possibility that his portfolio will exhibit more *short-term* volatility than the S&P 500—his benchmark—

since he invests in only about 10 percent as many stocks. He would have to match the index statistically to avoid that, which would require giving up the ability to significantly outperform the index over time. However, even with fifty stocks, Bill believes with good stock selection he should be able to achieve lower *long-term* volatility than the index while maintaining returns that match or beat the benchmark.

International Research

Ever since he joined Thornburg, Bill has researched firms on a global basis. In fact, he started the Thornburg International Value Fund because his research for the Thornburg Value Fund turned up a significant number of intriguing investments located in foreign countries. Bill manages both funds with the same style except for the geographical locations of the portfolio holdings.

While Bill invests primarily in large-cap stocks, he is free to purchase smaller companies if they meet his criteria—no synthetic guidelines restrict the size of firms that he can buy. However, "I'm not going to get carried away and have a portfolio full of illiquid small holdings," Bill says.

SUMMARY

The following summarizes the main points of Fries's investment philosophy:

Asset Allocation

- Bill divides his Thornburg Value Fund and Thornburg International Value Fund portfolio into three categories of stocks to "go to where the value is":

    Basic Value: Financially sound cyclical firms with well-established businesses.

    Consistent Earners: Blue-chip companies characterized by consistent earnings and dividend growth, stable revenues, and products with steady demand.

Emerging Franchises: Rapidly growing businesses that are in the process of establishing a leading position in a significant product, service, or market. Because of their higher risk, Fries limits exposure to these firms to 25 percent of portfolios. Additionally, each position size is typically less than 2 percent at time of purchase.

Security Selection

- Fries invests in stocks whose characteristics include promise and a value proposition. Promise refers to a company's ability to improve its profitability and business growth. That growth can stem from management correcting a problem or continuing to execute its business plan. Value characterizes a business that sells at a significant discount to its true worth.
- Fries looks for new investments by first screening for firms that are cheap according to traditional valuation measures, such as forward PE, dividend yield, and price-to-trailing twelve-month cash flow. Next, he screens for companies that have experienced a positive earnings surprise. Finally, the resulting stocks are narrowed down to a small group of survivors by subjecting them to a rejection process.
- Before investing in a company, the Thornburg team identifies its path to future success, develops an investment thesis, and lists all of its significant positives and negatives.
- Fries and his group consider subjective factors when analyzing firms, specifically their business models, competitive positions in the marketplace, and corporate cultures.
- He then develops a fair market value for each business being considered. That figure becomes the target price the stock is expected to achieve within the next twelve to eighteen months.
- Fries sells a stock when its price approaches its intrinsic value, its fundamentals do not develop as expected, or a better opportunity surfaces.

CHAPTER 6

John Calamos Sr.

Portfolio Manager, Calamos Growth Fund

John Calamos Sr. has developed an exceptional reputation as both a convertible securities manager and an equity manager. While this chapter focuses on his equity management process, it is worth noting that his Calamos Growth and Income Fund, a hybrid equity and convertible bond fund that John comanages with his nephew, Nick Calamos, was named as a winner of Standard & Poor's/Business Week's Excellence in Fund Management award in both 2003 and 2004.

As of year-end 2003, Morningstar rated the Calamos Growth Fund, an equity fund, in the top 1 percent of funds in its category over a five-year period and in the top 5 percent over a three-year period. Even more impressive, the fund ranked as the top performing open-end mutual fund for the previous ten years.[1]

John built that long-term record of success with strong relative performance in both good and bad markets. During the heady years of 1996 to 1999, the Calamos Growth fund (A shares) outperformed the S&P 500 index by a total of over 132 percent. In the ensuing three bear market years, the fund outperformed the same index by almost 36 percent.[2] According to Morningstar, the equity fund placed in the top third of its category every year throughout that seven-year stretch. It landed in the top 20 percent of its peers four times and in the top 10 percent twice.[3]

PERSONAL BACKGROUND

Growing Up

John Calamos Sr.'s story is one of living the American dream. He was born in 1940 to Greek immigrants who started their lives in America with virtually nothing. The young couple bought a grocery store on the west side of Chicago shortly after John's birth, which they ran until they retired. John grew up with his two sisters on the second floor of the little two-story building that housed the business. His parents labored diligently to support their family, often working seven days a week.

The Greek community in Chicago functioned in similar fashion to that of many other cities. Because it was difficult for poor immigrants to obtain money from banks for business ideas, vendors from within the community often provided the capital to start businesses. In the case of Calamos's parents, that vendor was the "egg man."

John recalls what it was like when the lender would visit. "I remember we kids would be playing around the house. The egg man would come in and sit down with my dad, have a little drink, and go through the store's numbers. My parents would pay a little on the debt every time he visited. It was obviously a terrific relationship. I guess we'd call that private equity today."

Although they had to borrow the funds to buy the store, owing money went against his parents' grain. So they paid extra on the debt whenever they could and disposed of it in five years.

Finding Hidden Treasure

A surprise discovery during his early teenage years gave John his first exposure to stocks. While rummaging through the basement of the grocery store one day, he came across some old boxes that contained stock certificates and confirmations from the 1920s and 1930s. They belonged to an uncle who had stored them there and then moved to the East Coast. Thinking he'd found a treasure, young John researched

SAVING SILVER DOLLARS IN A CIGAR BOX

America was just coming out of the Depression when Calamos was a young child. In spite of some lean times early on, his parents saved diligently. The fear created by the stock market crash and the collapse of numerous banks years earlier still lingered in their minds. So instead of depositing their money in a financial institution, they devised a unique method of saving: Every time a silver dollar crossed the counter, they threw it in a cigar box. They hid these cigar boxes all over the store—in the rice, under the counters, and so on. Only after years of saving in this manner did they open a bank account and start buying conservative instruments such as savings bonds and war bonds.

His parents' example taught John a powerful lesson about frugality and hard work. He credits much of his success to the work ethic they instilled in him.

each of the companies, just sure one of them had multiplied his uncle's original investment many times over! Instead, he discovered all the shares were worthless.

The only thing of material value that Calamos carried away from that incident was a unique stock certificate from Pierce Arrow Automotive Company, which hangs in his study today. More importantly, however, that experience sparked what soon became a passion for the financial markets and investing.

College

After graduating from high school, John went to the Illinois Institute of Technology, which is known primarily for its engineering and mathematics programs. Attending the institute held a particular significance for Calamos—out of all his immediate and extended family in the Chicago area, he was the first to go to college. "I look back and that experience really changed my life. I support IIT to this day. In fact, I'll soon be a trustee of the university," John says.

Calamos originally planned on studying engineering—a popular major because of the space race—or architecture, but a lack of artistic ability convinced him to abandon both. Instead, finance, economics, and philosophy captured his interest.

Philosophy attracted John because it involved critical thinking and the discussion of ideas. You can't answer questions such as, "What is justice?" in a multiple-choice format—you have to discuss it through the Socratic method. Similarly, he enjoyed the political and philosophical aspects of economics much more than the technical side of econometrics.

John entered college as a liberal who believed in the extensive use of government programs to better people's lives economically. However, the writings of certain economists—Milton Friedman in particular—changed his mind. Friedman championed a conservative philosophy, teaching that free markets, individual liberty, and economic freedom are necessary for economies to grow and people to prosper. The logic behind those ideas convinced John that free enterprise provides the most benefits to the most people, and he converted to Friedman's way of thinking.

In fact, today when Calamos evaluates foreign investments for the firm's global products, he first looks for free enterprise attributes at the national level before he even considers the investment merits of individual companies. If a nation doesn't offer its citizens legal rights, individual freedom, and economic freedom, firms within that country have little chance of making it into one of Calamos's funds.

John eventually settled on an economics major and graduated in 1963 with an economics degree. He studied under several excellent professors at IIT—especially his last year and a half—who motivated him to dig deeper into the financial area. Some of those professors persuaded Calamos to attend graduate school there. So he stayed at the institute an extra two years and earned an MBA in finance.

Calamos reflects on his education as an excellent background for working in the investment world: "IIT taught me a unique combination of the philosophical aspects of finance and economics and the mathematical, analytical tools you need to understand companies' financial statements."

INVESTING HIS PARENTS' $5,000 NEST EGG

John's interest in the financial markets grew steadily once he began studying finance and economics. In 1957, he talked his mother, who ran the family finances, into giving him $5,000 to invest on her behalf. He bought equal dollars of a few quality growth companies, such as Texas Instruments, Beckman Instruments, and Thiokol Chemical. "I did take one stock tip from a cousin of mine, and that quickly went to zero," John says. That latter experience taught Calamos to do his own research.

John remembers looking back at the market when he made those investments and thinking he had arrived late to the party. He figured the time to make big gains had surely passed. "It's tempting to get perspective on one time frame and say, 'If I could have done this two or three years ago, look at the returns I could have achieved.' Of course, look at what the market has done since that time," he reflects.

In those days, $5,000 was a substantial amount of money, equaling about a year's income for his parents. Knowing how they had sacrificed to save that money made it all the more important to John to preserve the capital and make the funds grow. John initially used a buy and hold strategy. He started managing the portfolio more actively after he left the military. Those funds grew considerably over time and became the major portion of his parents' retirement savings.

Flying Combat Missions in Vietnam

MBAs typically pursued management trainee positions at banks or other large companies after they left college. That sounded boring to John, so he looked to the military for a greater challenge. Having participated in the Reserve Officers Training Corps (ROTC) for two years in undergraduate school, he joined the Air Force in 1965 as a second lieutenant.

John immediately went through pilot training and flew active duty in the Air Force for five years. He spent one of those years flying bombing missions in B-52s over Vietnam, where he logged over eight hundred hours of combat time. Calamos achieved the rank of major and was awarded the Distinguished Flying Cross, as well as over twenty other medals, for his valiant service.

Preparing for the Markets

John spent his last year of duty as a B-52 pilot on alert, which essentially meant he sat in a ground silo waiting for someone to ring a bell signaling the beginning of World War III. Should that have occurred, his mission was clear: fly a B-52 to Russia and bomb Moscow.

Pilots on alert went on duty for as many as seven days at a time—just sitting in a hole and waiting. The boredom was almost unbearable at times. John decided to take advantage of the situation and prepare for life after the Air Force in case World War III never came about, so he passed much of the time reading investment books. His studies led to a strong interest in convertible bonds—corporate debt instruments that can be converted into shares of the company's common stock. Those relatively conservative instruments blend characteristics of both fixed income and equity securities, making them a great way to control risk and still participate in the equity markets. Relatively few financial advisors dealt in this area, which gave John the ability to set himself apart from the crowd. While knowing the theory was good, Calamos spent a lot of time contemplating how to apply what he was learning.

Launching His Investment Career

When John left the Air Force in 1970, he figured he could make a living either selling securities or flying airplanes. A nasty recession at the time made it an easy choice. Airline jobs were in short supply, so he signed on as a stockbroker with duPont, where H. Ross Perot, the famous Texas billionaire, was staffing the firm with a number of former military officers. "I've never talked to the man, but I assume he thought ex-military officers had the right kind of value system for the company's operations," Calamos says. Unfortunately, the firm filed for Chapter 11 a short while later.

Bankruptcy became an all too common occurrence for brokerage firms during that era. Most of the brokerage businesses were organized as partnerships and invested their own capital in the markets. When a firm started losing money, the partners often yanked their capital and bankrupted the company. Largely because of such experiences, John worked at a total of five brokerage firms between 1970 and 1977.

"That was a horrendous era," John explains. "Most advisors and investors today don't have a clue how bad things were unless they lived through it. The Dow started at 1,000 when I got into business in 1970. By 1974, it had plunged to just over 500." A confluence of factors contributed to the economic and financial crisis, including Vietnam, Watergate, the oil crisis, and coming off the gold standard. Additionally, double-digit inflation ravaged the value of our currency. Even some traditionally safe investments such as government bonds saw their value slashed by half in a matter of two or three years. The moribund stock market came to symbolize an attitude of helplessness that assaulted the national psyche. "So I cut my teeth in a very volatile era," John remembers.

Calamos rode that time by trying to preserve capital during market downturns and make money during the precious cyclical upturns. He developed a number of convertible bond strategies, similar to modern hedge-fund strategies, to help him accomplish that goal. "It sounds trite, but the way to create wealth is to not lose money. I don't take the attitude that if the market is down, that's okay because it'll come back," John says.

Calamos believes investors generally understand the Benjamin Franklin idea of how compounding can grow wealth exponentially over time. Fewer investors, however, appreciate the flip side—that wealth can get destroyed the same way. Losing 50 percent requires you to make 100 percent just to break even. So John's philosophy early on focused on preserving capital using whatever tools were available—convertibles, warrants, shorting stocks—in addition to standard risk management practices, such as diversifying and buying undervalued securities. "Whatever made sense, I used."

When the options exchange was birthed in 1974, all the work John had done up to that point became even more relevant. The new market solved the major problem with warrants: a lack of supply; only a minority of stocks offered them. Options were the functional equivalent of warrants, only the new exchange offered greater liquidity and more choices. While traders bought the new instruments enthusiastically, John mostly sold them (known as *writing options*) because his work showed they were significantly overvalued.

Starting His Own Firm

John initially attracted clients by teaching seminars on hedging stock market risk with options. He had a strong vision of what he wanted to accomplish in his business, but he recognized that achieving his goals would be difficult in a typical broker setting. "I was not a very good broker. I didn't care about the new issue calendar. I didn't want to rely on others' research. I wanted to do my own research and manage money my way," John says. So in 1977, the former fighter pilot mortgaged his house and left the small firm where he worked to start his own money management firm. His convertible bond strategy became the core business of the new investment advisor.

The business grew steadily. In 1980, the money management firm obtained its first institutional account: a $5 million investment from a major airline. His nephew, Nick Calamos, joined the firm in 1983. In 1985, John launched one of the first open-end convertible security mutual funds. His son, John Jr., came to the firm in 1987.

Managing convertible security portfolios remained the firm's focus throughout the 1980s and 1990s. During that time, John went on a crusade to persuade the investment world that convertibles were a separate asset class every investor ought to use. He even wrote a book on the topic (*Investing in Convertible Securities: Your Complete Guide to the Risks and Rewards*, Dearborn Trade Publishing, Chicago, 1988) and authored numerous articles.

By the year 2000, Calamos's firm had become one of the largest, if not the largest, convertible bond managers in the world, supervising close to $9 billion. "The reason I like convertibles is that they allow you to control risk, and I always wanted to offer a risk-averse invest-ment product," John says. "Our clients want to make money when the markets are cooperating, but they also want to preserve capital during the market's down cycles. So all our convertible strategies re-volve around that."

The Evolution of the Equity Process

In the mid-1980s, Calamos became an early pioneer in using option price theory to value convertible securities. He applied the academic community's ideas to the real world of money management and de-veloped the Calamos Convertible Model, which he detailed in his book. "Valuing convertibles is no secret—it's simply a matter of doing the math," John explains. "That model has held us in good stead over the years. It allows us to determine a security's risk/reward charac-teristics and analyze its upside versus its downside."

Learning to value convertible securities led Calamos to the next question: "Do I like the underlying stocks?" He felt a better under-standing of companies' common stocks would improve his convertible securities analysis. So he went to work on developing a process to analyze and value equities. John completed the project in 1990.

As Calamos anticipated, the stock evaluation process enhanced his understanding of firms' convertible securities. However, as he thought about his new process, it struck him that the convertible market made up only a small subset of the total market. Perhaps, he thought, the new strategy would make a formidable stand-alone product. He figured the best way to find out was to take his own assets—pension fund money and personal money—and seed an equity mutual fund. So John launched the Calamos Growth Fund in 1990.

For the first few years, the fund attracted relatively little attention and even less money. Calamos had established his reputation as a con-vertible manager, not an equity manager. However, several consecu-tive years of returns in the top third of his peer group made his equity performance hard to ignore. In the late 1990s and early 2000s, money poured into the stock fund. Today, Calamos Investments manages about $33 billion, with convertibles comprising only about a quarter of its total asset base. Amazingly, most of the growth in assets from $6 billion to $33 billion occurred during the worst stock market downturn since the Great Depression.

CALAMOS'S INVESTMENT PROCESS

As you might expect from an analytical manager with a strong philosophical bent, John has considered virtually every aspect of investing and developed a number of guiding principles that govern each step of his process.

Two Investment Beliefs

Two core philosophies pervade Calamos's strategy. First, in order to create wealth, you have to give up some of the upside to preserve capital on the downside. "I have always said that I'm long-term bullish, short-term scared, all the time," John quips. What does that mean? While he believes strongly in the ability of the economy to create significant prosperity over time, he understands the stock market can drop unexpectedly at almost any moment. When that happens, he wants to maintain his principal reasonably intact, even if that means missing out on some of the market's growth during the good times.

Second, no strategy works very well for very long, so you have to keep evolving your process. There is no magic quantitative equation that works all the time. If such a formula existed, everyone would use it and it would no longer work. What works at any point in time constantly shifts, so he believes you have to take a broader view and adjust your research to adapt to the current macroeconomic environment.

Four additional principles establish the foundation of John's investment process:

1. Perform extensive research.
2. Maintain long-term perspective.
3. Stay fully invested at all times.
4. Manage risk.

Perform Extensive Research.   Calamos underpins his investment process with detailed, comprehensive research. Sophisticated analytical models developed over a period of years give the Calamos team the ability to simulate a variety of situations regarding individual companies, the markets, and the economy. John continuously refines his research process based on his experience in order to avoid repeating mistakes and to spot opportunities before everybody else sees them. This depth of research applies to each step of the process and is required to yield the level of information John needs to understand a security and what is happening in the market.

Maintain Long-Term Perspective.   John believes you need a certain view of the world to be a growth manager—or investor. If you are not long-term bullish, don't put money in a growth fund. "Our economy is very vibrant and the envy of the world," John explains. "Regardless of the self-serving political debate that goes on, we're the envy of the world. We create jobs, we create opportunities. We're not a riskless society, but we create more good things economically than any other nation."

Stay Fully Invested at All Times.   Short-term market timing is one avoidable hazard that threatens strong long-term results. One mistake in either direction can cost you a great deal of earlier gains. You also risk being whipsawed in and out of the market, which runs up trading costs and generates higher-taxed short-term gains. John believes other methods of managing short-term risk work better while allowing you to capture the market's long-term benefits.

Manage Risk.   Experience has convinced Calamos that the way to create wealth is to manage risk effectively; good returns will follow naturally. "The way we manage money—what we are all about—has risk management at its core," John explains.

John's attitude about risk stems from his military experience. When he flew fighters, his goal was not to avoid risk but rather to understand and control it. How do you control risk as a pilot? "By knowing as much as possible about your airplane, especially the emergency procedures," John says. "If a fire breaks out, you don't have time to get the manual out and study what to do. You've got to know what to do, which means preparing before the event. That's risk management."

John treats investing the same way: he does not shun risk; he tries to understand it. His entire process hinges on assessing a security's risk, quantifying it if possible, and comparing it to the investment's potential rewards. "Risk management to us is making sure we're executing the process consistently. We've got to make sure everybody adheres to that."

To make good on his commitment to keep risk as low as possible, Calamos implements a number of risk-control measures throughout his process, beginning with diversification. Instead of searching for a few growth companies he can ride to the moon, John runs a very well-diversified portfolio and avoids concentrated positions. He has seen a lot of investors make the mistake of wagering their future returns on finding the modern equivalent of IBM in the 1930s or Qualcomm in early 1990. Instead, he strives to capture at the *portfolio* level what he thinks are the best overall growth attributes the stock market offers at any particular time.

KEY POINT

The characteristics of the *total portfolio* are much more important than those of any single security in the portfolio.

His portfolio emphasis directly contradicts the attitude of the popular media and financial press, who fixate on analysts' opinions of individual companies. They do so because individual names make attention-grabbing headlines. Few commentators want to talk about stocks in a comprehensive way because they can't do it in a thirty-second sound byte—it requires a discussion. Reporters don't want discussions; they want sound bytes.

John carries over a hundred positions in the Calamos Growth Fund to ensure no single security unduly influences the portfolio's overall results. While some investors think that many holdings might hurt the fund's performance, John disagrees. In fact, the size of the fund may actually have improved its returns because he can take advantage of more opportunities. Furthermore, he runs liquidity screens on all the stocks he buys to make sure he can sell them quickly without influencing their prices. "We watch that closely," he says. "If we feel our opportunity set gets diluted, we'll simply close the fund to new money."

Calamos also diversifies broadly across asset classes and industry groups. In fact, *even if he does not like an asset category, he will still hold a position in it.* This discipline keeps him from making sector bets. John notes that maintaining a small position in a category forces him to stay informed about it. Then when the situation improves, he is positioned to move quickly to a neutral or overweight position. "I think we've added a lot of value in our sector weightings over the years," he says.

John strives to maintain a consistent risk posture throughout an entire market cycle, as opposed to typical investors who let the market dictate their risk tolerance. As stocks rise, average investors become increasingly aggressive, making them most vulnerable to losses at the peak of the market. Conversely, those same individuals become very defensive at the trough of the cycle, unwittingly positioning themselves to miss the next upturn. Keeping risk constant means taking some chips off the table on the way up and raising your stakes as the market drops. This adjustment process helps you take advantage of the market's ebbs and flows.

A Science and an Art

Individuals often try to reduce investing to a science—a set of formulas that consistently produce winning stock picks. While John has developed his share of formulas, he stresses that investing is both a science and an art. The science is the quantitative aspect of money management; it's all the numbers and ratios you absolutely must know to understand companies' financial statements and how the market works. The art is judgment. You need an equal dose of both to invest successfully.

The quantitative part is academic and somewhat mechanical in its application. You learn it by studying textbooks. Art, however, comes from experience, making mistakes, and losing money. "All the enhancements we've made to our investment process over the last twenty years," John says, "resulted from times where we scratched our heads and said, 'If we were better stock pickers, we wouldn't have gotten caught here,' or, 'If we would have paid more attention to our credit homework, we would have seen that problem. Let's enhance that.' It's an iterative process of trying to get better and better and take more and more factors into account going forward."

The Calamos investment team uses numerous models to analyze firms and the market. However, some models work better than others at any given time depending on what is happening in the macroeconomic environment. The art is knowing which models will work best at any particular time; it is about understanding what is happening in the market and the economy so that you can adapt your research to the current environment.

Identifying Growth Companies

Calamos wants to be invested in the best growth companies in the United States at any point in time. He looks specifically for businesses with strong balance sheets that he believes can sustain rapid earnings growth.

John begins his search by screening according to a variety of factors, such as top-line growth, margin expansion, and forward-looking earnings, which help him ferret out the leading growth firms from a large starting universe. This quantitative process produces a much smaller subset of businesses on which John will focus his analysis efforts.

Next, he assesses the growth potential of those firms and determines if their growth is sustainable for the foreseeable future. Calamos looks at a host of qualitative factors in addition to examining the hard data. His analysis covers four areas:

1. Credit analysis
2. Equity analysis

3. Risk/reward profile
4. Fit of the security within the portfolio

Credit Analysis.   This is where Calamos's background as a convertible bond manager gives him a real edge in understanding a company's operations. John first looks at how rating agencies score the firm's bonds, but only to get a preliminary indication of the company's creditworthiness. He conducts his own thorough analysis from that starting point to determine the financial soundness of the business and evaluate its financing needs. He evaluates every security in the company's entire capital structure during that process.

Remember that Calamos is looking for companies with *sustainable* earnings growth. The financial condition of a company plays a key role in its ability to continue growing. Is the business able to fund its expansion from its current cash flow, or will it need to keep tapping the credit markets with new security offerings? If the company still has significant borrowing needs, Calamos must determine if the capital markets are likely to continue extending credit to the firm. The company may not even survive, much less grow, if investors turn the money spigot off.

Equity Analysis.   John looks at a number of models to quantify a firm's growth prospects. He also searches for potential catalysts that might move a stock's price.

As a critical first step, Calamos modifies the company's financial statements from standard accounting to cash-on-cash accounting. Why? He wants to know the bottom line on how much money a firm generates. "In the grocery store, we had a cigar box. If we wanted to know how we were doing, we looked at the cigar box. It's the same concept with big companies," he explains. "I don't want to know earnings after they've been manipulated by accounting gimmicks. Give me the cash flow number."

Calamos reclassifies specific line items within a company's financial statements to properly reflect the effect of those transactions on the firm's cash flow. Those adjustments frequently involve leases and R&D expenditures, although he examines other revenue and expense items as well. Because there is no one correct way to classify many of these transactions, he must make subjective judgments based on his knowledge of a firm's operations and unique circumstances—one formula does not fit all companies. "The more you know about a business, the better you can evaluate those types of situations," John says. "Classifying a company's transactions properly so we can assess its true cash flow is critical to our process. That's the qualitative aspect of cash flow analysis."

Calamos likes to illustrate this step with an example involving a beverage manufacturer. The business showed an expense on its income statement for advertising in India. However, a little detective work turned up the fact that the business could not sell its products in India at the time. So why would it advertise there? It was planning for the future! Should the company then have classified that charge as an advertising expense or research and development? Moving the charge from an expense account to a capital account increased the firm's earnings and gave Calamos a better understanding of the company's real performance.

In similar fashion, Calamos revises a firm's balance sheet, if necessary, to calculate the amount of capital being used in the business. He includes a company's net debt in that figure. What does he mean by net debt? Corporations use a variety of techniques to move monies owed off their balance sheets (known as off–balance sheet financing). For instance, some businesses such as airlines finance a high percentage of their assets with leases, which do not show up as liabilities on their balance sheets. Failing to capitalize those leases—place a debt-equivalent value on them—and modify the firms' balance sheets accordingly can artificially inflate the returns generated on the companies' capital by wrongfully reducing their capital invested figures.

To illustrate why John includes a firm's net debt as part of its invested capital, assume you invest $100—$50 of your own money and $50 that you borrowed—in a project. When calculating your personal return, you base your figures on the $50 out of your pocket. However, when you compute the return generated by the project irrespective of financing decisions, you should base your calculations on the entire amount of capital invested in the project, not just on the $50 out of your pocket. Likewise, Calamos wants to know the return a business is generating apart from its financing to help him gauge the quality of the company's earnings.

Calamos divides the cash earnings figure he developed by the firm's total capital invested to compute the company's cash flow return on invested capital.

KEY POINT

The company's cash flow return on total capital (CFROTC) ratio becomes John's benchmark measure of the firm's performance and a key tool in determining the sustainability of the business's growth.

John develops a historical series of a firm's CFROTC stretching back several years to see what trends have developed in the company's performance: Has it improved, deteriorated, or remained stable over time? He also compares the business's CFROTC to its industry average to determine how the company is performing relative to its peers. Firms that are performing better than their industry, but whose prices do not yet reflect their superior returns on capital, often represent excellent buying opportunities.

Calamos also uses the industry comparison to evaluate the sustainability of a firm's growth. If a company earns a below average return on its total capital, he tries to determine if it will continue to underperform or improve to the industry average. If the latter scenario plays out, the business might generate above average growth on its way to average performance. Conversely, if the business is performing above the industry's norm, John assumes its CFROTC will eventually revert to the industry average and estimates over what period of time this will occur.

Calamos synthesizes all the information developed from this analysis into cash flow projections for the company to help him determine how long its above average growth will continue.

Risk/Reward Profile.   Ultimately, Calamos wants to populate his portfolio with those companies that offer the best risk/reward characteristics. Thus, he wants stocks with lots of upside potential and little downside risk. How does he identify those opportunities?

In the previous step, John whittled his universe down to a group of companies with exceptional growth potential. Those firms only represent good buys, however, if their prices do not already reflect their outstanding prospects. To make that determination, Calamos must establish what a business is worth. The cash flow projections from the previous step help him do that.

When John projects a firm's cash flows, he asks himself two questions: (1) What is the best thing that could happen to this company? (2) What is the worst thing likely to happen to this company? He uses the answers to these questions to build best-case and worst-case scenarios. He then estimates the stream of cash flows that each situation would produce. He discounts the cash flows for each scenario back to present values to compute the firm's intrinsic value under each set of circumstances. The result is a range of fair values that quantifies the probable upper and lower boundaries for the company's near-term price action. Comparing those boundaries to the stock's current price allows John to build a risk/reward profile for each security.

To illustrate, say John determines that a firm's intrinsic value ranges between $20 and $40 a share. If the price resides at the top end of its range, the market has fully valued the business, limiting its upside potential—it's a great company and everybody knows it. However, because the firm's valuation is stretched, if the business hiccups, its price could fall off the table. Is it a great company? Yes. However, Calamos is not just looking for great companies—he's looking for great companies at bargain prices with little downside risk.

Now assume the same business is hovering around $23 a share. John has already determined it offers above average growth potential, but the market has priced it as a below average company. The stock is worth $20 in a worst-case scenario, limiting its probable downside to $3 a share. However, it could appreciate to as much as $40 once the market recognizes the firm's value, giving the security considerable upside potential. While the intrinsic value figures represent only probable price boundaries, this methodology gives John a way to quantify a company's risk/reward characteristics.

Determining a firm's real worth serves as a check on other areas of Calamos's analysis. Even if another part of the process erroneously leads him to invest in a below average business, buying the stock near the bottom end of its intrinsic value range should limit the damage from mistakes.

AMAZON.COM

Amazon.com, a company in which Calamos invested a few years ago, serves as an excellent example of his thinking and investment process. He first looked at Amazon in the late 1990s when it came out with a 4¾ percent convertible bond—an abysmal coupon, John thought, for such a low-rated bond issue. The stock price vacillated between $60 and $70 a share at the time, and the conversion price was $85.

The company had not made any money yet, so it had a negative cash flow. To Calamos, that meant it would need access to a lot more capital in the future. The company would not only have to issue this convertible, but it would need to keep going back to the well for a while. If Wall Street cut off Amazon's access to capital, it wouldn't survive, which echoed the story of a lot of tech firms at the time.

In order to value the convertible security, Calamos first had to value the company. To do so, he needed to determine in which sector to place the company. If he listened to Wall Street, Amazon was an Internet company—it was *technology*, code for "everybody is supposed to buy it and don't worry about the price." Instead of getting caught up in the tech hype, Calamos asked, "What does Amazon do?" It sells things, John thought, so he evaluated the business as a retail company, not a technology firm. As opposed to brick and mortar stores, the Internet simply served as the company's delivery system.

(Continued)

Next, John asked, "What is the best-run retail company in the world?" Most analysts would answer Wal-Mart. So Calamos valued Amazon assuming it eventually achieved the same margins, financial ratios, and cash flow return on total capital as Wal-Mart. So if Amazon became as good as the world's most dominant, best-run retailer, what would it be worth? The answer—$12! Calamos passed on the convertible bond and the stock.

After the tech bubble burst a couple of years later, Amazon's stock hit a low of about $6 a share. John looked again at the same convertible bond, then trading at well under half its par value with a current yield in the range of 11 to 12 percent. He believed the stock was at least fairly valued, if not undervalued, and he figured the bondholders would get paid first if the company generated any cash flow. That sounded like a good deal, so he bought the bond in the Calamos High Yield Fund and the stock in the Calamos Growth Fund.

While John eschews short-term market timing, neither does he believe in buying a company and holding it forever. Instead, he asks, "At what price do I want to own the firm, and at what price should I sell it because its above average risk/reward profile is no longer in place?" "People see *Fortune* magazine's report on the best-run companies in America and think they must be good buys," John says. "Well, if everybody knows a company is great, is that fact priced in? If it's not, then how far off is the price from its fair value? Those are the questions investors ought to ask."

Valuing securities provides an additional benefit: it allows you to see what assumptions are built into a stock's price. Then you can determine if those assumptions make sense. When John evaluated many of the technology stocks in 1999, he calculated how far out investors were discounting the companies' current growth rates to justify the stocks' prices. In many cases, the answer was *forever*.

Assume investors price a company based on the notion that it will grow at 30 percent indefinitely. If the firm's growth drops over time to 18 percent—still considered outstanding—the stock's intrinsic value could drop by half. Is that a risk you want to take? The business only does as well as a premier growth company and you lose 50 percent of your money? That kind of analysis allows John to quantify firms' risk/reward trade-offs from another angle and determine which risks make sense.

A stock's fair value range is dynamic and changes every time a company reports its quarterly earnings. Just because a stock doubles in price after six months does not mean you should sell it—the security may still be undervalued based on improved earnings and prospects. Therefore, John continually makes the decisions to hold or sell positions based on their current risk/reward profiles.

Fit of the Security within the Portfolio.   According to Calamos, any security that survives the process to this point should make an excellent investment. It is financially strong, exhibits above average growth potential, and possesses exceptional risk/reward traits. However, one final hurdle must be cleared before John will buy the stock: it must "fit" the rest of the portfolio.

The portfolio as a whole must meet certain risk management guidelines. In particular, John wants to keep the fund very diversified to moderate the impact of volatile markets. Therefore, he analyzes each security's influence on the fund's sector and industry design. If he believes adding a company would endanger the portfolio's risk profile, he will forgo the investment.

"Same Team, Same Process"

John uses that slogan to describe the unique way the approximately fifty analysts at his firm divide duties: the same investment team manages all the various strategies using the same process. That arrangement differs markedly from most money management firms, where analysts specialize in certain aspects of the process or certain strategies. For instance, a typical structure would divide the analysts into teams of fixed-income specialists and equity specialists. Within the fixed-income area, some analysts would focus on convertible securities while others would focus on high-yield securities, and so on. In the equity area, analysts frequently specialize by sector.

In contrast, Calamos likes analysts who are generalists rather than focused on specific areas. He believes that structure brings a lot of thinking into the investment process. "We work in this environment as a team concept, almost a think tank. A couple of years ago, we recognized our asset base was getting bigger and explored if we needed to change our structure," Calamos recalls. "We ultimately decided we would lose too much of the value our current structure offers. Plus, I think the cross-fertilization of the team makes for a better cultural atmosphere."

Calamos strives for consistently strong relative performance in both up and down markets. He believes teams can achieve that goal better than individuals over the long term. Individuals who get hot hands might do better over short periods of time. Every once in a while, you might even find a Michael Jordan who performs at a high level for a long while. Over time, however, teams will usually generate more consistent results than individuals.

Calamos Investments' team structure fits John's philosophy of evaluating firms. He believes if you can properly assess the enterprise value of a company, then you can value each security within that company—whether it's a high-yield bond, a convertible bond, or any other credit on the capital structure—because all the securities derive their values from the same cash flow stream. Having the same team cover the entire spectrum of a firm's operations improves members' knowledge of each specific area and gives them a better understanding of the common stock.

Having the team involved in the whole process yields another advantage: each area serves as a check on the others. Suppose a company reports strong earnings growth. From the perspective of the equity analysis, the firm looks promising. So Calamos examines the business from the viewpoint of its high-yield and convertible securities—instruments that reveal important information about a firm's need to access capital. That analysis indicates the company will face problems accessing capital in the future. The firm will never be able to maintain its performance going forward because it will have to apply any new capital to servicing existing loans, not growing the business. If the two areas of analysis were performed by different individuals, the equity analyst might miss the impact of the credit situation on the company's growth.

That kind of comprehensive analysis helped the Calamos team sit out much of the technology debacle. This scenario described many of the tech stocks in 1999, when Calamos had reached his maximum weighting in the technology sector. John sliced the Growth Fund's allocation to tech in half over the next twelve months, not because he thought the tech bubble would burst, but because his multidiscipline analysis warned that many of those companies could not sustain the growth needed to support their prices.

What's Working

Does John somehow combine all this information into a score to grade stocks? "We tried doing that, but it really doesn't work that well," John says. "You can say, 'I want this factor to have a 20 percent weighting and another factor be 10 percent,' but the market's too smart. It doesn't allow that to work very well for very long. At any point in time, it's more a matter of determining what's working, what isn't working, and what we should do about it. It's very subjective, and that's where keeping your finger on the market's pulse day to day helps in the selection process. I don't know of too many successful businesses where you can set up a formula and then be completely hands off. Money management is surely not one of them."

What does John mean by "determining what's working"? According to the master investor, there is a continual churning of ideas in the marketplace. At various times, different ideas dominate investors' thinking as to what matters. John refers to those dominant ideas as the "combined wisdom of the market." To be successful, investors have to respect that combined wisdom and get in sync with it rather than fight it.

In John's words, "The law of large numbers kicks in and somehow the combined wisdom of investors makes the financial markets work. Much of our effort centers around trying to get a sense of what the combined wisdom is doing." As opposed to buying undervalued stocks and holding them for years, Calamos adapts swiftly to changes in market conditions based on his understanding of what the market is saying.

To get a handle on what's working, John tries to measure and quantify the market's combined wisdom to the extent possible. As part of this exercise, he uses attribution analysis. He analyzes the common traits of the best-performing stocks to determine what characteristics the market currently favors. Sometimes the market looks forward; sometimes it looks back. Sometimes it values top-line growth; sometimes it rewards rising net earnings. "That's what we're constantly trying to figure out," John explains. "So we measure that as best we can."

Much of the work in this area is subjective; however, the subjective analysis must fit within the bounds of John's quantitative requirements. The quantitative work grounds the qualitative work and keeps the process from becoming too subjective.

A factor that is working often becomes a catalyst to move stocks' prices—something Calamos will try to take advantage of. For example, say a company is undervalued, but it has languished in that condition for three years. It's like dead money. If the market is currently rewarding earnings momentum and the firm's earnings start to accelerate, John will try to pick up on that situation and use the opportunity to buy the stock.

Remember that John believes no single strategy works very well for very long, which explains why he does not invest by formulas. Take earnings momentum, for instance. When it's working, it's very powerful. But the same is true on the downside when it quits working. Often, an investor who focuses exclusively on one strategy or one key factor doesn't sell in time and rides a stock down. That investor could time her sells better if she looked at more factors and had a better sense of why certain stocks' prices were rising.

Companies' Sizes

John believes that trying to keep your style in a box based on companies' sizes is a misguided concept. Rather, he views a firm's size more as a liquidity issue than a factor affecting the stock's investment potential. Calamos argues the biggest advantage of being in the public markets rather than the private markets is that you can sell a stock at

CALAMOS ON THE EFFICIENT MARKET THEORY

"I think it's a shame that people have really bought into this idea that markets are efficient. That notion started an indexing craze, which is silly to me. Indexing distorts the whole access to capital equation.

"What proponents of indexing are missing is that the efficient market hypothesis was just a convenience for schools to test people. It's a mathematical convenience, not a reality. Why do academics do that? Because they have too many kids in their classes. They don't have time to get into an intellectual discussion like you would in philosophy, so they'd rather give you a mathematical test.

"So finance is no longer about qualitative issues; it's about whether you know all the ratios. Economics is no longer about the political economy, which it should be about; it's about econometrics, which bores everyone to tears. If you were to read Adam Smith and study political economy, it has so much relevance to freedoms and how an economy's organized. That's interesting stuff. But unfortunately most academics prefer to focus on econometrics because that's easier to test.

"The same things apply to the financial markets. That's why the 1987 stock market crashed. That's not supposed to happen— it's a five standard deviation event. The Long Term Capital fiasco was not supposed to happen either. All the professors bought into their own theories, and then they said the market was wrong when they collapsed. The market was wrong? They leveraged up 90:1 and then they say the market's wrong? The market's going to whack you if you leverage up that much."

will. You lose that advantage if you impact a security's price when you sell it. Therefore, John analyzes the stock float (the number of shares held by the public and available for trading) of every security he buys to make sure he can liquidate holdings without affecting their prices. That allows him to maintain a very fluid portfolio—he can move in and out of positions at will.

John does not limit his investing activities to companies of any particular market capitalization: he looks for the best growth firms that meet his stringent criteria, period. In practice, however, Calamos tends to find many of his opportunities in the mid-cap sector. His requirements for rapid growth and high expected return filter out most large companies, while his insistence on a strong balance sheet and sustainable earnings growth disqualifies many small firms. Mid caps are often in that sweet spot—small enough to grow substantially but large enough to demonstrate a high quality of earnings.

Turnover

John strives to keep the portfolio very fresh. He wants a snapshot of the Growth Fund at any given time to reflect the best investment characteristics possible. Good ideas surface all the time in our dynamic investment markets, and yesterday's success can quickly become tomorrow's failure. So he is quick to sell a holding to make room for a better idea. As a result, Calamos's turnover ratio tends to range between 70 percent and 120 percent, making his average holding period about one year.

Investors often view a high turnover ratio in a negative light. John does not see it that way because two of the major costs of trading—the bid/ask spread and trading commissions—have come way down over the years. John believes investors profit more by keeping the portfolio fresh than by saving a little on trading fees.

Tax Efficiency

What about the third cost of high turnover: reduced tax efficiency in the form of a higher proportion of short-term gains? John does not want to let tax issues drive investment decisions, but he also understands the financial advantages of long-term gains and shareholders' desires for the best *after-tax* returns they can get. Therefore, he manages the fund to maximize its tax efficiency. For example, if he wants to sell a position he has owned for eleven months that has appreciated significantly, he'll try to hold it for another thirty days to make the gains long term. He'll watch those situations very closely, of course, because he doesn't want to lose principal trying to save taxes. Nevertheless, as a result of his tax emphasis, over 90 percent of the fund's capital gains have qualified for long-term status.

John also has a selfish motivation to manage the Growth Fund in a tax-wise manner—he invests his own money in the fund. In fact, the Calamos family has approximately $100 million invested in the firm's funds. As shareholders, they, too, want strong tax efficiency.

The War Room

Developing an investment strategy is one thing. Applying those ideas effectively in the actual buying and selling of securities is quite another. John borrowed an idea from the military to help bridge the gap between idea and execution—the war room. "I like to think of it like when I was in the military going to a command center. Large maps show where everything's going on all over the theater of battle. Then leadership can funnel down and focus on what they consider to be important. That's what we've tried to do."

Military leaders want voluminous amounts of information at their fingertips during a battle in order to make decisions. So John and his investment team meet in the war room to analyze all the information they have gathered about a security. Analysts bring all their models and openly discuss what's going on with a stock. Team members are free to debate, raise contradictory points, and suggest other data that need to be considered. That immediate access to huge quantities of information has proven extremely beneficial to their decision-making process.

Selling a Security

A well-defined sell strategy is as important to Calamos's investment process as his buy strategy. John will liquidate holdings for a variety of reasons, including:

- *Deceleration in relative CFROTC, revenue growth, or earnings per share growth*: John wants to be invested in companies that sport the best growth prospects at any point in time. A deceleration in any one of these factors indicates that a firm may no longer fit that category.

- *Expectations that a firm's operating margins, earnings, or revenue will fall short*: Stocks often tumble after they miss expectations on one of these factors in an earnings report. A shortfall in one of these categories also frequently presages problems that eventually cause earnings to decelerate.
- *Price can not be sustained by a company's growth*: The risk/reward profile becomes unfavorable when a stock's price reaches a point where the firm's expected growth no longer supports it.
- *A better opportunity*: John wants to keep the portfolio fresh with the best ideas at any given time. That requires liquidating current holdings to take advantage of new superior opportunities.
- *Balance sheet deterioration*: When a company's balance sheet weakens, firms lose financial flexibility, which can cost them future growth.
- *Significant management changes*: New leadership can introduce a significant risk to a business's future growth prospects. Look at what happened to Coca-Cola after Roberto Goizueta died. Calamos avoids situations where he cannot understand the risks involved.
- *Bad news*: This includes any information flow that leads Calamos to believe the firm's sustainability of earnings growth is at risk.
- *Industry problem*: Industry-level problems often affect the stock prices of all companies in the industry, even those not affected by the difficulties.

SUMMARY

The following summarizes the main points of Calamos's investment strategy:

- Two key philosophies should guide your investing activities: (1) Creating wealth over time requires that you give up some of the upside in order to preserve capital when the market drops. (2) No single investment technique works very well very long, so continually evolve your process.

- Do not try to time the markets. One mistake in either direction can cost you much of what you gained earlier. Instead, stay fully invested all the time.
- Investing is risky. Do not shun risk—try to understand and manage it. The characteristics of the *total portfolio* matter more than those of any single security; diversify by number of stocks and by business sector; and maintain a consistent risk posture throughout an entire market cycle.
- Investing is both a science and an art. The science is the quantitative aspect of money management, and it is learned from textbooks; the art is judgment and comes from experience and losing money.
- Strive to stay invested in top-quality growth companies at all times. Look for businesses with strong balance sheets and *sustainable* rapid earnings growth.
- Analyze a firm by first recasting its income statement to cash-on-cash accounting to arrive at the firm's cash flow. Also adjust its balance sheet to compute the total capital invested in the business. Divide the cash flow by the total capital to derive the business's cash flow return on total capital (CFROTC). Compare that figure to past trends and the industry average to determine whether the firm's growth is sustainable and to build a risk/reward profile for the company.
- Develop a range of intrinsic values for the business based on best- and worst-case scenarios. Ideally you want to buy companies with above average growth prospects that the market has priced as below average companies.
- Adapt swiftly to changes in market conditions based on what the combined wisdom of the market is saying.
- Strive to keep your portfolio fresh. Replace holdings quickly that no longer sport favorable risk/reward profiles, that give you reason to believe their growth is unsustainable, or when a better opportunity surfaces.

CHAPTER 7

Five Common Principles of the Professionals

BILL SAT DOWN IN THE MAROON WINGBACK CHAIR OPPOSITE ME. WE exchanged pleasantries, and he removed several papers from his briefcase, laying them on the conference table. A single forty-two-years-old engineer, he had spent most of his career accumulating assets. As I reviewed his paperwork, I was impressed by what I saw—no debt and $300,000 in savings. Not bad, I thought. Then Bill began relating his concerns to me.

"I know that looks like a lot of money for someone my age," he said. "But I'd have a lot more if I hadn't made some big mistakes."

"What mistakes?" I asked.

"I lost $60,000 in three investments."

He went on to explain how he had placed $20,000 in each of three investments—some index options, a stock his broker had recommended, and gold options—that had all gone bust.

As I listened to his story and further reviewed his paperwork, something else caught my attention. He had placed almost his entire savings in certificates of deposit and a money market account. He owned no stocks or equity mutual funds. Someone that young posturing his assets so conservatively struck me as odd, especially when I considered his goal of maximizing his assets. Sensing there was more to understanding Bill's situation, I asked about his apparent aversion to the stock market.

"About three years ago, I took all my money out of stocks because I thought the market was overvalued," he shared.

Bill had sold all his equity investments in early 1995, the beginning of a three-year period in which stock prices approximately doubled.

Doing the mental math, I calculated that if Bill had avoided the three losing investments and obtained average stock market returns the prior three years, he would have accumulated about $700,000 instead of $300,000. Fundamental errors had cost him almost a half-million dollars. Why had he consistently made such bad decisions?

INVESTMENT FRAMEWORK

As I pondered this question, I realized the mistakes Bill had made were by no means peculiar to him—investors all across the country lose money every day for exactly the same reasons. People pour money into investments that stand little chance of making money. Conservative investors unwittingly make risky wagers. Charged by the returns others have made, many individuals enter the market at the top, only to sell out at the bottom, fearful of ever investing in stocks again. Others avoid the stock market completely, failing to recognize the potential it offers long-term investors.

Bill's mistakes were not the problem—they were merely symptoms of something deeper. Like most investors, Bill had no strategy, no strict guidelines for making investment decisions. He simply acted on emotions, hunches, and recommendations from any salesperson who could tell a good story.

KEY POINT

Successful investing requires a consistent strategy, a *systematic* means of sifting through and analyzing potential investments. Each of our managers has developed such an investment framework.

Few readers, if any, will be able to implement the exact methodology of any of the professionals I interviewed. Money managers of their caliber possess extensive resources well beyond those available to nonprofessionals. Specifically, professionals utilize sophisticated (read expensive) software programs that provide vast quantities of data on companies, including historical financial information, real-time trading statistics, and current news items. Staffs of well-trained analysts perform extensive research for successful managers, allowing them to examine more businesses than laypersons can ever hope to look at. Top professionals have also developed far-reaching networks of contacts on Wall Street and with companies' managements, helping those professionals acquire insights into firms' operations that extend beyond the scope of most individual investors.

While you may lack the necessary means to duplicate the process of any particular money manager, you *can* learn principles from all of them that will help you invest more profitably. You can adapt what they have shared to your situation and develop your own investment process, *your* system for finding and selecting quality investments. You may not be able to afford a Bloomberg terminal for your home office, but the Internet and new computer technologies have made an abundance of excellent resources available at reasonable costs— free in many cases—allowing you to make educated and informed investment decisions.

FIVE COMMON PRINCIPLES

Each of the professional money managers I interviewed has carefully evolved his own unique *philosophy* of investing and developed a *process* by which he implements his philosophy. None of the managers totally agree with one another on how to invest, yet they are all successful. The lesson here is that no one correct investment strategy exists. No single approach ensures success while all others are destined to underperform.

That explains why investing often evokes many of the same passions as sports and other forms of competition. Every day it's you against the market, trying to discover something others have overlooked that can boost your returns above the average. Investing involves so much more than simply trying to make money—it is a channel for self-expression. Are you conservative and risk averse? Or are you a risk taker? Perhaps you are calculated and deliberate. Whatever your personality, investing allows you to assert your individuality within the parameters of a few time-tested disciplines.

Your mission is to develop an investment approach that works well over a complete investment cycle and stay with it. Problems come when you switch strategies midstream to match what is popular in the market at a particular time. You will undoubtedly refine your methodology as your investing skills mature, but don't completely abandon one strategy for another just because the market periodically goes against you.

Our five money masters are among the best at their craft (make no mistake about it—investing is a craft, a set of skills you can learn, practice, and improve on over time). Each continues to work hard at honing his expertise, constantly striving to improve his abilities. By spending time with them, I wanted to pinpoint what they each considered most important about investing and to understand why they were so passionate about their particular strategies. However, while that was important, I had an even more important goal in mind when I interviewed them: to learn what they *all* considered essential to investing! In other words, I sought to uncover their *commonalties*, those things they all do and believe that have helped them consistently perform above the pack. I felt that identifying those critical elements would help investors focus their efforts on the most profitable activities.

After combing through the copious amounts of information obtained from our experts, I discovered five principles common to all of them—five standards to which they each adhere. The experts vary in how they define those investing tenets. They differ in how they execute each element. But each manager holds fast to the following five principles in his own way:

1. Invest instead of speculate.
2. Develop a very defined investment philosophy.

3. Follow a detailed, repeatable process every time they analyze a security.
4. Limit their investment selections to quality companies.
5. Buy a corporation's stock only when it is selling at or below its fair market value.

Speculating Versus Investing

Individuals have developed a plethora of complex and confusing techniques for investing in securities. Many, if not most, of those methods neglect the fundamental purpose of buying stocks: to build wealth by allocating capital to those companies that will employ it most productively. How you view the stock market will dictate the strategy you ultimately develop to select stocks and manage your portfolio. To some, the market is a vehicle for *investing*. To others, it is a means of *speculating*.

Certain elements of investing and speculating are common to both activities. For example, they each entail placing capital at risk. With both, a dollar is forfeited today in hopes of getting back more than a dollar in the future. However, a vast gulf separates the two activities in spite of their similarities.

Webster's Universal College Dictionary (New York: Random House, 2001) defines *speculate* as "to buy or sell commodities, property, stocks, etc., especially at risk of a loss, in the expectation of making a profit through market fluctuations." This definition contains two noteworthy characteristics: it emphasizes risk of loss, and it specifies that speculators depend on fluctuations in the prices of assets to generate profits.

Webster's defines *invest* as "to put (money) to use, by purchase or expenditure, in something offering potential profitable returns." Note this definition does not reference the risk of loss or mention the necessity of price fluctuations to obtain a profit.

Benjamin Graham, the renowned patriarch of value investing and Warren Buffett's finance professor at Columbia University, differentiated investing and speculating by stating, "An investment operation is one which, upon thorough analysis, promises safety of principal and an adequate return. Operations not meeting these requirements are speculative."[1]

Speculating typically involves buying an asset simply because you believe you will be able to sell it later for a higher price. The underlying characteristics of the holding itself are generally not important. In fact, much speculation depends on a change in *external* circumstances to push the price of an asset higher. Speculators also tend to make relatively short-term bets. Timing is critical to successful speculating.

Investing normally entails placing money in an enterprise that generates income instead of depending solely on appreciation to earn a profit. It emphasizes the fundamentals of a business's operations and its future prospects. *Timing* is not as critical to an investor as is *time*.

Speculative Activities. Let me illustrate speculation with the example of buying precious metals. Think about what an ounce of gold is really worth. While you can argue that supply and demand determine its value in a free market, it is ultimately worth what someone else is willing to pay for it. Its price goes up if buyers decide to pay more, and its price drops if they decide to pay less. You have no control over what others are willing to offer for the asset, and gold generates no income while you hold it. Therefore, your purchase will produce a profit only if you can sell the metal later for a higher price than you originally paid for it.

Typically marketed as limited partnership units, Arabian horses were popular "investments" in the mid-1980s and provide another example of speculation. The story was simple: The partnership could purchase a foal for $3,500. Raising the foal to maturity cost about another $3,000 to $3,500, including food, board, grooming, and so forth. The horse would sell for about $10,000 at that point, generating a $3,000 profit on the $7,000 investment—not a bad return over a three-year period. Of course, that return hinged on the assumption that a buyer would still pay $10,000 for a mature Arabian horse after three years. Since the animal generated no income until someone bought it, investors lost money if the horse sold for less than $7,000.

Two individuals can place money in similar assets, yet one can be investing while the other is speculating. Take real estate, for instance. A speculator buys raw land in hopes of selling it later at a higher price. The investor purchases a rental property that generates income and a positive return over time regardless of whether it sells at a profit. Obviously the investor hopes her asset appreciates in value while she holds it, but she can realize a profit regardless.

Speculating in Stocks.   As with other assets, people can both invest and speculate in stocks. Legions of individuals acquired shares in grossly overvalued technology firms during the late 1990s, having no idea what the businesses were really worth. Many of those companies had never generated a profit. Buyers acquired shares solely because their prices had been rocketing upward, and purchasers expected those price trends to continue indefinitely (or at least until they sold their shares). They did not base their optimism on any value they perceived in the firms they bought; they simply hoped someone else would pay a higher price for their shares in the future. Those individuals were speculating.

Speculators commonly view the stock market as no more than a black box of numbers that oscillate up and down on a routine basis. They strive to discern patterns in the numbers' fluctuations in order to predict the directions and magnitudes of future price movements. The fundamental characteristics of the individual companies that comprise the market matter little to them.

While speculating is not inherently wrong or bad, as long as you realize you are doing it, neither is it a sound long-term wealth accumulation strategy. Therefore, you should limit funds dedicated to speculative activities to a small percentage of your total net worth.

Am I insinuating that speculating will never generate profits? Quite the opposite—if things go your way, it can pay quite handsomely. It just is not related to investing. In fact, speculating actually parallels gambling in many respects. Both can offer similar thrills and rewards.

This analogy exemplifies the perspective of professional stock market speculators and the goals of their techniques. When buying and selling stocks, they focus on such extraneous factors as price trends, trading volumes, and the levels of others' enthusiasm or pessimism regarding the shares. They bet on stocks' future movements based on how their prices have responded to those factors in the past.

Businesslike Investing.   Investors view the stock market differently than speculators. In his book, *The Intelligent Investor*, Benjamin Graham, stated "Investment is most intelligent when it is most businesslike."[2] That philosophy of analyzing securities from the perspective of a businessperson acquiring businesses is foundational to successful stock investing.

Let me contrast investing in the stock of a quality company with speculating as described earlier. A corporation generates earnings, or income, for its owners, the shareholders. A knowledgeable individual can forecast those earnings several years into the future with some level of confidence and calculate a current value for them. *An investor buys an expected stream of cash flow.* The business should generate positive returns for its owners over time from the income it generates, even if potential buyers never offer the owners a price above their original investment.

K E Y   P O I N T

When you buy shares of stocks, you are not merely accumulating sheets of paper—you are acquiring ownership in companies. You must view an investment as if you are a businessperson purchasing the entire business, even though you are buying only a small fraction of the enterprise.

Many individuals fool themselves into thinking they are investing in stocks when they are in fact speculating. For a variety of reasons, including a lack of knowledge and effort, those individuals fail to scrutinize such things as a firm's business model, competitive advantages, and quality of management. Instead, they buy the stock based on trading issues they believe will affect the security's price in the near term.

Investors, however, understand stock prices are unpredictable over short periods of time but tend to track companies' values over long periods. Therefore, as businesspeople acquiring businesses—a mindset that permeates every aspect of how they select stocks—investors focus on issues that affect companies' values instead of trying to predict future stock prices.

Developing an Investment Philosophy

Webster's defines philosophy as "the critical study of the basic principles and concepts of a particular branch of knowledge . . . a system of principles for guidance in practical affairs." Stated simply, a philosophy is a belief system, a way of thinking.

KEY POINT

Your investment philosophy states what you believe about investing. It determines how you will select stocks and manage your portfolio. The philosophy you develop should encompass virtually everything you know about investing and should establish the criteria by which you will make every buy and sell decision.

When you filter out companies based on objective standards, you will likely exclude firms that turn out to be good investments. That is not a problem. You are not trying to develop a philosophy that identifies every good investment; rather, you want to build a philosophy such that every investment it identifies is good. For example, assume the universe of superior investments consists of one hundred businesses. Your selection criteria filter out eighty of those companies, along with thousands of bad ones. As long as the twenty firms that pass muster are quality selections, you have accomplished your goal of constructing a portfolio of winners.

KEY POINT
It is better to miss a good opportunity than to make a bad investment.

Some money managers only invest in companies below a certain size as part of their philosophy. That is not to say they believe larger businesses never make good investments. They have just decided to limit their purchases to the small-cap market, perhaps because they believe the best growth opportunities reside there, or possibly they feel this area offers exceptional valuations. By excluding large firms from their consideration, they hope to develop greater expertise in the small-cap sector and spot opportunities missed by others.

Some managers exclude firms that have not grown their earnings by at least some minimum rate over a number of years. By doing so, those professionals don't even look at high-quality, slower-growing corporations selling for half their value. Even though those firms might produce excellent returns, their characteristics do not match the philosophies of the growth-oriented managers, so the companies get rejected.

Investors often needlessly suffer losses from failing to develop and abide by strict buy and sell guidelines. In an effort to chase short-term performance numbers, even professionals can fall into this trap. During the great technology bubble, I periodically read statements by analysts similar to this: "You can't justify the price for this security, but you just have to own it." In other words, "This security is overvalued and no longer meets my criteria, but its price continues to rise for some inexplicable reason and I'll look bad if I don't urge investors to buy it. So I am ignoring my philosophy and recommending it anyway."

If you purchase a stock that doesn't meet your buy criteria, how will you know when to sell it? When everyone else decides to sell it? When its price drops a certain percent? A lower price might actually make the security more appealing instead of turning it into a sell candidate. You leave the realm of investing to speculate when you violate your investment philosophy.

Rather than base their decisions on objective criteria, individuals often buy and sell solely because of the opinions of others, again moving them from investing to speculating. Accepting someone else's analysis is fine *if you understand and agree with his or her philosophy*. However, most people don't know the reasoning behind a recommendation when they embrace it.

An investment philosophy anchors your decision making and stabilizes your portfolio during turbulent times. It acts as both a map and a compass that provide direction and guide you through stormy investment markets. Great investors do not change what they believe to match whatever is popular. They are willing to risk missing a good investment to avoid bad ones.

Developing a Repeatable Process

Once you have developed your philosophy and determined what types of companies you want to own, you must develop a repeatable process, or set of procedures, designed to search for and identify firms that match your investment criteria. You should also include procedures for identifying holdings you need to sell because they no longer meet your requirements. *Your process implements your philosophy and moves you from the idea phase into the action phase.*

KEY POINT

Following the same process every time you analyze a stock ensures you give adequate attention to each firm you examine. This prevents you from overlooking important details because you are in a hurry and fail to spend the necessary time evaluating a security. It also guarantees you judge all investments by a consistent set of criteria.

Specific data must be gathered, organized, and analyzed, and particular calculations must be made *every time* you examine a company.

As I emphasize throughout this book, no single correct way to invest exists. The process I develop over the next several chapters is not *the* correct process; it is simply *a* process that employs many sound investing principles. The important thing is that you establish a set of procedures that puts your philosophy into action and you follow those procedures faithfully.

Buying Quality Businesses at Reasonable Prices

Bill Nygren, Lead Manager of the Oakmark and Oakmark Select funds, stated the last two principles succinctly during a conference call in which I participated: "I buy businesses that are growing their intrinsic values when they are selling at sizable discounts to their intrinsic values." His statement makes two things clear about his strategy. First, he buys firms that are growing their values, implying he looks for quality companies. Second, he waits to purchase them until they sell for significantly less than they are worth. Those two standards exemplify businesslike investing.

Ask yourself these two questions each time you consider investing in a company: (1) Does this firm qualify as a quality business? (2) Can I buy it at a price that will allow me to earn a strong return over time? Do not purchase shares of the business unless you can answer *both* questions affirmatively.

Defining a Quality Business.   A cheap price alone does not justify buying a company. A corporation may sell at a bargain price for good reasons, such as incompetent management or waning demand for the company's products. You should disqualify the firm as an investment candidate if company-specific factors that are structural in nature drive its depressed price.

Superior businesses possess certain common characteristics, including robust profit margins, strong earnings and revenue growth, a clean balance sheet, and competent management.

Profit Margins.   High profit margins help a business weather negative circumstances. Such circumstances may be economy-wide, such as a recession; industry-wide, such as airlines after 9/11; or company specific. Poor margins have forced many corporations to fold or sell

---

KEY POINT

The professionals are especially adept at distinguishing between long-term problems and temporary issues and picking up early on positive changes taking place in a company's operations. Until you develop your skills to the point you feel comfortable making those calls, I suggest you stay with businesses that have exhibited *consistently* strong historical performance. I base recommendations I make throughout the book on that principle.

---

to competitors during business downturns, as low-margin firms can easily generate bottom-line losses when their revenues take a hit.

The larger a firm's net profit relative to its revenues, the greater the probability it will generate positive earnings for the foreseeable future, offering investors a higher margin of safety. While there are exceptions, companies with large, ongoing capital requirements and firms that produce commodity items with little pricing flexibility tend to operate at relatively low margins. Service-oriented businesses and those with pricing power, due to either strong demand for their products or a lack of competition, frequently operate at higher margins.

Historical Earnings Growth.   Look for businesses that exhibit historically strong and consistent earnings growth. Strong previous growth adds credibility to the notion that the firm has a product line and management team capable of generating future earnings increases. Be wary of any business projecting a sizable income expansion that has never attained such growth in the past.

Consistent earnings growth allows you to project a company's future cash flow with greater confidence. Since a firm's worth depends on its projected income, you can more accurately value a business with a reliable earnings stream.

Does this eliminate cyclical firms, whose earnings rise and fall periodically based on external factors such as interest rate cycles? Not at all. However, understand that investing in those businesses adds another factor that you have to get right—timing! If you feel confident that a company is coming out of a cyclical downturn and entering a period of rapid growth, the principles I discuss apply.

There are a few ways to determine the consistency of a company's historical earnings growth. The first involves running a regression analysis on a firm's previous earnings per share. The formulas can get quite complex, so I recommend using another method.

Second, the Value Line Investment Survey computes an earnings predictability factor for businesses it covers. This measure, which runs between 1 and 100, indicates how reliable and therefore predictable a firm's earnings stream is. I recommend looking for businesses with factors of 75 and higher.

Third, you can eyeball a company's prior years' earnings figures and make an informed judgment about how consistently a firm has grown its earnings. For example, compare the five-year earnings history for O'Reilly Automotive and General Motors:[3]

	O'Reilly Automotive	General Motors
1999	$0.92	$8.52
2000	$1.00	$8.58
2001	$1.26	$3.23
2002	$1.53	$6.81
2003	$1.84	$5.68

Quite obviously, O'Reilly has generated more consistent growth. Investors would likely place a higher degree of confidence in their forecasts for O'Reilly's future earnings than GM's.

Projected Earnings Growth.   Strong historical growth does not guarantee a healthy expansion in a firm's future income. New technologies make older products obsolete, demographic changes alter consumers' purchasing habits, and buyers' preferences shift over time. Before investing, make sure you understand a company's products well enough to develop confidence in its future demand. Ask yourself if the firm's products are trendy, or if they exhibit *growing* demand regardless of changing fads. You want businesses that can sustain their earnings growth.

You cannot simply extrapolate prior earnings trends indefinitely into the future when projecting a firm's growth—another mistake technology investors made in the late nineties. Then corporations upgraded equipment early and expanded their IT spending dramatically in 1998 and 1999 to avoid potential Y2K problems, resulting in huge earnings growth for tech firms. A drop in business spending occurred after the turn of the millennium. Investors, however, had projected years of unsustainable earnings growth to justify prices for technology companies.

Historical and Projected Revenue Growth.   Top-line growth is just as critical to a company's long-term success as increasing its bottom line. Firms can temporarily cut costs to expand their net profits without growing sales. At some point, however, businesses must grow their revenues to achieve long-term earnings growth.

Balance Sheet.   Producing a unique product with a strong demand will not ensure a company's success. A weak financial situation can prevent a firm's management team from executing its business plan effectively. Two factors dominate when determining the health of a company's balance sheet: liquidity and debt level. A strong balance sheet with plenty of liquidity and low debt gives a company flexibility and fortifies it against business downturns.

Liquidity refers to the amount of assets a business can convert to cash in a relatively short period of time. A company may have lots of assets, but if they cannot be converted to cash, the firm may not be able to pay its bills. Liquid assets are referred to as *current assets*. Bills that come due within a year are known as *current liabilities*. The absolute amount of liquid assets a business has on hand does not matter as much as its current assets relative to its current liabilities. Therefore, you compute a key measure of a company's liquidity, known as its *current ratio*, as current assets/current liabilities.

Excessive debt has plunged many corporations into bankruptcy because steep payments strangled the firms' cash flows. High fixed expenses also reduce a company's ability to adjust to changes in its operating environment.

Analysts refer to a firm's debt as borrowings with at least a year before they must be paid back. Again, a company's absolute debt level is not as important as its debt level relative to the company's size, often measured by its equity. Therefore, investors often look at a company's debt/equity ratio as the most relevant measure of the firm's debt.

Competent Management.   The future success of a company hinges on the quality of its leadership team. A corporation with a great product line will never fulfill its potential without a management team capable of developing and executing a well-designed business plan. Qualities to look for in management include experience, integrity, shareholder orientation, honest and forthright communication, and the ability to consistently allocate the firm's resources into high-return projects.

Although this area is somewhat subjective, measuring the return the business has earned on its capital can help determine the competency of a firm's leaders and how effectively they have allocated the company's resources. Understanding a firm's return on capital also helps you project how fast the company is likely to grow its future earnings. The most common figure used in this regard, the return on equity (ROE), divides the net income of a business by its equity.

Buying Reasonably Valued Companies

Great businesses do not necessarily make great investments. For example, a firm may possess an accomplished management team, claim the leading shares of the markets in which it competes, and manufacture products for which strong demand is projected several years out. Yet all these positive factors may be built into the stock's current price, leaving little room for shareholders of the fully valued corporation to experience above average returns. In fact, enthusiastic investors often *overprice* outstanding businesses.

To quote Andy Stephens, "Statistically there is a correct price to pay for a company." Christopher Davis says, "No business is worth buying at any price."

KEY POINT

Overpaying for a business, even a superior one, generally yields mediocre investment results. Therefore, you want to buy a stock when it sells at a substantial discount to its value. This should increase your return over time and give you a *margin of safety* if the business experiences unforeseen difficulties, a concept popularized by Benjamin Graham.

Valuing a business plays such an important role in successful investing that I devote two chapters to it. I not only discuss the factors that influence a firm's worth, but I also build a simple model to calculate that figure. As you will learn, however, a couple of issues make it difficult, if not impossible, to determine one precise value for a company.

First, investment experts do not agree on one correct methodology to calculate a firm's fair market value. Money managers have experienced great success using a variety of techniques.

With little dispute, a corporation's worth depends primarily on the size of its future cash flows. However, professional investors and analysts disagree on what measure of cash flow should be used. Some formulas focus on operating earnings, whereas others consider dividends most pertinent. Still other methods emphasize some variation of a firm's free cash flow (net income + depreciation − capital expenditures).

Second, a company's future income stream is uncertain. Even if they use the same methodology, investors will likely calculate numerous fair market values for a firm because they anticipate different levels of earnings. Only time will tell whose numbers were correct.

You can solve this dilemma a couple of ways. First, you can determine a *range* of possible values for a business instead of trying to calculate one exact figure. You might utilize multiple earnings growth rates, such as for best- and worst-case scenarios, or you could use more than one method of computing a firm's worth to develop this range. Instead of stating that XYZ Corporation is worth $75 a share, you might determine the company's value lies somewhere between $70 and $85, then buy the stock when its price is at or below the lower end of that range.

Second, you might look at a number of factors in determining a corporation's fair value, as already discussed, and synthesize the information into one intrinsic value figure. You then only buy the firm's stock when the market prices it at a significant discount to that figure in order to give yourself a large margin of safety.

IN WRITING THIS BOOK, I DID NOT WANT TO JUST FILL YOU WITH GOOD ideas and then frustrate you by not showing you how to apply them. Therefore, I develop a detailed yet simple investment process in the remaining chapters that virtually every investor who has use of a computer and access to the Internet can learn and follow to make intelligent investment decisions. The strategy does not correspond exactly to any particular manager's methodology or philosophy, but it does incorporate the five common principles of our money masters. Implementing the process requires a few minor expenditures, and you must be willing to spend some time and effort analyzing securities and managing your portfolio. However, the potential payoffs more than justify the costs. Investing in stocks can produce substantial rewards, and learning to invest skillfully may very well be your ticket to financial independence.

SUMMARY

The following summarizes the five common investment principles of our elite managers:

- Invest instead of speculate. Speculating involves buying an asset because you believe you will be able to sell it later for a higher price. It is usually shorter term in nature and timing is critical. Speculators attempt to profit from fluctuations in an asset's value. The underlying characteristics of the asset itself matter little, if at all.

Investing involves placing money in an enterprise that generates earnings. It emphasizes the operations of the underlying business and does not require fluctuations in the value of an asset to generate a positive return. Time is more important than timing to an investor.

- Develop an investment philosophy. Your philosophy states what you believe about investing and should encompass virtually everything you know about the subject. It establishes the criteria by which you will make every buy and sell decision.
- Follow a defined process every time you analyze a security. Your process implements your philosophy—it moves you from the idea phase to the action phase and ensures that you give adequate attention to each investment considered.
- Limit your investment selections to quality companies. Quality firms possess healthy profit margins, strong earnings and revenue growth (both historical and projected), clean balance sheets, and competent management. A poor business selling at a great price usually makes a bad investment.
- Buy a corporation's stock when it is selling well below its fair market value. Overpaying for a superior business generally yields mediocre investment results. Buying a stock at a discount to its intrinsic value should increase your return and offer a margin of safety if the firm experiences unexpected problems.

CHAPTER 8

The Artist Meets the Technician

Developing an Investment Philosophy and Process

AS I SPOKE WITH EACH PROFESSIONAL ABOUT HOW HE INVESTED, TWO common traits clearly stood out: (1) all the managers had developed very defined investment processes, and (2) they were able to clearly articulate how they invested. They plainly laid out how they analyze stocks and the characteristics of what they consider strong investments. They discussed their typical holding periods and how those play into their strategies. They talked about the particular triggers that cause them to liquidate holdings. They even occasionally mentioned alternative stances other managers took on specific issues and explained why they believed their ways were better.

During our interviews, I peppered them with questions about how they would handle various hypothetical situations: What if a company grows its earnings but its price doesn't change? What if a firm doesn't meet your requirements in one area but is exceptionally strong in others? Would you sell a business that still has sound fundamentals if its macroenvironment deteriorates? Each manager answered my questions in a way that reflected depth of thought and consistency.

PROCESS COMES FROM PHILOSOPHY

It became clear that all the managers had thoroughly considered each step of their investment processes. They had considered alternative methodologies and deliberately settled on their respective strategies.

As I delved further, however, I realized their processes were more than just the results of book learning—they reflected deeply held beliefs about investing. Those beliefs were the roots and the managers' processes grew from them. They had built entire systems of investing around their convictions. While they respected how other managers did things and they were open to learning, any new ideas they implemented needed to fit within their basic belief systems.

The managers adopted different philosophies for a variety of reasons, their ideas often stemming from attitudes they developed growing up. For instance, Andy Stephens was raised in a very challenging financial environment. As a result, he places a strong emphasis on preserving assets during market downturns. Value investing made sense to Bill Nygren because it corresponded to what his mother taught him about shopping as a young child. Chris Davis saw his grandfather develop almost a billion-dollar net worth by investing a certain way. Regardless of how they developed their ideas, each manager held strong beliefs that formed the foundation for his investment process.

Your investment philosophy should express *your* beliefs about investing—it should encompass virtually everything you know about the field and establish a framework for making all your decisions.

Your philosophy goes hand in hand with your goals. What do you want to accomplish through investing: To generate income for retirement? To accumulate assets to achieve financial independence twenty-five years down the road? To become very wealthy?

One major factor that will affect your strategy is how much risk—short-term loss of principal—you feel comfortable with. Andy Stephens rejects a concentrated portfolio because he believes it will create more volatility than he wants. To the contrary, reflecting an attitude held throughout Harris Associates, Bill Nygren believes that concentrating his portfolio helps him outperform the markets.

BUILDING YOUR PHILOSOPHY

So what types of issues should your investment philosophy address? Begin by answering two basic questions: (1) What standards must a company meet for you to buy it? (2) What developments will cause you to sell a firm you own?

Buy Criteria

The first question, which addresses your buy criteria, encompasses several areas. At a minimum, you should consider these factors:

Company Size.   What size companies do you want to own—large, small, midsize, or all of these? Investors gauge the size of companies by two primary measures: revenue and market capitalization (market cap). You calculate a firm's market capitalization by multiplying its number of shares outstanding by its price per share.

Smaller companies in the early stages of their business cycles exhibit different characteristics and carry different risks than larger, more mature businesses:

- While smaller firms' earnings may fluctuate more than those of larger businesses, the earnings of small companies often grow faster.
- The leaders of larger businesses may have proven their abilities to manage big companies. Those managements may also have shown they can compound capital at high rates of return for long periods of time—something the leaders of small firms may not have accomplished yet.
- Smaller firms do not come under as much scrutiny from the investment world as larger, more established businesses, creating greater potential for fraud and other financial abuses.
- Small companies often face liquidity issues with regard to their daily trading volumes, which can make their prices more volatile.
- Once a small firm has proven the market demand for its product, the business may face the threat of competition from a larger, better capitalized firm.
- While a young business may be showing positive accounting earnings, it usually takes a while for companies to generate positive free cash flow. Until that occurs, they may be dependent on the credit markets to sustain their growth. Therefore, the quality of earnings for larger companies is often better.
- The overall risk of failure is greater for small firms.

Financial Strength.   What financial standards must firms meet for you to buy them? Determining a company's overall financial strength is complex and requires a strong financial background. Fortunately, several ratings agencies score the financial conditions and historical earnings reliability of publicly traded companies as part of their services. Two such agencies are Value Line and Standard & Poor's. Therefore, you might evaluate a corporation's financial wherewithal simply by the grade one of those firms assigns to the company.

You may also want to set hurdles based on specific financial metrics. For example, you might reject businesses that exceed certain debt thresholds or fall short of minimum liquidity levels. Since the rate at which a firm compounds capital is an important element of the company's financial strength, you might establish a return on equity requirement.

Growth.   Investors generally measure companies' growth rates in terms of earnings per share, top-line revenues, and/or book values. Rapidly growing firms typically behave differently and carry different risks than slower-growing businesses. Companies that do not grow at all risk losing value over time. You should set a standard that holdings must meet. For example, Bill Nygren generally requires that a firm's value growth plus dividends at least match that of the market.

Valuation.   A firm's market price may or may not reflect the company's fair value. At how steep of a discount to its intrinsic value must a business sell for you to buy it?

Number of Stocks.   The number of stocks in your portfolio will significantly impact its risk/return characteristics. Larger portfolios tend to be less volatile, but you may find yourself investing more money in lesser-quality ideas. You must determine for yourself what size portfolio offers the best risk/return attributes relative to your investment goals. Academic research suggests that you need at least fifteen to twenty stocks to diversify away between 90 and 95 percent of the risk that can be diversified away, known as *unsystematic risk*. Bill Nygren runs about twenty to twenty-five positions in the Oakmark Select Fund, while John Calamos owns over a hundred positions in the Calamos Growth Fund.

Also decide how large you will let a position become before trimming it back. Bill Fries generally limits a security to between 4 and 5 percent of the portfolio, depending on the type of company. Chris Davis will go up to about 8 percent, whereas Nygren will let a holding take up 20 percent of Select.

Keep in mind you need to invest across several market sectors to maximize the benefits of diversification. Fifteen tech stocks do not constitute a diversified portfolio.

The amount of time you can devote to investing also influences how many securities you should place in your portfolio. If you only have time to follow twenty stocks, don't invest in thirty.

Sell Criteria

Your sell criteria should provide guidance in at least these areas:

Company Fundamentals.   This one is hard to quantify, but it encompasses several factors, all of which threaten the sustainability of the firm's earnings growth. Businesses that were once healthy can develop a variety of problems, some of which are short term and others that are longer term or permanent. Some negative situations are company specific, while others relate to a firm's macroenvironment. Even if a problem can be fixed, remember a question Bill Fries asks: Is the fix doable in a time frame that's relevant to current investors?

Also remember that some problems relate more to perception than reality. Investors drove Tyco to under $10 a share on the belief it was another Enron or WorldCom. This ultimately proved to be a false view. Tyco actually had several solid operating businesses and generated legitimate free cash flow. Investors eventually realized their error, and the company's share price rebounded to over $30 in less than two years.

Think about the types and severity of problems that would prompt you to liquidate a holding. Some important reasons include declining market share or waning demand for its product(s), increasing debt and interest payments, legal issues, management changes, and negative developments in the macroenvironment.

Valuation.   Just like when you buy a stock, a company's valuation should play a significant role in your decision to sell a security. Set a price target where you think the business no longer offers a favorable risk/return trade-off. Adjust that price over time as the firm's earnings and expected growth rate change.

Superior Opportunities.   Stocks with better prospects than one of your present holdings will periodically surface. *Superior* can be defined in a number of ways, but this issue typically centers on valuation. Since valuation is not an exact science, you probably do not want to sell a holding that is 30 percent undervalued for one that is 35 percent undervalued. You must decide at what point a superior opportunity justifies liquidating a stock.

While this framework is not comprehensive, it gives you a good idea of the kinds of questions your philosophy should answer and the areas it should address. You should fine-tune and add elements to your philosophy as your experience increases and you face new issues. Unfortunately, lessons you learn from losing money will likely play a major role in this refinement process. Since you're going to make mistakes, at least try to learn from them and avoid making the same mistake twice.

True professionals develop their belief systems and stick with them when the market moves contrary to their ways of investing. The pros will alter aspects of their philosophy if they uncover legitimate flaws, and they may emphasize certain aspects of their analysis over others at different times. However, that fine-tuning is vastly different from periodically changing their styles to justify buying into the latest investment fads.

SAMPLE PHILOSOPHY

This section illustrates a philosophy I believe makes sense for many, if not most, investors. I assumed readers are not professional money managers or financial experts, and they have a limited amount of time to devote to investing. I designed this philosophy only as a starting point that you can use immediately to make sound investment decisions. Customize it to fit your situation and refine it as you gain experience.

Goal

My goal is to accumulate wealth over a period of several years by compounding money at a rate equal to or higher than the broad stock market represented by the S&P 500 index. I want to accomplish this goal by investing in financially sound companies with sustainable strong earnings growth when they are significantly undervalued.

Buy Criteria

Company Size. *Purchase companies with market capitalizations greater than $1.5 billion based on my calculations of their intrinsic values.*

You can avoid many potential risks by insisting firms reach this size before investing in them.

Base companies' market caps on your calculations of their intrinsic values, which means a corporation with a $750 million market cap that is 50 percent undervalued would meet your $1.5 billion threshold. You don't want to exclude a firm as too small only because its price is undervalued.

Financial Strength. *Invest in businesses with the following characteristics*:

- *S&P Earnings and Dividend Ranking[1] of B+ or higher, or Value Line Financial Strength Rating[2] of B+ or better*
- *Debt/equity < 1*
- *Current ratio > 1*
- *Return on equity of 15 percent or greater*

Growth. *Buy firms that are expected to grow their earnings per share by at least 10 percent annually.*

You want to buy businesses that are not only undervalued, but growing their values as well.

Valuation. *Only buy businesses when they sell for less than 65 percent of their intrinsic values.*

Number of stocks.   *Develop a portfolio of between twenty and twenty-five stocks diversified across at least six different industries. Trim positions by at least 2 percent when they grow to more than 8 percent of my portfolio.*

Sell Criteria

Company Fundamentals.   *Liquidate a position if its fundamentals deteriorate.*

Valuation.   *Sell a holding when the stock price reaches 90 percent of its fair value.*

Superior Opportunities.   *Sell a stock when another opportunity comes available that is at least 25 percent more undervalued.*

For example, sell a 15 percent undervalued stock only to replace it with one that is at least 40 percent undervalued.

EXPLANATORY NOTE

Valuation plays a role in both your buy and sell criteria. By definition, the valuation gap between where you buy a stock and where you sell it is your *hold zone*—that is, you hold positions when they are priced above 65 percent of their intrinsic values until they reach 90 percent of their full values. At that level they are too expensive to invest more money in them but not close enough to full value to sell.

A company that meets all of your criteria except valuation should go on a watch list. You've done the research and know you like the business, so you simply wait for the price to drop low enough to buy it.

DEVELOPING AN INVESTMENT PROCESS

As I stated previously, your process transforms the *ideas* of your philosophy into *actions*, which explains why you cannot begin to invest successfully without first defining what you believe and establishing your investment goals. The process spells out how you will accomplish your philosophy. As you develop your process, write it down and develop a checklist to help you form the discipline of following the same steps every time you analyze a security. This ensures your portfolio maintains consistent investment traits based on characteristics you deem important.

Your process should encompass three important areas: screening, analysis, and ongoing portfolio management.

Screening

Where can you get investment ideas? Perhaps you read an interview of your favorite mutual fund manager touting a recent stock pick. You might see a well-known market strategist on a financial news show talking about his favorite companies. You might hear a news reporter discuss a demographic trend that sparks your thinking about firms that might profit from it. Be alert and you can pick up on potential investments from a variety of sources.

Peter Lynch, the legendary former manager of the Fidelity Magellan Fund, suggests looking at the stocks of companies where you shop. You know about their products and reputations, and you can directly observe how much business the stores do. He strongly advocates investing in firms you know.

INVEST WHERE YOU SHOP

You can learn much about potential investments by patronizing their stores. On a Saturday afternoon early one holiday season, my fifteen-year-old daughter and I traveled to a local shopping center strip mall. An office supply superstore had advertised a $79 CD burner for only $19. When we walked into the store at about 5:30 P.M., I was immediately struck by the fact that only two other customers were shopping there. One checkout lane was open. After spending a few minutes searching fruitlessly for the item, I found a clerk who could assist me. She informed me

(Continued)

that the store had sold out of the CD burners that morning. Must have been a huge rush, right? Wrong! The store had only stocked ten of them, which they sold during the first hour after opening.

Seeing my frustration, the teenager let me know I could special order the item, and it would arrive with the store's next shipment. I gave her my credit card, and she disappeared through a door in the back. After ten minutes she reappeared and said I could call the store on Tuesday to make sure it had received my order (nobody would call me to let me know).

Taking advantage of the object lesson, I rehearsed with my daughter what we had just experienced: bad inventory management and poor customer service! The store's inability to handle any significant volume of business efficiently had become a self-fulfilling prophecy.

We then walked next door to an electronics retailer to pick up another item on our shopping list. The store was full of customers and uniformed, easy-to-identify sales personnel to service them. Eight checkout lines moved the shoppers through quickly. I stopped a salesperson who answered my question and showed me where the part I needed was located. I grabbed the item, paid for it, and walked out of the store within ten minutes of when I had entered.

Dutiful father that I am, I reviewed our second shopping venture with my daughter. The store had plenty of inventory, knowledgeable salespeople, and was geared to service a lot of customers in a short period of time—an unusually pleasant experience during a hectic shopping period.

When we got home, I ran some financial numbers on both companies. The figures confirmed my suspicions! The office supply store had maintained an average return on equity of only 4 percent for the previous five years and actually lost money the prior year. The electronics retailer, however, boasted an ROE of over 15 percent and had actually grown its earnings throughout the recession. Too bad it didn't sell $79 CD burners for $19!

Shopping offers the opportunity to check out companies first-hand. However, with all its benefits, this method of finding potential investments suffers from two major weaknesses. First, a lot of businesses you will never patronize might make great investments. When was the last time you purchased a Boeing 757 or took advantage of a great deal on a Patriot missile? Second, you will likely waste a lot of time researching firms that don't meet several of your criteria.

Investors need a methodology for *consistently* generating quality investment ideas. Screening answers that need. Thousands of businesses trade publicly, most of which you would not consider investing in. Proper screening rapidly eliminates companies from consideration that don't come reasonably close to meeting your investment requirements, saving you valuable analysis time. On the positive side, screening generates a list of ideas that might make suitable investments and are worth taking the time to examine further.

Numerous software programs can aid you in the screening process. Some are online and others reside on your local hard drive as part of more extensive analytical systems. Importantly, some programs allow you to filter the investment universe on more extensive sets of variables than others, permitting a higher level of precision for your initial search.

Screening requires that you determine what minimum requirements a company must meet for you to consider investing in it, which you did when developing your philosophy. I recommend setting the filters slightly under what you really want on most factors for a couple of reasons. First, if you set your criteria too tight, you might filter out some excellent candidates that barely miss your standards in one or two areas. Second, exceptional strength in one area may offset a slight weakness in another. For instance, if you want firms with returns on equity of 15 percent or greater, you might list 14 percent for this criterion to avoid filtering out businesses that may score slightly low on ROE but are 45 percent undervalued and growing exceptionally fast. If a company meets your requirements in every area, you will likely have to pay a premium price for it.

The factors on which you screen should relate to elements we used earlier to define excellent companies, although you will probably not be able to filter on every element you would like due to limitations of your software. The hurdle levels should correspond to your philosophy. But keep in mind that a screen is designed to generate investment ideas, not to replace research. A lot of analysis will have to be done outside the screen.

In the following, I recommend some initial screening requirements. Again, customize these filters to fit your goals and refine them as your skills increase. Also, you will find that the same set of filters will generate a significantly different number of companies at various times, largely due to macro issues. If your screen produces an abundance of firms, you can tighten the filters. Conversely, if you don't find enough businesses to populate your portfolio from the results, you can loosen some of the requirements and rerun the screen.

Suggested Screen

- *Market capitalization*: $700 million or larger.
- *Projected earnings growth*: 10 percent or higher.
- *Historical earnings growth*: 8 percent or higher.
  Using a lower hurdle rate than for projected earnings growth may keep you from filtering out good companies that are experiencing a rebound from a temporary slump. However, I have my doubts a business will grow at 10 percent in the future if it has not managed to grow at 8 percent historically.
- *Historical revenue growth*: 6 percent or higher.
  Many firms can increase their earnings faster than their revenues because their margins are growing. Therefore, revenues do not necessarily have to grow at 10 percent to generate that same level of earnings growth.
- *Overall financial strength*: Value Line Investment Survey Financial Strength Rating[3] of B+ or higher, or S&P Earnings and Dividend Ranking[4] of B+ or better.
- *Competent management*: Screen for an ROE of at least 14 percent. While management influences virtually every aspect of a firm's operations, no rating exists to judge the quality of leaders. You cannot screen on integrity and other subjective factors—that analysis must occur outside the screening process.

Analysis

You must next analyze companies that make it through your screening process to determine if they would make suitable investments. The information you need depends on the depth of your analysis. Professional money managers who perform exhaustive research need detailed financial information on every firm they analyze. They typically get that information from the company's quarterly and annual financial reports to the SEC. I assume most readers have little financial experience and lack the ability to do in-depth analysis of corporations' financial statements. Fortunately, our screening criteria should eliminate the bulk of weak companies whose financial problems might pose undue risk to investors.

KEY POINT

The more you learn about financial statements, the better an investor you will become. A number of excellent books for laypeople have been written on this topic. Even gaining an understanding of the basics will go a long way toward increasing your skills. I highly recommend you take some time to develop your aptitude in this area.

You will have no problem finding an abundance of data about companies on the Internet. Additionally, plenty of information is available for a fee from a number of providers. I list several sources of information, both free and fee-based, in Appendix 1 at the back of the book. I believe you will find the Value Line Investment Survey especially helpful. Virtually all of a company's financial information needed to implement this process is contained in its one-page summaries. Those summaries also provide a number of financial ratios and other analyses as well as analysts' comments. The print edition of the service can be found in most major public libraries.

At a minimum, you should collect and analyze the following information:

Financial Data.   You need enough financial information to value firms (discussed in the next two chapters) and to calculate a few important financial ratios discussed earlier:

- Debt/equity
- Current ratio—current assets/current liabilities
- Return on equity—net income/equity

Calculating those ratios for the last few years will help you spot any trends that may prompt you to look closer at key areas. Although debt levels may be acceptable today, a growing level of capital needs may portend future problems. Rapidly rising liquidity could indicate a lack of investment opportunities. Slowing returns on equity might presage a decline in earnings growth.

Reviewing key lines from the last few years' financial statements in the concise format provided by a number of services also lets you spot possible trends in such areas as earnings, revenues, margins, and cash flow.

Analysts' Comments.   You should review a few analysts' comments about companies you analyze. You are not very interested in their *opinions* of stocks as investments, but analysts may bring up potential problems, lawsuits, and other significant items affecting businesses that you missed in your research. Analysts also often have insight into the likely impact of competition and other macro factors affecting firms' operations.

Miscellaneous Business Data.   Much of your research at this point will involve learning as much about the business operations of potential investments as you can, including their products, business models and strategies, markets, and competition. You can gather a good bit of this information by visiting firms' web sites.

Articles about Businesses.   Writers for various business publications often write articles analyzing important aspects of companies' operations. Those revealing third-party accounts often take the form of investigative journalism and can provide you with invaluable information about businesses.

News.   Read through press releases that companies have issued over the last several months as well as other news articles concerning the firms. A corporation may look great on paper—until you find out the CEO resigned yesterday over fraud charges brought by the SEC!

Monitoring

Once you have built your portfolio, you must constantly monitor it to know when you need to make changes. Companies' fortunes fluctuate and new opportunities constantly emerge, forcing you to continually decide whether to hold or sell specific securities.

Monitoring your investments requires that you stay abreast of any significant news concerning businesses you own. Companies regularly issue press releases that talk about significant happenings relevant to their operations. Such happenings include new business won, earnings guidance, management changes, acquisitions, spin-offs, and so on. Most corporations allow you to sign up to receive their press releases automatically via e-mail.

Businesses report their quarterly earnings every three months. Analysts and shareholders alike eagerly await those informational reports. Beyond communicating their earnings for the previous quarter, corporate leaders usually discuss whether their firms met, missed, or exceeded expectations; reveal factors affecting their companies' performance; and provide guidance for future earnings.

Corporations submit detailed audited financial statements every quarter to the Securities and Exchange Commission. Reviewing those reports (or a summary of them as provided by a data service) will help you determine if any financial developments, good or bad, require further investigation. In fact, I recommend using those reports as triggers to rerun your entire financial analyses on current holdings, especially your valuation calculations. With the updated guidance available, your intrinsic value figures may well change.

Finally, screen for new potential investment candidates on a regular basis, such as weekly or monthly. Companies that did not meet your criteria earlier might have reported new numbers to the SEC and may now fulfill your requirements. This regular screening will help keep your portfolio fresh with excellent investment ideas.

SUMMARY

The following summarizes how to develop an investment philosophy and process:

- Your philosophy goes hand in hand with your goals. Before you can develop your philosophy, you must determine what you want to accomplish through investing.
- Establish a set of standards that a business must meet for you to buy it. It should at least take into account company size, financial strength, growth rate, and valuation.
- Your buy criteria should also address the number of stocks you want in your portfolio, which will significantly impact its risk/return characteristics. Along the same lines, you should decide how big you will allow a position to grow before trimming it back.
- Liquidate a holding if its fundamentals deteriorate, its price approaches full value, or a superior opportunity becomes available.
- The investment process you build should encompass three areas: screening, analysis, and portfolio management.
- Screening provides a methodology for consistently generating quality investment ideas and rapidly eliminates firms that don't come reasonably close to meeting your investment requirements. The factors on which you screen should relate to elements we used to define excellent companies. The hurdle levels should correspond to your philosophy.
- You should collect and analyze the following information for firms that your screen generates: financial data; analysts' comments; miscellaneous business data, including information on firms' products, business models and strategies, markets, and competition; articles; and recent news.

- You must monitor the companies in your portfolio on an ongoing basis to recognize when you need to make changes. Monitoring requires you to stay abreast of any significant news concerning businesses you own. You should also review firms' quarterly earnings announcements and reports to the SEC. Finally, screen for new potential investment candidates on a regular basis.

CHAPTER 9

Finding the Blue Light Specials

I OFTEN WENT SHOPPING WITH MY MOTHER WHEN I WAS A YOUNG BOY. Sometimes those trips took us to K-Mart. I always enjoyed going there because of the snack bar stocked with popcorn, candy, and other assorted goodies. While we traipsed through the store, inevitably an announcement similar to the following came across the public address system: "Attention K-Mart shoppers. On aisle nine, our large golf umbrellas have been temporarily reduced to $4.50 from $7. This sale will only last for the next twenty minutes." A blue light situated on aisle nine then flashed for the next twenty minutes to alert shoppers where the special value was located.

Unfortunately, no blue light flashes on Wall Street to alert investors where the bargains are. But they're out there . . . you just have to find them.

PRICE VERSUS VALUE

In the last two chapters I discussed characteristics of quality businesses and I developed a process for finding companies that possess those traits. Now we move to the second element of businesslike investing: buying stocks when they sell below their fair market values.

Since investors of all experience levels will read this book, let's start with the basics and define some terms. The *value* of a corporation refers to what it is truly worth—what the business would sell for in an arm's-length transaction to an informed, willing buyer. Put another way, it is the maximum amount a purchaser could pay for a company and still achieve an adequate return on her investment. Investors also use the terms *intrinsic value, private market value*, and *fair market value* to describe a firm's worth. Dividing a corporation's value by the number of its outstanding shares gives its per share value. Thus, money managers will often make statements such as, "XYZ Company has an intrinsic value of $25 a share."

A firm's *price* denotes what other investors, collectively referred to as the *market*, are currently willing to pay for a share of the company's stock. While a firm's price tends to follow its value over a long period of time, the two may diverge widely during shorter periods, as illustrated by Figure 9.1.

When businesses prosper, overenthusiastic investors often push their prices well above their true values. Conversely, when companies experience adversity, pessimism frequently drives their stock prices considerably below their actual values. The latter situation often creates buying opportunities that afford smart investors the ability to achieve long-term market-beating returns.

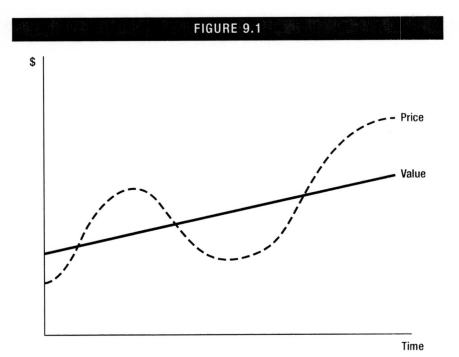

FIGURE 9.1

FLYING SAUCERS, BIGFOOT, AND STOCK MARKET BARGAINS

Because they have accepted modern portfolio theory (MPT) as the gospel of investing, many financial professionals and most academicians question whether stocks ever sell for less than their intrinsic values. Taught in almost every college investment class in the country, MPT preaches that the stock market efficiently prices all securities at all times based on all publicly available information. Thus, individual stocks never become undervalued, making it virtually impossible for an individual to consistently outperform market averages over a long period of time. Investors can only beat the market by increasing their risk levels to above those of the market or by gaining access to important information before it becomes public.

If modern portfolio theory is true, then almost all security analysis is a waste of time. As the yarn goes, a monkey tossing darts at the stock page could do as well over time as a knowledgeable investor who expends considerable effort analyzing companies' data.

Benjamin Graham flatly rejected this notion! In *The Intelligent Investor*, Graham states that the rate of return for which an investor should aim is not "more or less proportionate to the degree of risk he is ready to run. . . . The rate of return sought should be dependent, rather, on the amount of intelligent effort the investor is willing and able to bring to bear on his task."[1] This bold declaration flies in the face of MPT, which confidently asserts an investor's return correlates directly to the risk she assumes. Instead, Graham believed that achieving exceptional results is not a matter of plugging in a desired return on one side of an equation that spits out the required risk on the other. Rather, he said investors obtain outstanding returns by exercising "intelligent effort" to expose undervalued gems overlooked by others.

Lining up behind Graham, none of our managers believe that stock market bargains rank with flying saucers and Bigfoot as a modern-day myth. Like bumblebees that never bought into the notion that they can't fly, the masters have outperformed their peers and the broader market by relentlessly searching for securities that sell for less than their fair values.

VALUE INVESTING VERSUS GROWTH INVESTING

Unfortunately, many investors skip the valuation step because they believe buying stocks at discounted prices limits their investment choices to troubled businesses. After all, if you want to buy a high-quality fast-growing firm, you have to be willing to pay up for it. Right?

Actually, even well-managed, rapidly growing businesses sometimes sell for considerably less than they are worth. Buying stocks at bargain prices does not limit your investment choices to particular kinds of companies—it simply ensures you do not overpay for the companies you buy.

What then separates value investing from growth investing? According to common typecasts, value investors single-mindedly focus on buying businesses that sell for cheap prices, regardless of the quality of the firms. A cheap price is usually defined as one that produces a low PE or price-to-book value. Conventional value investors do not generally care about companies' growth rates. To the contrary, stereotypical growth investors focus on buying rapidly growing businesses without regard to their prices.

Although delineating investment styles into one category or the other makes the financial world nice and orderly, our managers emphasize that applying such broad labels can be very misleading. For instance, Bill Nygren considers himself a staunch value investor, yet he loves to purchase fast-growing companies. However, in keeping true with his discipline, he only buys them when they sell at a large discount to their fair market values.

KEY POINT

Since the price you pay for a security matters regardless of how fast the company is growing, in a sense all investing should be value investing. Even growth investors benefit by not overpaying for their investments.

ANALYZING COMPANIES AS
INVESTMENT OPPORTUNITIES

Sometimes the thought of analyzing and valuing a huge corporation with thousands of employees and multinational operations intimidates investors. However, you should treat such an investment in essentially the same way you would the purchase of a small, entrepreneurial business, such as a local cleaners. As a reasonable buyer, you would take certain steps to determine its investment potential before making an offer.

You would scour the company's accounting statements to determine its financial status, looking for answers to such questions as: How dependable and consistent is the firm's income? Is the business liquid or drowning in debt? How old is the equipment? How rapidly have the firm's revenues grown over the last five years? You would study recent demographic changes of the community in which the business is located to determine if adverse trends are developing. Since the company owns the building and land on which the business operates, you would familiarize yourself with the local real estate market. Numerous other items might also figure into your analysis.

What is the ultimate goal of this exercise? To assess the future earnings potential of the business. Why is a company's income potential so important? *Because a firm's earnings drive its value.*

Earnings Create Value

When you invest in a corporation, what are you buying that you hope will increase in value over time? Equipment? Buildings? Intellectual property? Management's reputation? While all those things impact a firm's value, they play only a supporting role to the real star—the company's earnings. Stated simply, *you buy a stock to capture its future earnings.* Granted, in some instances you may also acquire some important assets, but assets typically add value only to the extent that they support the generation of income or cut costs, both of which impact a firm's profits. It is those profits that create wealth for the company's owners. That principle forms the basis for determining a business's value.

You must answer two questions when you consider what is an appropriate price to pay for a business: (1) What rate of return do you need to earn from the investment? (2) What is the highest price you can pay and still earn that return? You buy the business only if you can get it for less than that price; otherwise, you pass.

Compare this way of thinking to that of typical investors, who mostly fly blind and just hope to make the best return they can. They achieve largely random returns determined by luck. To the contrary, businesslike investing is purposeful, deliberate, and informed: the whole process is well planned. While you will still make mistakes, you will err mostly because of unforeseen events. Businesslike investing avoids many of the problems that plague average investors by properly analyzing what is known about a company.

Two aspects of a corporation's earnings impact its value: size and growth rate. Imagine you have the opportunity to buy one of two legal money-printing machines. Machine A prints $10 a day and machine B cranks out $20. Obviously you expect to pay more for the higher-yielding device.

Now suppose both pieces of equipment print $10 a day. However, machine A grows its output by 10 percent each year and machine B increases its production by 20 percent yearly. Even though both machines currently generate the same amount of money, machine B's faster growth makes it worth more.

Think of a company as a machine that prints money, only instead of printing it, the business generates cash by manufacturing or selling goods and/or services.

KEY POINT

Like a money machine, the level and growth rate of a corporation's earnings drive its value. The higher its earnings and the faster they grow, the more the business is worth.

Relating a Firm's Earnings to Its Fair Value

How would knowing a company's future cash flows help you determine a fair price for the business? That price must somehow relate to the return you could earn from investing your money elsewhere, known as your *opportunity cost*. For example, if a bond of acceptable quality yields 10 percent, purchasing the cleaners ought to generate a higher return. Otherwise, you are better off buying the bond. So if you expect to earn $25,000 net income each year from the business, you should pay something less than $250,000 for it.

If the bond yields a lower rate, you could pay more for the company and still generate a comparable return, and vice versa. For example, a purchase price of $312,500 yields the same return as an 8 percent bond, whereas you could invest only $208,333 in the business to match the income of a 12 percent bond.

KEY POINT

The price at which you purchase a business determines the return it will generate. An adequate return and therefore a fair value for the company should correlate to what other investment options yield.

Look for the Flashing Blue Light

Suppose you determine the cleaners is worth $250,000. If the owner is in no hurry to sell and is asking $350,000 for the business, should you buy it? Obviously not. Why? Because it is a bad business? To the contrary, you concluded it is an excellent business with strong profit potential. Then why would you not buy the cleaners? Because the price is too high.

Instead of dealing with a patient seller, let's assume an opposite scenario. Suppose the owner died recently and her estate contains insufficient liquid assets to pay estate taxes that are due shortly. Her executor is liquidating the business in order to raise cash and has priced the cleaners to sell quickly, asking only $200,000. Should you buy the operation? As quickly as you can sign the paperwork! Why? Because you can get it for a price well below what you believe it is really worth. That type of deal is what you are hunting for—a bargain!

Evaluating a publicly traded corporation for investment purposes does not differ in concept from analyzing the local cleaners. The corporation's numbers are bigger and its operations are more complex, but the principles and process remain essentially the same: examine the company to determine if it meets your investment criteria. Assuming an affirmative answer, determine the firm's fair market value. As a purposeful businessperson, only buy the company's shares when they sell at a sufficient discount to that value. The bigger the gap between the firm's price and its worth, the higher the return your investment will ultimately generate.

SUMMARY

The following summarizes the topics covered in this chapter:

- *Value* denotes what a company's stock is truly worth, whereas *price* refers to what other investors are currently willing to pay for it. A firm's price tends to track its value over a long period of time, but a sizable chasm may separate the two at any given time.
- The price you pay for a stock ultimately determines the rate of return you will earn from your investment. If you pay too much for even a high-quality firm, you will likely obtain a mediocre return at best.
- Determining a company's intrinsic value ranks as one of the most important steps in analyzing a potential investment. That value is driven by the level of the company's earnings and the anticipated growth rate of those earnings.
- Only buy a stock when the market has priced it below its fair value. The bigger the gap between the worth of a company and the price you pay for it, the higher the return you will earn from your investment.

CHAPTER 10

Valuing Stocks

MOST INVESTORS UTILIZE SIMPLISTIC VALUATION TECHNIQUES THAT RE-
quire little time and effort. As we will see shortly, most of those methods are flawed and frequently yield inaccurate results.

Faulty analysis can produce two types of poor investment decisions: Valuing a company too richly increases the probability you will
overpay for it. Conversely, significantly undervaluing a security may
cause you to pass on a compelling investment opportunity because
you think its price is too high. Without a reasonable idea of what a
firm is worth, obtaining a strong return from an investment becomes
a matter of chance.

Computing a stock's fair value does not so much establish a single
number that represents the company's exact worth as it helps you determine the business's worth to you—it tells you what you can pay for
the firm and still generate the return you need. Stated differently, the
intrinsic value figure places a worth on a security's projected cash flow
based on the available alternatives. Calculating stocks' fair values also
lets you compare the relative valuations of companies to each other.

Since the cash flows of corporations drive their values, a time-
tested method for determining a firm's worth involves calculating a
current value for all of its expected future income. The math used to
calculate the present value of a firm's future earnings is relatively simple, but it requires an understanding of two basic concepts: (1) the
future value of a present sum of money and (2) the present value of
a future income stream.

THE FUTURE VALUE OF MONEY

Would you rather receive $1 today or $1.10 a year from now? The answer depends on the return you can earn on $1. If you can earn 7 percent, today's $1 would be worth $1.07 a year from now, making the guaranteed $1.10 more attractive. Conversely, if you can invest at 15 percent, taking the $1 now makes more sense.

Let's assume you can invest at 7 percent. The *future value* of $1 in one year would be $1.07. The $1 would grow to $1.14 in two years, and so on. By varying the interest rates and time periods, you can develop a future value table, such as the one found in Table 10.1.

While a future value table offers convenience, that convenience limits the table's usefulness. For instance, you may need to calculate values involving fractional years or fractional interest rates, or you may want to know future values beyond the time period covered by the table. This formula for calculating future values gets around those limitations:

$$FV = PV(1 + i)^n$$

where:
FV = future value
PV = present value
i = interest rate
n = number of future time periods

For example, if you want to find the value of $1 five years from now invested at 10 percent, the calculations look like this:

$$
\begin{aligned}
FV &= \$1 \times (1 + 10\%)^5 \\
&= \$1 \times (1 + 0.1)^5 \\
&= \$1 \times (1.1)^5 \\
&= \$1 \times 1.61 \\
&= \$1.61
\end{aligned}
$$

TABLE 10.1

Future Value of $1

Interest Rate

# Years	5%	6%	7%	8%	9%	10%	11%	12%	13%	14%	15%
1	1.0500	1.0600	1.0700	1.0800	1.0900	1.1000	1.1100	1.1200	1.1300	1.1400	1.1500
2	1.1025	1.1236	1.1449	1.1664	1.1881	1.2100	1.2321	1.2544	1.2769	1.2996	1.3225
3	1.1576	1.1910	1.2250	1.2597	1.2950	1.3310	1.3676	1.4049	1.4429	1.4815	1.5209
4	1.2155	1.2625	1.3108	1.3605	1.4116	1.4641	1.5181	1.5735	1.6305	1.6890	1.7490
5	1.2763	1.3382	1.4026	1.4693	1.5386	1.6105	1.6851	1.7623	1.8424	1.9254	2.0114
6	1.3401	1.4185	1.5007	1.5869	1.6771	1.7716	1.8704	1.9738	2.0820	2.1950	2.3131
7	1.4071	1.5036	1.6058	1.7138	1.8280	1.9487	2.0762	2.2107	2.3526	2.5023	2.6600
8	1.4775	1.5938	1.7182	1.8509	1.9926	2.1436	2.3045	2.4760	2.6584	2.8526	3.0590
9	1.5513	1.6895	1.8385	1.9990	2.1719	2.3579	2.5580	2.7731	3.0040	3.2519	3.5179
10	1.6289	1.7908	1.9672	2.1589	2.3674	2.5937	2.8394	3.1058	3.3946	3.7072	4.0456
11	1.7103	1.8983	2.1049	2.3316	2.5804	2.8531	3.1518	3.4785	3.8359	4.2262	4.6524
12	1.7959	2.0122	2.2522	2.5182	2.8127	3.1384	3.4985	3.8960	4.3345	4.8179	5.3503
13	1.8856	2.1329	2.4098	2.7196	3.0658	3.4523	3.8833	4.3635	4.8980	5.4924	6.1528
14	1.9799	2.2609	2.5785	2.9372	3.3417	3.7975	4.3104	4.8871	5.5348	6.2613	7.0757
15	2.0789	2.3966	2.7590	3.1722	3.6425	4.1772	4.7846	5.4736	6.2543	7.1379	8.1371

16	2.1829	2.5404	2.9522	3.4259	3.9703	4.5950	5.3109	6.1304	7.0673	8.1372	9.3576
17	2.2920	2.6928	3.1588	3.7000	4.3276	5.0545	5.8951	6.8660	7.9861	9.2765	10.7613
18	2.4066	2.8543	3.3799	3.9960	4.7171	5.5599	6.5436	7.6900	9.0243	10.5752	12.3755
19	2.5270	3.0256	3.6165	4.3157	5.1417	6.1159	7.2633	8.6128	10.1974	12.0557	14.2318
20	2.6533	3.2071	3.8697	4.6610	5.6044	6.7275	8.0623	9.6463	11.5231	13.7435	16.3665
21	2.7860	3.3996	4.1406	5.0338	6.1088	7.4002	8.9492	10.8038	13.0211	15.6676	18.8215
22	2.9253	3.6035	4.4304	5.4365	6.6586	8.1403	9.9336	12.1003	14.7138	17.8610	21.6447
23	3.0715	3.8197	4.7405	5.8715	7.2579	8.9543	11.0263	13.5523	16.6266	20.3616	24.8915
24	3.2251	4.0489	5.0724	6.3412	7.9111	9.8497	12.2392	15.1786	18.7881	23.2122	28.6252
25	3.3864	4.2919	5.4274	6.8485	8.6231	10.8347	13.5855	17.0001	21.2305	26.4619	32.9190
26	3.5557	4.5494	5.8074	7.3964	9.3992	11.9182	15.0799	19.0401	23.9905	30.1666	37.8568
27	3.7335	4.8223	6.2139	7.9881	10.2451	13.1100	16.7386	21.3249	27.1093	34.3899	43.5353
28	3.9201	5.1117	6.6488	8.6271	11.1671	14.4210	18.5799	23.8839	30.6335	39.2045	50.0656
29	4.1161	5.4184	7.1143	9.3173	12.1722	15.8631	20.6237	26.7499	34.6158	44.6931	57.5755
30	4.3219	5.7435	7.6123	10.0627	13.2677	17.4494	22.8923	29.9599	39.1159	50.9502	66.2118

Note: This table shows what a $1 investment would grow to over different periods of time at various rates of interest.

A financial calculator makes even easier work of the math. Here are the steps for computing future values using a Texas Instruments BA II Plus:

Step	*Keystrokes*
1. Set periods per year equal to one	2nd, P/Y, 1, Set
2. Change calculator mode	2nd, Quit
3. Enter the current lump sum (as a negative number)	−1, =, PV
4. Enter the annual interest rate	10, I/Y
5. Enter the number of periods	5, N
6. Compute the future value	CPT, FV

Voilà! The calculator produces the value of 1.61.

THE PRESENT VALUE OF A FUTURE INCOME STREAM

To paraphrase Yogi Berra, the *present value* is a similar concept—only different. Instead of calculating the future value of a current sum, you start with a future lump sum and compute its worth today, known as *discounting* the future sum. The interest rate used is called the *discount rate.*

KEY POINT
Understanding how to discount future sums of money to present values is essential to valuing stocks.

To illustrate the present value concept, let's revisit Table 10.1. Assuming a 7 percent discount rate, you can see that a dividend of $1.07 in one year equates to a $1 dividend today. Just as $1.07 is the future value of today's $1, $1 is the *present value* of next year's $1.07. Similarly, at a 10 percent discount rate, $1 is the present value of $1.61 received five years from now. Using different discount rates and time periods, you can develop a present value table, such as the one found in Table 10.2.

To find today's equivalent of $100 received 10 years from now, assuming a 10 percent discount rate, find the number in Table 10.2 that intersects the 10% column and 10 years row, which is 0.386. Multiply 0.386 by $100 to arrive at the present value of $38.60.

A present value table has the same limitations as a future value table. Therefore, you should become familiar with the following formula for calculating present values:

$$PV = \frac{FV}{(1+ i)^n}$$

where:
- PV = present value
- FV = future value
- i = discount rate
- n = number of future time periods being discounted

Computing the present value of $150 to be received three years from now using a 7 percent discount rate:

$$
\begin{aligned}
PV &= \$150 \ / \ (1 + 7\%)^3 \\
&= \$150 \ / \ (1 + 0.07)^3 \\
&= \$150 \ / \ 1.225 \\
&= \$122
\end{aligned}
$$

Present values can also be calculated quickly using your trusty Texas Instruments BA II Plus by following these steps:

Step	*Keystrokes*
1. Set periods per year equal to one	2nd, P/Y, 1, Set
2. Change calculator mode	2nd, Quit
3. Enter the number of periods	3, N

TABLE 10.2

Present Value of $1

# Years	5%	6%	7%	8%	9%	10%	11%	12%	13%	14%	15%
1	0.9524	0.9434	0.9346	0.9259	0.9174	0.9091	0.9009	0.8929	0.8850	0.8772	0.8696
2	0.9070	0.8900	0.8734	0.8573	0.8417	0.8264	0.8116	0.7972	0.7831	0.7695	0.7561
3	0.8638	0.8396	0.8163	0.7938	0.7722	0.7513	0.7312	0.7118	0.6931	0.6750	0.6575
4	0.8227	0.7921	0.7629	0.7350	0.7084	0.6830	0.6587	0.6355	0.6133	0.5921	0.5718
5	0.7835	0.7473	0.7130	0.6806	0.6499	0.6209	0.5935	0.5674	0.5428	0.5194	0.4972
6	0.7462	0.7050	0.6663	0.6302	0.5963	0.5645	0.5346	0.5066	0.4803	0.4556	0.4323
7	0.7107	0.6651	0.6227	0.5835	0.5470	0.5132	0.4817	0.4523	0.4251	0.3996	0.3759
8	0.6768	0.6274	0.5820	0.5403	0.5019	0.4665	0.4339	0.4039	0.3762	0.3506	0.3269
9	0.6446	0.5919	0.5439	0.5002	0.4604	0.4241	0.3909	0.3606	0.3329	0.3075	0.2843
10	0.6139	0.5584	0.5083	0.4632	0.4224	0.3855	0.3522	0.3220	0.2946	0.2697	0.2472
11	0.5847	0.5268	0.4751	0.4289	0.3875	0.3505	0.3173	0.2875	0.2607	0.2366	0.2149
12	0.5568	0.4970	0.4440	0.3971	0.3555	0.3186	0.2858	0.2567	0.2307	0.2076	0.1869
13	0.5303	0.4688	0.4150	0.3677	0.3262	0.2897	0.2575	0.2292	0.2042	0.1821	0.1625
14	0.5051	0.4423	0.3878	0.3405	0.2992	0.2633	0.2320	0.2046	0.1807	0.1597	0.1413
15	0.4810	0.4173	0.3624	0.3152	0.2745	0.2394	0.2090	0.1827	0.1599	0.1401	0.1229

16	0.4581	0.3936	0.3387	0.2919	0.2519	0.2176	0.1883	0.1631	0.1415	0.1229	0.1069
17	0.4363	0.3714	0.3166	0.2703	0.2311	0.1978	0.1696	0.1456	0.1252	0.1078	0.0929
18	0.4155	0.3503	0.2959	0.2502	0.2120	0.1799	0.1528	0.1300	0.1108	0.0946	0.0808
19	0.3957	0.3305	0.2765	0.2317	0.1945	0.1635	0.1377	0.1161	0.0981	0.0829	0.0703
20	0.3769	0.3118	0.2584	0.2145	0.1784	0.1486	0.1240	0.1037	0.0868	0.0728	0.0611
21	0.3589	0.2942	0.2415	0.1987	0.1637	0.1351	0.1117	0.0926	0.0768	0.0638	0.0531
22	0.3418	0.2775	0.2257	0.1839	0.1502	0.1228	0.1007	0.0826	0.0680	0.0560	0.0462
23	0.3256	0.2618	0.2109	0.1703	0.1378	0.1117	0.0907	0.0738	0.0601	0.0491	0.0402
24	0.3101	0.2470	0.1971	0.1577	0.1264	0.1015	0.0817	0.0659	0.0532	0.0431	0.0349
25	0.2953	0.2330	0.1842	0.1460	0.1160	0.0923	0.0736	0.0588	0.0471	0.0378	0.0304
26	0.2812	0.2198	0.1722	0.1352	0.1064	0.0839	0.0663	0.0525	0.0417	0.0331	0.0264
27	0.2678	0.2074	0.1609	0.1252	0.0976	0.0763	0.0597	0.0469	0.0369	0.0291	0.0230
28	0.2551	0.1956	0.1504	0.1159	0.0895	0.0693	0.0538	0.0419	0.0326	0.0255	0.0200
29	0.2429	0.1846	0.1406	0.1073	0.0822	0.0630	0.0485	0.0374	0.0289	0.0224	0.0174
30	0.2314	0.1741	0.1314	0.0994	0.0754	0.0573	0.0437	0.0334	0.0256	0.0196	0.0151

Note: This table shows what a dollar received at different points in the future would be worth today using various discount rates.

Step	*Keystrokes*
4. Enter the annual interest rate	7, I/Y
5. Enter the future lump sum	150, FV
6. Compute the present value	CPT, PV

As expected, the calculator yields $122.

Discounting a future amount of money is straightforward and easy to understand. However, a company does not generate just one year of income. Rather, it produces an ongoing stream of annual earnings. To calculate the present value of multiple years of income, simply discount each year's earnings back to the present using an appropriate discount rate, then sum the results.

DEVELOPING A VALUATION MODEL

Now that you know how to discount future cash flows, we can develop a model for calculating companies' intrinsic values. The information this model provides will help you uncover excellent investment opportunities and avoid disastrous decisions. Building the model step by step and explaining each concept as I introduce it takes more time than if I just presented the final product, but understanding each of the factors involved and how they interact will make you a savvier investor. A worksheet at the end of the chapter (Table 10.6) organizes the model into an easy-to-use format.

Valuing a Bond

Valuing a stock is similar in concept to valuing a bond, so let's start by looking at a simplistic example of how to compute a bond's worth. Assume you invest $1,000 in a five-year bond that pays 5 percent interest. Table 10.3 illustrates the cash flows the bond will generate. *Note that those cash flows consist of two parts*: five *annual interest payments* of $50 each and the *return of your principal* when the bond matures. Those six payments constitute the bond's projected cash flows.

TABLE 10.3

Value of a Bond

Original Investment:	$	1,000
Interest Rate:		5%
Time Periods:		5

Year	Cash Flow Type	Cash Flow		(Table 10.2) Present Value Factor	Present Value
1	Interest	$	50.00	0.9524	$ 47.62
2	Interest	$	50.00	0.9070	$ 45.35
3	Interest	$	50.00	0.8638	$ 43.19
4	Interest	$	50.00	0.8227	$ 41.14
5	Interest	$	50.00	0.7835	$ 39.18
5	Principle	$	1,000.00	0.7835	$ 783.53
Total:		$	1,250.00		$1,000.00

Note: This illustration assumes the bond pays out all interest, so the annual payments remain static.

As the example shows, the present value of the bond's future income stream equals your purchase price of $1,000. In essence, you pay that amount to capture $1,250 in future cash flows.

Since the interest rate remains fixed throughout the bond's life, you can use a shortcut and calculate the bond's value by simply dividing its annual payments by its interest (discount) rate:

$$\$50 \ / \ 5\%$$
$$= \$50 \ / \ .05$$
$$= \$1,000$$

A stock's projected income stream differs from a bond's in one key way: a company's cash flows will hopefully increase over time, whereas a bond's interest payments typically remain fixed. A firm's value reflects this anticipated growth in earnings. If not for this important difference, you could calculate the fair value of a stock simply by dividing its annual dividends per share by an appropriate discount rate.

Why do corporations' profits generally escalate over time? Because instead of distributing all their profits to shareholders each year, most firms reinvest some or all of their earnings to expand their operations, causing their revenues and profits to grow. As their earnings rise, companies' intrinsic values generally increase as well.

For valuation purposes, a corporation that reinvests its earnings is comparable to a bondholder who reinvests her interest payments in the bond's principal (I know bonds do not normally allow this— humor me for this example). The bond's income would rise over time, just as a corporation's income increases, because its fixed interest rate would apply to a larger principal amount each year. I demonstrate this concept in Table 10.4a.

Does the fact that the annual interest payments rise each year because you reinvest them affect the bond's present value? Table 10.3

TABLE 10.4A

Value of a Bond with Interest Reinvested

Original Investment: $ 1,000
Interest Rate: 5%
Time Periods: 5

Year	Cash Flow Type	Cash Flow	Cash Flow Reinvested	Cash Flow Received	Principal Value
1	Interest	$50.00	$50.00	$0.00	$1,050.00
2	Interest	$52.50	$52.50	$0.00	$1,102.50
3	Interest	$55.13	$55.13	$0.00	$1,157.63
4	Interest	$57.88	$57.88	$0.00	$1,215.51
5	Interest	$60.78	$60.78	$0.00	$1,276.28
5	Principal	$1,276.28		$1,276.28	

This bond is sold at the end of year five for: $ 1,276.28
Present Value Factor (year 5, 5%):   0.7835
Present Value: $ 1,000

showed that to compute a bond's value you discount both its interest payments and its principal at maturity. Thus, *you discount the cash flows you actually receive from investing in the bond.* If you reinvest the interest payments instead of collecting them, the only cash flow you actually receive is the return of your principal when the bond matures. Therefore, you discount only that cash flow when valuing the bond, as shown in the bottom shaded area of Table 10.4a. Note that as long as the reinvested interest continues earning 5 percent, the present value of the bond remains $1,000 even though the security's income rises each year.

Table 10.4b illustrates this same principle assuming the bondholder reinvests only part of her interest payments and collects the rest. Once again, we see that taking the interest or reinvesting it does not change the bond's $1,000 value as long as the reinvested interest earns 5 percent.

TABLE 10.4B

Value of a Bond with Interest Reinvested

Original Investment: $ 1,000
Interest Rate: 5%
Time Periods: 5

Year	Cash Flow Type	Cash Flow	Cash Flow Reinvested	Principal Value	Cash Flow Received	Present Value Factor	Present Value
1	Interest	$50.00	$30.00	$1,030.00	$20.00	0.9524	19.05
2	Interest	$51.50	$30.90	$1,060.90	$20.60	0.9070	18.68
3	Interest	$53.05	$31.83	$1,092.73	$21.22	0.8638	18.33
4	Interest	$54.64	$32.78	$1,125.51	$21.85	0.8227	17.98
5	Interest	$56.28	$33.77	$1,159.27	$22.51	0.7835	17.64
5	Principal	$1,159.27			$1,159.27	0.7835	908.32
Total:		$1,424.73			$1,265.46		$1,000.00

From this example, we derive the following principle:

BOND VALUATION PRINCIPLE

When valuing a bond, you compute the current value of interest payments *received* by discounting them to a present value. *You do not discount interest payments that you reinvest in the principal.* Rather, they are accounted for by a corresponding increase in the bond's principal value, which you discount to a present value at the bond's maturity.

Dividend Discount Model

Just as a bond's worth equals the present value of all its future cash flows, it is fair to say *the intrinsic value of any financial instrument equals the discounted value of all the future cash flows it will generate.* While most analysts agree with this principle, they often disagree on how to apply it. When calculating a company's worth, even many professional investors mistakenly discount all the future earnings the business will produce instead of just the cash flows its shareholders will receive. That mistake results in too high of a valuation if the firm reinvests any of its earnings, as almost all do.

Like the bondholder in our example, corporations can either reinvest their earnings to generate higher future cash flows or distribute current income as dividends. When analysts project a firm's net income to increase over time, they almost always assume the company will reinvest at least some of its profits to fund that growth. If you discount *all* the projected annual earnings of that firm when valuing it, you include the reinvested profits twice in your calculations: once as annual income and again when you discount their positive impact on the company's earnings and future value.

Just as a bond generates two types of income—annual interest payments and the return of principal—so does a stock. The dividends a corporation pays correspond to a bond's interest. A stock's selling price at the end of your assumed holding period, known as its *terminal value*, is analogous to a bond's principal at maturity. Both components of a stock's cash flow must be discounted to properly compute the company's fair value, which leads to a second valuation principle:

> ## STOCK VALUATION PRINCIPLE
>
> The intrinsic value of a company equals the present value of its future dividends over some period of time plus the discounted value of the stock's terminal value at the end of that period. This method of valuing stocks is commonly known as the dividend discount model (DDM).

Now you understand the logic behind the dividend discount model, which I will illustrate shortly. Many professional investors use variations of this model to value equities.

Choose the Discount Rate

Investors use two main methods to select an appropriate discount rate. The first states that the discount rate should equal the interest rate on a risk-free investment (known as the *risk-free rate of return*) plus a premium to compensate investors for assuming the risk of owning stocks. For example, if a Treasury bond and a stock offer identical returns, you would buy the Treasury bond because it involves no risk: the government guarantees both the interest payments and the principal as long as you hold the bond to maturity. A stock must therefore offer a higher potential return than a Treasury bond to justify taking on the equity's risk. This method of determining the discount rate recognizes that principle.

Although there is no consensus, those who use this approach often use the interest rate on the thirty-year Treasury bond as the risk-free rate and add a 3 percent risk premium to arrive at their discount rate.

I suggest making one change if you use this approach. Bond investors' inflation expectations drive the level of long-term interest rates. Interest rates fluctuate considerably more than inflation, however, and sometimes become misaligned with their fair value level. That means the starting point for your discount rate may whipsaw sharply over short periods of time, causing you to alter your discount rate frequently.

Instead of basing your discount rate on the long-term Treasury bond, I suggest basing it on the inflation rate as measured by the consumer price index (CPI). Since the long-term Treasury yield has traditionally hovered about three percentage points above the twelve-month CPI figure, I recommend using a risk-free rate that equals the twelve-month CPI plus 3 percent. Adding a 3 percent risk premium to this number produces a discount rate equal to 6 percent above inflation.

Paying fair value for a business generates a return equal to your discount rate if the firm's actual earnings meet your projections. Therefore, the second philosophy suggests simply using a discount rate that equals your desired return. Using this method, you would buy firms that sell for your calculated fair value or less as opposed to buying companies *only* at significant discounts to their intrinsic values.

As with many other aspects of stock analysis, there is no single correct method for choosing a discount rate. I am merely providing you with two valid philosophies on which to base your selection. Just be aware that your intrinsic value figures may vary considerably based on the discount rate you use. A higher rate results in a lower valuation, and vice versa.

When I asked Chris Davis how he chose his discount rate, he replied, "It really does not matter as long as you use the same rate for every company. That way, as you measure the valuation of one stock against another, your comparison will be valid on a relative basis, if not an absolute basis." Then he added, "I generally use 10 percent."

For my model, I use a discount rate equal to 6 percent above inflation as measured by the trailing twelve-month CPI figure. That currently equals about 8 percent.

Value a Stock as You Would a Bond

Since the cash flows of both stocks and bonds drive their values, you can value a stock with the same methodology used to value a bond. Our equity valuation formula, therefore, looks like this:

$$IV = PV_{D,T} + PV_{TV,T}$$

where:

IV = intrinsic value of the company

$PV_{D,T}$ = present value of dividends received over time period T

$PV_{TV,T}$ = present value of stock's terminal value at the end of time period T

This formula looks simple enough. The challenge is developing the three required pieces of information: an assumed holding period, the dividends the business will pay during that time, and the stock's selling price at the end of that period.

While there is no single correct holding period for valuing firms, I recommend using ten years. The further out you go, the less visibility you have regarding companies' earnings. However, using too short of a period may not give corporations enough time to realize the potential of their business strategies. Ten years offers an acceptable compromise.

Unfortunately, you cannot predict either of the latter two factors with certainty, which is what makes valuing businesses part art as well as part science. However, you can estimate a company's dividends and terminal value based on reasonable assumptions. Armed with those estimates, you can then develop a sensible idea of a firm's real worth.

Projecting a Company's Earnings Stream

Since the dividends and terminal value of a corporation are both functions of its future income, valuing a business begins with projecting its earnings for the next ten years. The other pieces fall easily into place once you have developed this forecast.

To project a company's earnings, you must make some assumptions about its future growth. Keep two things in mind: (1) Your projections become less accurate the further out you forecast. Therefore, you should estimate a firm's growth conservatively—you would rather value a business too low than too high, which will keep you from overpaying for its stock. (2) No corporation will increase its earnings at an above average pace forever. Rather, all companies' growth rates eventually revert to the mean—that is, as businesses mature, their growth ultimately slows to some average rate. Why is this?

First, it is mathematically impossible for a firm to expand its income abnormally fast forever. If a company were to do so, it alone would eventually account for the majority of our nation's gross domestic product. As much as Bill Gates would love that, it's just not going to happen.

Second, and more importantly, when an innovative firm offers a groundbreaking good or service and experiences extraordinary growth, the company's above average returns attract competition. Other corporations swarm to the business like a defensive line going after a fumble. The new entrants steal market share from the original provider, slowing its rate of expansion. The market eventually becomes saturated with the new product, and opportunities to reinvest profits at above average returns vanish. At that point, the growth rates of surviving companies subside to some average level. This process may take many years or it may happen quickly.

For those two reasons, you must somehow factor a deceleration in earnings growth into your forecasts. To accomplish this, I assume all businesses regress to an average growth rate after ten years. Remember also that companies do not expand at one rate for ten years and then instantly revert to the mean. Rather, firms slow their growth *during* this ten-year period.

Two-Stage Earnings Model

To account for decelerating growth, I recommend using a two-stage model to project a corporation's ten-year earnings (Table 10.5a). Begin your calculations with two figures: the firm's expected earnings per share for the next four quarters and its projected long-term growth

TABLE 10.5A

Ten-Year Discounted Cash Flow
Valuation Model
Company X

Prior Year's Earnings:	$ 1.00
Earnings Estimate, Next Four Quarters:	$ 1.20
Earnings Growth Rate (1st five years):	20%
Earnings Growth Rate (2nd five years):	12%

Year	Projected Earnings
1	$ 1.20
2	$ 1.44
3	$ 1.73
4	$ 2.07
5	$ 2.49
6	$ 2.79
7	$ 3.12
8	$ 3.50
9	$ 3.92
10	$ 4.39

rate. Excellent sources for this information are companies' earnings guidance and analysts' estimates.

While analysts' estimates are certainly not flawless, they provide important information for making earnings projections. At a minimum, they let you know what Wall Street professionals think about a company's growth prospects. However, always compare analysts' expectations to a corporation's historical numbers to see if the two conflict. If the analysts appear too optimistic or pessimistic, research why and determine if you agree with their reasoning. If you do not agree, consider adjusting their numbers to conform more closely to the firm's past record. Do not be afraid to disagree with analysts if you have expertise in an area. However, exercise caution in using numbers

WHERE TO GET THE DATA

A number of Web sites offer analysts' earnings estimates, along with other financial information, free of charge. In fact, a company's Web site makes a great place to start your research on the firm's financial data.

Most businesses provide guidance for their future earnings and expected growth when they report their quarterly results. The majority of publicly traded corporations post the press releases for their recent earnings announcements in the Investor Relations area of their Web sites.

All publicly traded corporations are required to submit quarterly and annual financial reports to the Securities and Exchange Commission (SEC). Those treasure troves of information include not only financial data but also managements' commentaries on their businesses. Most companies archive those reports as well on their Web sites.

The bulk of corporations also post analysts' projections for their future earnings and long-term growth rates, or they include links to sites that provide that information. Those growth projections normally encompass a five-year period.

A multitude of Web sites offer free financial information on publicly traded corporations. Those sites' sponsors typically offer premium services to which they hope you will subscribe, or you may have to put up with numerous pop-up ads. However, the information provided can be very useful. Examples of such sites are www.moneycentral.msn.com, www.cbsmarketwatch. com, and www.morningstar.com. Even the sites of some brokerage firms, including www.schwab.com, www.fidelity.com, and www.waterhouse.com, make excellent data and research available to their clients.

The information available over the Internet at no charge will suffice for most investors. However, various data services also provide corporate financial information for a fee. Fee services justify their charges by offering efficiency—they normally provide the desired data in a well-organized format through a convenient delivery system, saving you significant research time. They also typically supply proprietary information and more comprehensive data than many of the free sites.

If you want detailed information about corporations' financial histories along with analysts' comments, popular fee services include Value Line Investment Survey, Morningstar StockInvestor, and Standard & Poor's Outlook. If you don't care to spring for the cost of those services, you can find the print edition for at least one of them in most large public libraries.

significantly above their consensus projections. Remember, erring on the conservative side is better than overestimating earnings.

Apply the firm's long-term expected growth rate to its next year's forecasted income to project its earnings per share for each of the next five years. Repeat this process for a second five-year period, only this time reduce the anticipated growth rate by 40 percent. That may sound drastic, but it makes sense for a couple of reasons.

First, five years is a long time, and a corporation will likely experience unforeseen adversities during that period. Unanticipated negative developments, which may be company-specific, industry-wide, and/or at a macro level, could easily hinder a firm's growth. Competition can spring up from unexpected places, consumers' tastes may change, new technologies might emerge, and so on. For instance, few analysts expected corporate spending to fall off a cliff as it did in late 2000 to early 2001. The economic downturn that ensued set back many companies' business plans by at least three years.

Second, a corporation's growth rate may slow quicker than anticipated as the company matures. Estimating a firm's earnings growth conservatively helps you develop a solid valuation figure that offers you a margin of safety. Buying a stock below that figure may allow you to obtain a satisfactory return even if the company does not perform as well as you expect.

Company X in Table 10.5a earned $1 per share last year and expects to earn $1.20 over the next twelve months. Analysts project the business to grow by 20 percent annually. Our model assumes 20 percent growth continues five years, then slows to 12 percent the following five years. These figures produce tenth-year earnings of $4.39 per share.

Project a Company's Dividends

Now use your earnings projections to forecast the company's dividends for the next ten years. Corporations typically distribute dividends out of their net profits. Investors call the percentage of earnings a firm distributes to shareholders its *dividend payout ratio*. This ratio tends to remain fairly constant over time for most corporations, so you can reasonably assume a firm's dividends grow at the same rate as its earnings.

Table 10.5b demonstrates how to project a corporation's dividends. Start by calculating an average dividend payout ratio (annual dividend/earnings) for the firm over the past three years. I use 10 percent in our example. Next, multiply each year's projected earnings by that figure to get annual dividend numbers.

Finally, discount each year's dividend to a present value (assuming an 8 percent discount rate) and sum the total. The present value of company X's projected dividends over the next ten years equals $1.64.

Congratulations! You're halfway through the valuation model!

What Will the Stock Be Worth in Ten Years?

The second part of the valuation model requires you to calculate a company's ten-year terminal value. Obviously, no one knows at what price a firm's stock will sell that far in the future. However, you *can* calculate a fair value for the business ten years out based on your earnings projections and assume the stock then sells for that price.

To compute a corporation's terminal value, you must make some assumptions about the firm's *permanent growth rate* and *dividend payout ratio* beyond ten years. You should once again use conservative assumptions to help you determine the minimum amount a firm should be worth at that time. Providing such a floor for your terminal value estimate helps ensure the business is worth at least the intrinsic value you calculate.

TABLE 10.5B

Ten-Year Discounted Cash Flow Valuation Model
Company X

Discount Rate:	8%
Prior Year's Earnings:	$ 1.00
Earnings Estimate, Next Four Quarters:	$ 1.20
Earnings Growth Rate (1st five years):	20%
Earnings Growth Rate (2nd five years):	12%

Year	Projected Earnings	Payout Ratio	Dividends	Discount Factor	Disc Value Dividend
1	$ 1.20	10%	$ 0.12	0.9259	$ 0.11
2	$ 1.44	10%	$ 0.14	0.8573	$ 0.12
3	$ 1.73	10%	$ 0.17	0.7938	$ 0.14
4	$ 2.07	10%	$ 0.21	0.7350	$ 0.15
5	$ 2.49	10%	$ 0.25	0.6806	$ 0.17
6	$ 2.79	10%	$ 0.28	0.6302	$ 0.18
7	$ 3.12	10%	$ 0.31	0.5835	$ 0.18
8	$ 3.50	10%	$ 0.35	0.5403	$ 0.19
9	$ 3.92	10%	$ 0.39	0.5002	$ 0.20
10	$ 4.39	10%	$ 0.44	0.4632	$ 0.20

Discounted Value of Dividends:	$ 1.64

Permanent Growth Rate and Dividend Payout Ratio

A corporation should retain earnings when it can generate a return on that money higher than the company's cost of capital. The firm should distribute income above that as dividends. As a result, rapidly expanding businesses often forgo paying dividends to conserve cash and support their growth. As a company matures, however, its opportunities to reinvest capital profitably diminish and its pace of expansion slows. At some point, the firm typically either starts paying a dividend or increases an existing one. As its investment opportunities continue to shrink, the company will likely increase the percentage of profits it pays out to shareholders even further. The dividend payout ratio of a corporation, therefore, both *affects* its rate of expansion and *reflects* management's perception of its growth potential.

Microsoft provides an excellent example of this principle. The software behemoth maintained the reputation of being a premier growth company for many years, at one point claiming the throne from GE as the largest corporation in the United States based on market capitalization. However, by the early 2000s, it became apparent that the mature company's rate of expansion was permanently slowing and significant investment opportunities were becoming scarcer. By June, 2004 the business had accumulated over $60 billion in cash and short-term investments—enough to buy all of major league baseball with several billion dollars to spare! Recognizing it was unfair to investors to stockpile so much capital in low-yield instruments, Microsoft announced a plan in July 2004 to return up to $75 billion to shareholders by doubling the company's regular dividend, paying a special dividend, and buying back up to $30 billion in stock over a four-year period.

So two things happen simultaneously in a textbook world as a firm ages: its earnings growth slows while its dividend payout ratio increases. At the logical end of that process, the company's growth reverts to an average rate and the business distributes the bulk of its entire net income to shareholders as dividends. At the extreme end, the company ceases to grow and pays out its entire net earnings. How long does it take for a firm to reach that point? The answer varies for different businesses. Some companies grow at above average rates for decades, whereas others do so for only short periods. My model assumes companies exhaust their opportunities to reinvest earnings profitably over our ten-year holding period. At the end of that time, businesses merely maintain the existing sizes of their operations, manufacturing or selling the same number of product units year after year. Once a firm reaches that point, I assume its earnings grow at the long-term rate of inflation—about 3 percent. Here's why.

Because the company no longer increases its level of production, the revenue of the firm rises only because it raises its product prices in line with inflation. Likewise, the expenses of the firm rise 3 percent annually because its costs of production move up with inflation. Since the company's revenue and expenses both grow at the rate of inflation, the corporation's net earnings (revenue minus expenses) must by definition grow at the same rate.

Since companies pay all their net income out as dividends at that time, I also assume corporations maintain a 100 percent dividend payout ratio at the end of ten years. Let me reiterate—these are very conservative assumptions.

Terminal Value

The highlighted areas of Table 10.5c illustrate how to calculate a stock's terminal value using our assumptions. Begin with the firm's tenth-year projected earnings and grow them by 3 percent a year from that point forward. *Since the dividend payout ratio of the company equals 100 percent, its dividends equal its earnings each year.* The stock's terminal value equals the discounted value of this infinite stream of future dividends. How do you calculate that?

A stream of income that grows forever at a steady rate is known as a *perpetuity*. The field of mathematics supplies us with an easy formula for calculating the present value of a perpetuity:

$$\text{Present Value} = \frac{I}{D - G}$$

where:
   I = income
   D = discount rate
   G = growth rate

Assuming a 9 percent discount rate—6 percent above the 3 percent long-term inflation rate—and 3 percent annual earnings growth yields a denominator of 6 percent. Increasing the firm's tenth-year earnings by 3 percent gives a numerator of $4.52. Dividing $4.52 by 6 percent produces the terminal value for company X of $75.33.

TABLE 10.5C

Ten-Year Discounted Cash Flow Valuation Model
Company X

Discount Rate:	8%
Prior Year's Earnings:	$ 1.00
Earnings Estimate, Next Four Quarters:	$ 1.20
Earnings Growth Rate (1st five years):	20%
Earnings Growth Rate (2nd five years):	12%
Permanent Growth Rate:	3%

Year	Projected Earnings	Payout Ratio	Dividends	Discount Factor	Disc Value Dividend
1	$ 1.20	10%	$ 0.12	0.9259	$ 0.11
2	$ 1.44	10%	$ 0.14	0.8573	$ 0.12
3	$ 1.73	10%	$ 0.17	0.7938	$ 0.14
4	$ 2.07	10%	$ 0.21	0.7350	$ 0.15
5	$ 2.49	10%	$ 0.25	0.6806	$ 0.17
6	$ 2.79	10%	$ 0.28	0.6302	$ 0.18
7	$ 3.12	10%	$ 0.31	0.5835	$ 0.18
8	$ 3.50	10%	$ 0.35	0.5403	$ 0.19
9	$ 3.92	10%	$ 0.39	0.5002	$ 0.20
10	$ 4.39	10%	$ 0.44	0.4632	$ 0.20
				Total:	$ 1.64
11	$ 4.52	100%	$ 4.52		

10-Year Terminal Value:	$4.52	=	$4.52	=	$ 75.33
(Perpetuity Formula)	9%-3%		6%		

Moving the numbers around simplifies the terminal value formula even more:

$$\frac{\$4.52}{6\%} = \$75.33$$

$$\frac{\$4.52}{\$75.33} = 6\%$$

$$\frac{\$75.33}{\$4.52} = 16.67$$

This formula tells us that the fair value price of the company divided by its eleventh-year earnings equals 16.67. *Thus, this entire formula simplifies to the assumption that firms sell for a forward PE of 16.67 at the end of year ten.*

Quick Note: You probably noticed that I used an 8 percent discount rate for computing present values, but I used 9 percent to compute the ten-year terminal value. That was not an oversight. I base the 8 percent rate on current inflation of about 2 percent. However, regardless of what it presently runs, I assume that in ten years inflation reverts to its average long-term rate of about 3 percent for computing the terminal value.

Put It All Together and Calculate the Intrinsic Value

You now have all the information you need to compute a stock's intrinsic value. Table 10.5d shows you how to finish the job.

You already know the present value of the projected dividend stream for company X equals $1.64. Now multiply the year-ten discount factor (0.4632) by the firm's terminal value of $75.33 to obtain its present value of $34.89. Add these two figures together and you find that company X is currently worth a little over $36 a share.

I provide you with a blank valuation worksheet in Table 10.6. You can make all the necessary computations using our present value table (Table 10.2) or a financial calculator. However, programming the model into an electronic spreadsheet will save you significant analysis time by making it easy to run what-if scenarios.

Let me reiterate that the valuation model I have developed is not *the* correct way to value companies. Professional money managers use *various* means to determine the intrinsic values of businesses, but most of those methods have at their core the principle of discounting firms' anticipated cash flows. Therefore, our model contains a tremendous amount of valuable information that will help you make informed, knowledgeable investment decisions.

TABLE 10.5D

Ten-Year Discounted Cash Flow Valuation Model
Company X

Discount Rate:	8%
Prior Year's Earnings:	$ 1.00
Earnings Estimate, Next Four Quarters:	$ 1.20
Earnings Growth Rate (1st five years):	20%
Earnings Growth Rate (2nd five years):	12%
Permanent Growth Rate:	3%

Year	Projected Earnings	Payout Ratio	Dividends	Discount Factor	Disc Value Dividend
1	$ 1.20	10%	$ 0.12	0.9259	$ 0.11
2	$ 1.44	10%	$ 0.14	0.8573	$ 0.12
3	$ 1.73	10%	$ 0.17	0.7938	$ 0.14
4	$ 2.07	10%	$ 0.21	0.7350	$ 0.15
5	$ 2.49	10%	$ 0.25	0.6806	$ 0.17
6	$ 2.79	10%	$ 0.28	0.6302	$ 0.18
7	$ 3.12	10%	$ 0.31	0.5835	$ 0.18
8	$ 3.50	10%	$ 0.35	0.5403	$ 0.19
9	$ 3.92	10%	$ 0.39	0.5002	$ 0.20
10	$ 4.39	10%	$ 0.44	0.4632	$ 0.20
				Total:	$ 1.64
11	$ 4.52	100%	$ 4.52		

Terminal Value:	Year 11 Dividend	Terminal Value PE	Terminal Value	Discount Factor	Disc Terminal Value
	$ 4.52	16.67	$75.33	0.4632	**$34.89**

Discounted Value of Dividends:	$ 1.64
Discounted 10-Year Value:	$ 34.89
Intrinsic Value:	$ 36.53

TABLE 10.6

Ten-Year Discounted Cash Flow Valuation Model

Date: ___/___/___

Company: _____

1. Price: _____
2. Intrinsic Value: _____
3. Price/Intrinsic Value (#1 / #2): _____
4. Discount Rate: _____
5. Prior Year's Earnings: _____
6. Earnings Estimate, Next Four Quarters: _____
7. Earnings Growth Rate (1st five years): _____
8. Earnings Growth Rate (2nd five years) (#7 x .6): _____
9. Permanent Growth Rate: 3%

Year	Projected Earnings	Payout Ratio	Dividends	Discount Factor	Disc Value Dividend
1	_____	_____	_____	_____	_____
2	_____	_____	_____	_____	_____
3	_____	_____	_____	_____	_____
4	_____	_____	_____	_____	_____
5	_____	_____	_____	_____	_____
6	_____	_____	_____	_____	_____
7	_____	_____	_____	_____	_____
8	_____	_____	_____	_____	_____
9	_____	_____	_____	_____	_____
10	_____	_____	_____	_____	_____
					Total
11	_____	100%	_____		

10-Yr Terminal Value:	Year 11 Dividend	Terminal Value PE	Terminal Value	Discount Factor	Disc Terminal Value
	_____	16.67	_____	_____	_____

Discounted Value of Dividends: _____

Discounted 10-Year Value: _____

   Intrinsic Value: _____

Also keep in mind that a model is only as good as its input. Our model might lead you to pass up a good opportunity if a business performs better than the model anticipates. If you suspect that could occur with a particular firm, adjust your cash flow projections to match your expectations. Of course, you should similarly adjust your numbers in the other direction if you believe a firm will underperform the model's assumptions.

In the next chapter, I show you a real-world example of how you could have applied this model to spot a great investment opportunity in one of America's finest companies.

SUMMARY

The following summarizes the topics covered in this chapter:

- Computing a company's intrinsic value places a worth on the firm's projected cash flow, taking available investment alternatives into account. Knowing stocks' fair values helps you decide at what prices you are willing to buy securities and compare the relative valuations of businesses to each other.
- Since the cash flows of a corporation drive its value, an often-used method for determining a firm's worth involves calculating a current value for all the company's anticipated future cash flows.
- Using the dividend discount model, the intrinsic value of a company equals the present value of its future dividends over some period of time plus the present value of the stock's terminal value at the end of that period. Our valuation model assumes a ten-year holding period.
- Investors use two primary methods of choosing discount rates. The first technique adds a risk premium—normally about 3 percent—to the risk-free rate of return. Since interest rates tend to track with inflation over time, I recommend adding 6 percent to the inflation rate. The second philosophy suggests using a discount rate that equals your desired return.
- Use a two-stage model to project a corporation's earnings over ten years. Apply the firm's long-term expected growth rate to its next

year's estimated income to forecast its earnings per share for each of the next five years. Repeat this process for a second five-year period, only this time reduce the anticipated growth rate by 40 percent. After that, assume all businesses grow at the rate of inflation and pay out 100 percent of their net earnings as dividends.

- Use your earnings forecasts to project the firm's ten-year dividend stream and to calculate the company's terminal value.
- Add the present values of a company's ten-year dividend stream and terminal value to arrive at the firm's intrinsic value.

CHAPTER 11

A Big Value in an Orange Box

NOW THAT YOU UNDERSTAND THE BASICS OF VALUING A CORPORATION, let's look at how this knowledge might have helped you spot a profitable opportunity in Home Depot stock.

COMPANY BACKGROUND

Based in Atlanta, Home Depot is the national leader in the do-it-yourself home improvement field. Founded by Bernie Marcus and Arthur Blank in the late 1970s, the company entranced Wall Street with its performance for many years—and for good reason. The business set several records on the way to claiming the title of the fastest-growing retailer in American history, reaching $50 billion in sales quicker than any other domestic corporation. For the five-year period ending in 2000, the company's annual percentage growth rate averaged in the upper twenties.

Even with Home Depot's success, management knew the business was entering a new era and cracks were surfacing in the company's operations. In 2001, the firm's return on equity dropped 2 percent from the prior year, its net profit margin fell, and earnings per share growth slowed to 10 percent.

MANAGEMENT

The ranks of loyal Home Depot employees loved and revered Marcus and Blank. The company's decentralized organizational structure had produced a highly motivated workforce and a unique job environment where hardworking people could thrive. Store managers essentially ran their own businesses. Under the duo's leadership, the company's stock generated significant wealth for multitudes of ordinary workers. However, as the legendary founders grew older, they knew that management succession was becoming an increasingly important issue. So in the summer of 2000, having determined that no one in the corporation's ranks was ready to assume responsibility for leading the giant retailer, they began searching for a new CEO.

Their search ended when Robert Nardelli, formerly the president and CEO of GE Power Systems, was passed over for the top spot at General Electric. Nardelli had been one of a select group being groomed to succeed another legendary manager, Jack Welch. When GE named Jeffrey Immelt as Welch's replacement in late November 2000, Arthur Blank pounced on the opportunity. Within two weeks, Nardelli agreed to take the helm at Home Depot, and Blank, the CEO since 1997, resigned his position and assumed the post of cochair with Marcus.

CHANGING OF THE GUARD

The transition to a new CEO faced numerous challenges and did not go as smoothly as the board and investors hoped. Not only had Home Depot recruited an outsider who was unfamiliar with the company's operations, but the change took place as external pressures were on the rise. Consumers were spending less on home improvement projects as the country headed into its first recession in a decade, and Lowe's, a well-financed competitor with a deep management team, was eating into Home Depot's market share.

General Electric's management development program is reputed to be the best among American corporations. With his GE training and knowledge of Six Sigma principles, Nardelli brought strong management skills to the table. However, he lacked retail experience.

To make matters worse, Mark Baker, the executive vice president of merchandising, left in the summer of 2001. Baker was a talented manager who had served Home Depot in several high-profile capacities. Because of his rapid rise through the ranks, many felt he was being groomed for big things, perhaps even running the company one day. The loss of his experience dealt a further blow to the already embattled company.

CHANGING THE COMPANY AND THE CULTURE

The new CEO brought about many changes quickly at the retail behemoth—perhaps too quickly. Nardelli played to his strengths and focused immediately on tightening the company's operations. However, in the process of improving operations, he failed to recognize the extent to which he was transforming Home Depot's culture. Some of his actions hurt employees and caused morale to suffer. His lack of merchandising prowess also caused some missteps that turned off customers.

Among the more sweeping changes, he replaced the decentralized organizational structure with a centralized model. This increased operational efficiencies and allowed Home Depot to negotiate better terms with its vendors, evidenced by a shortened cash conversion cycle. It also took away store managers' autonomy, sparking discontent and resentment among many in their ranks.

Additionally, Nardelli cut inventory levels at stores. While this improved profit margins and cash flows, it hurt the shopping experience, the lifeblood of a retail operation. Customers often found the products they needed were sold out, so they began shopping elsewhere.

He also replaced many full-time employees with part-timers, which saved money and increased the flexibility of staffing operations. However, the part-time employees could not match the product knowledge of the full-time staff, causing a further deterioration in customer service. The full-time employees who lost hours were upset, and morale declined further.

Business operations at Home Depot had undoubtedly improved, but the cost was heavy. A culture of efficiency replaced the growth culture that had dominated the company for so many years. Many employees felt that upper management no longer respected their role in making the company successful and was treating them like a commodity.

OPPORTUNITY OR HEAD FAKE?

Against this backdrop, earnings per share growth slowed to a paltry 1 percent in the twelve months ending July 2001. The stock price plunged to about $30 early that fall—down more than 50 percent from its peak of about $70 a year and a half earlier. Although growth started to rebound after that point, critics and frustrated investors joined together in voicing their doubts about Nardelli's ability to manage the business. Talk abounded that the board would need to own up to its mistake and search for a new CEO unless things turned around quickly. Many believed that Nardelli's lack of retail experience rendered him incapable of solving Home Depot's problems.

In spite of the morale issues and negative press, internal operations continued to get better. Cash jumped from $170 million in January 2000 to $2 billion two years later. Due largely to the efficiencies gained from the centralized buying structure Nardelli had implemented, the cash conversion cycle declined from fifty-two days at the end of fiscal year 2001 to thirty-nine days at fiscal year-end 2003. The board continued to voice support for the changes taking place and remained resolute in keeping the new CEO.

Then in early January 2003 came a bombshell announcement that sent Home Depot stock plunging to new lows. Nardelli made official what some analysts had suspected: 20 percent annual earnings growth was no longer sustainable. Instead, he predicted that once the company worked its way through its current problems, growth would average no higher than 14 percent. That announcement caught the investment community flatfooted. Before the market opened the next day, several analysts had already issued sell recommendations.

Home Depot's stock fell from the opening bell. Over the next several days, the stock price settled in the low twenties. What should investors do—buy shares at those levels, simply hold tight what they already had, or sell out?

The answer focuses on what Home Depot was worth based on the new information. Two questions had to be answered: (1) Had the company's fundamentals deteriorated to a point where it was no longer wise to hold the company's stock? (2) If not, was the current price attractive?

ANALYSIS

Investors could not definitively answer the first question, but they could form a reasonable opinion from the available information. Earnings had grown under Nardelli, not shrunk. Operations were tighter. The company was in better financial shape than at any other time in its history and had billions stockpiled in cash to invest in solving its problems. While Nardelli had made some mistakes, he was quick to admit them and take corrective action. For instance, after realizing the problems associated with employing too many part-timers, he reversed course and beefed up the roster of full-time employees. He also increased inventory to more appropriate levels. It was a stretch to believe the company was about to go down the tubes.

Let's face it—14 percent annual earnings growth does not sound like a company on the brink of disaster. As Bill Nygren told me, "I wish all my companies had that problem!" It only sounded bad because investors were used to 20 percent.

Based on the available information, it was not unreasonable to assume Home Depot would attain Nardelli's 14 percent growth target. If it did grow at that rate, did the stock's price offer a bargain?

Table 11.1 reflects the information available for Home Depot in late January 2003. The company had earned $1.56 per share in the prior twelve months, and analysts expected the company to earn $1.62 in the coming twelve months. Assume Nardelli's 14 percent growth figure held for the next five years. Home Depot paid out about 15 percent of its earnings in dividends. Based on those assumptions, our model calculates a fair value for Home Depot at the time of $35.20 per share. Considering that the stock sold for close to $20 a share, the company was selling for less than 60 percent of its intrinsic value—a bargain!

A 40 percent discount to intrinsic value gives investors a large margin of safety in case a firm does not perform as expected. To verify this, let's see what happens if we assume the business would grow its earnings at only 10 percent annually, as illustrated in Table 11.2. Even under this very conservative scenario, the corporation was worth over $27 per share—still well above its selling price. That means Home Depot could miss its earnings projections by a wide margin and you

TABLE 11.1

Ten-Year Discounted Cash Flow Valuation Model

Date: January, 2003

Company: Home Depot

1. Price:	$ 20.60
2. Intrinsic Value:	$ 35.20
3. Price/Intrinsic Value (#1 / #2):	59%
4. Discount Rate:	8%
5. Prior Year's Earnings:	$ 1.56
6. Earnings Estimate, Next Four Quarters:	$ 1.62
7. Earnings Growth Rate (1st five years):	14%
8. Earnings Growth Rate (2nd five years) (#7 x .6):	8.4%
9. Permanent Growth Rate:	3%

Year	Projected Earnings	Payout Ratio	Dividends	Discount Factor	Disc Value Dividend
1	$ 1.62	15%	$ 0.24	0.9259	$ 0.22
2	$ 1.85	15%	$ 0.27	0.8573	$ 0.23
3	$ 2.11	15%	$ 0.31	0.7938	$ 0.25
4	$ 2.40	15%	$ 0.36	0.7350	$ 0.26
5	$ 2.74	15%	$ 0.40	0.6806	$ 0.28
6	$ 2.97	15%	$ 0.44	0.6302	$ 0.28
7	$ 3.22	15%	$ 0.48	0.5835	$ 0.28
8	$ 3.49	15%	$ 0.52	0.5403	$ 0.28
9	$ 3.78	15%	$ 0.56	0.5002	$ 0.28
10	$ 4.10	15%	$ 0.61	0.4632	$ 0.28
					$ 2.63
11	$ 4.22	100%	$ 4.22		

10-Yr Terminal Value:	Year 11 Dividend	Terminal Value PE	Terminal Value	Discount Factor	Disc Terminal Value
	$ 4.22	16.67	$ 70.32	0.4632	$ 32.57

Discounted Value of Dividends:	$ 2.63
Discounted 10-Year Value:	$ 32.57
Intrinsic Value:	$ 35.20

TABLE 11.2

Ten-Year Discounted Cash Flow Valuation Model

Date: January, 2003

Company: <u>Home Depot</u>

1. Price:	$ 20.60
2. Intrinsic Value:	$ 27.53
3. Price/Intrinsic Value (#1 / #2):	75%
4. Discount Rate:	8%
5. Prior Year's Earnings:	$ 1.56
6. Earnings Estimate, Next Four Quarters:	$ 1.62
7. Earnings Growth Rate (1st five years):	10%
8. Earnings Growth Rate (2nd five years) (#7 x .6):	6.0%
9. Permanent Growth Rate:	3%

Year	Projected Earnings	Payout Ratio	Dividends	Discount Factor	Disc Value Dividend
1	$ 1.62	15%	$ 0.24	0.9259	$ 0.22
2	$ 1.78	15%	$ 0.26	0.8573	$ 0.23
3	$ 1.96	15%	$ 0.29	0.7938	$ 0.23
4	$ 2.16	15%	$ 0.32	0.7350	$ 0.23
5	$ 2.37	15%	$ 0.35	0.6806	$ 0.24
6	$ 2.51	15%	$ 0.37	0.6302	$ 0.23
7	$ 2.67	15%	$ 0.39	0.5835	$ 0.23
8	$ 2.82	15%	$ 0.42	0.5403	$ 0.23
9	$ 2.99	15%	$ 0.44	0.5002	$ 0.22
10	$ 3.17	15%	$ 0.47	0.4632	$ 0.22
					$ 2.28
11	$ 3.27	100%	$ 3.27		

10-Yr Terminal Value:	Year 11 Dividend	Terminal Value PE	Terminal Value	Discount Factor	Disc Terminal Value
	$ 3.27	16.67	$ 54.50	0.4632	$ 25.24

Discounted Value of Dividends:	$ 2.28
Discounted 10-Year Value:	<u>$ 25.24</u>
Intrinsic Value:	**$ 27.53**

could still justify buying it. Therefore, it appears the stock was significantly undervalued and represented an excellent buying opportunity.

With the benefit of hindsight, we can see that the market agreed with our analysis. By early July 2003, less than six months later, the stock price had rebounded to over $34 a share—within $1 of our fair value calculation.

Not every situation works out as favorably as Home Depot. However, by assigning a value to a business based on the best earnings forecasts available, you can determine how the market is valuing the firm's stock relative to other available opportunities. Our valuation model also reveals the margin of safety offered by a firm's stock price. This information will help you make better investment decisions and improve your chances of finding long-term winners!

CHAPTER 12

PEs, PEGs, and IRRs

PE RATIO

The price-to-earnings ratio (PE), typically calculated by dividing a firm's stock price by its prior year's earnings per share, is one of investors' favorite valuation tools. This figure tells you how much individuals are willing to pay for a dollar of the company's current earnings in order to capture its future earnings, revealing the market's level of enthusiasm about the firm's prospects. Investors also compare the PEs of businesses to determine their relative valuations. Companies with low PEs are generally thought to represent better values than firms with high PEs.

While most investors use this measure on a regular basis, a company's PE ratio is almost worthless by itself. To appreciate the information it provides, you must understand how two other factors influence it: the company's growth rate and market interest rates. Otherwise, you are likely to misuse the PE and arrive at wrong investment conclusions.

Growth Rates

Let's examine how corporations' growth rates affect their fair value PEs. Suppose two businesses each earned $1 a share last year, but company B is growing considerably faster than company A. For simplicity, assume both firms generate only the five years of cash flows shown in Table 12.1.

TABLE 12.1

Comparison of Two Companies' Future Five-Year Earnings Stream

Prior Year's Earnings: $ 1.00
Discount Rate: 8%

Company A				Company B			
EPS Growth Rate: 10%				EPS Growth Rate: 15%			
Year	Earnings Per Share	P.V. Factor	Present Value	Year	Earnings Per Share	P.V. Factor	Present Value
1	$ 1.10	0.9259	$ 1.02	1	$ 1.15	0.9259	$ 1.06
2	$ 1.21	0.8573	$ 1.04	2	$ 1.32	0.8573	$ 1.13
3	$ 1.33	0.7938	$ 1.06	3	$ 1.52	0.7938	$ 1.21
4	$ 1.46	0.7350	$ 1.08	4	$ 1.75	0.7350	$ 1.29
5	$ 1.61	0.6806	$ 1.10	5	$ 2.01	0.6806	$ 1.37
Total	$ 6.72		$ 5.30	Total	$ 7.75		$ 6.06

Note: Even though both companies have the same prior year's earnings, company A's earnings are projected to grow 10% annually, whereas company B's earnings are projected to grow 15% annually. Therefore, company B is worth more than company A.

The present value of company B's future income equals $6.06 versus $5.30 for company A, making B more valuable and giving it a higher fair value PE. This shows that firms with faster growth rates *deserve* to sell at higher PEs: investors are willing to pay more for a dollar of current income the faster a company's profits are growing.

Carrying this one step further, it follows that each earnings growth rate has a corresponding fair value PE (if we ignore the impact of dividends) based on our valuation model. Table 12.2 shows these PE calculations for three different discount rates.

Realistically, too many factors affect a company's worth to simply equate a particular growth rate to a fair value PE. However, if we ignore those other dynamics and look only at the influence of a firm's growth on its intrinsic value, this table provides some valuable insight. We see that a high PE does not necessarily mean a business is overvalued, and a low PE does not automatically signal a firm is a bargain.

TABLE 12.2

Intrinsic Value PEs for
Various Earnings Growth Rates

| | Discount Rate | | |
| | 8% | 10% | 12% |
Earnings Growth Rate	Intrinsic Value PE	Intrinsic Value PE	Intrinsic Value PE
6%	12.7	10.6	8.8
7%	13.7	11.4	9.5
8%	14.8	12.3	10.3
9%	15.9	13.3	11.1
10%	17.1	14.3	11.9
11%	18.4	15.4	12.8
12%	19.8	16.5	13.8
13%	21.3	17.8	14.8
14%	22.9	19.0	15.9
15%	24.6	20.5	17.1
16%	26.4	22.0	18.4
17%	28.3	23.6	19.7
18%	30.4	25.3	21.1
19%	32.6	27.1	22.6
20%	34.9	29.0	24.2
21%	35.9	29.9	24.9
22%	36.9	30.7	25.6
23%	37.9	31.6	26.4
24%	39.0	32.5	27.1
25%	40.0	33.4	27.9

Note: This table shows the fair value PEs for various earnings growth rates and discount rates using our discounted cash flow model.

> **KEY POINT**
>
> A fast-growing company with a high PE may be a better bargain than a slow-growing firm selling at a low PE. This shows the danger in valuing firms based solely on their PE ratios.

Interest Rates

Table 12.2 also illustrates how altering the discount rate can significantly change firms' intrinsic value PEs. For example, if a business is growing its earnings by 15 percent annually, raising the discount rate from 8 percent to 10 percent cuts the company's intrinsic value PE from 24.6 to 20.5, slicing the firm's worth by almost 17 percent! What would cause you to raise your discount rate? Higher interest rates, which increase the risk-free rate of return. Remember, you must relate a stock's fair value to returns available from alternative investments.

You can extend the influence of interest rates on fair value PEs from individual stocks to the overall market. Assume corporate earnings are growing at an average rate of 7 percent a year. The Federal Reserve Board becomes concerned about inflation, so it tightens monetary policy by gradually raising interest rates two percentage points, lifting the discount rate from 8 percent to 10 percent. Then the overall fair value level of PEs and stock prices would decline almost 17 percent. Conversely, if interest rates decline, a lower discount rate would lift the general value of stocks. Thus the saying, "Don't fight the Fed."

The impact of rising interest rates, or at least the lack of declining rates, on stock prices explains why many market pundits believe average stock market returns over the next several years will fall short of those of the last two decades. In the early 1980s, interest rates reached deep into double-digit territory, creating average PEs that were abnormally low. As rates declined over the next twenty years, rising PEs lifted stock prices, resulting in unusually high stock market returns.

Since interest rates likely bottomed in 2003, market PEs should stabilize, or even decline if rates rise, resulting in lower average returns going forward.

Uneven Earnings Growth

Another problem with using PEs to value businesses is that firms' earnings do not increase in straight lines—they grow unevenly or rise and fall with cyclical factors, such as interest rates. Therefore, the earnings used to calculate this measure may not reflect a company's normal level of income. For example, the best buying opportunities for cyclical businesses normally occur near the bottoms of their earnings cycles. At those times, PEs are typically very high because firms' earnings are so low. That makes their stock prices look expensive precisely when they are bargains. Bill Fries notes you must be careful to compute PEs for cyclical companies based on *normalized* earnings, which may be the firm's projected earnings a couple of years out.

For another example, suppose a business had a bad year last year and its earnings temporarily stumbled, falling by half. However, analysts expect the company's income to rebound to normal levels this coming year and continue growing thereafter. Calculating the firm's PE on last year's earnings will make the firm look twice as expensive as basing the measure on this year's earnings. Therefore, in order to better understand the firm's valuation picture, money managers often calculate a company's PE based on its projected earnings for the coming twelve months, known as its forward PE, as well as its last year's earnings.

The Light Side of the Force

I've discussed lots of problems with valuing firms using the PE ratio. So when is it useful to calculate PEs? Primarily in two situations. First, this tool can help you spot trends in a firm's relative valuation by comparing its current PE to its historical averages. Second, this measure can help you compare the valuations of two companies with the same growth rate.

PEG RATIO

Because the fair value PE of a company correlates to its growth rate, many investors try to assess the valuation of a firm by simply dividing its PE ratio by its earnings growth rate (G), yielding a figure commonly known as the PEG ratio. Investment advisors frequently tout the PEG as a means to compare businesses with different growth rates and suggest that, other things equal, companies with identical PEG ratios represent comparable investment opportunities. Many of those same advisors also recommend that you buy a stock only when its price yields a PEG of no greater than one to ensure the firm is adequately undervalued.

The PEG ratio is popular largely because of its ease of use. If it indeed accurately measures companies' values, then much of what I have discussed about how to value stocks becomes unnecessary. Unfortunately, comparing the fair value PEGs for several firms growing at different rates shows this measure is a very blunt tool that is too imprecise for serious use.

Let's examine two businesses. Company A is growing at 7 percent a year and sports a seven PE. Company B grows at 15 percent annually and sells for a PE of fifteen. Supporters of the PEG ratio would argue that both firms represent comparable values since they have identical PEGs. Let's work through the numbers and see if our calculations support that notion. The computations are found in Table 12.3a.

As you can see from the example, the businesses do not offer equivalent investment values. Company A, the slower-growing of the two firms, sells at a 49 percent discount to its intrinsic value. Company B sells for a smaller, although still sizable, 39 percent discount to its fair value.

If we change the discount rate from 8 percent to 10 percent, as shown in Table 12.3b, we come to the same conclusion. Under that scenario, company A sells at a 39 percent discount to its intrinsic value, while faster-growing company B sells at a slimmer 27 percent discount.

Table 12.3a also shows there is no basis for buying only businesses whose prices yield a PEG of one or less. If company A sold for its in-

TABLE 12.3A

PEG Ratio Illustration

	Company A	Company B
Price:	$ 7.00	$ 15.00
Prior Year's Earnings:	$ 1.00	$ 1.00
P/E:	7.0	15.0
Growth:	7%	15%
PEG:	1	1
Discount Rate:	8%	8%
Earnings Estimate, Next Four Quarters:	$ 1.07	$ 1.15
Earnings Growth Rate (1st five years):	7.0%	15.0%
Earnings Growth Rate (2nd five years):	4.2%	9.0%
Permanent Growth Rate:	3.0%	3.0%
Intrinsic Value:	$ 13.70	$ 24.61
Intrinsic Value PE:	13.70	24.61
Intrinsic Value PEG:	1.96	1.64
Price/Intrinsic Value:	51%	61%

TABLE 12.3B

PEG Ratio Illustration

	Company A	Company B
Price:	$ 7.00	$ 15.00
Prior Year's Earnings:	$ 1.00	$ 1.00
P/E:	7.0	15.0
Growth:	7%	15%
PEG:	1	1
Discount Rate:	10%	10%
Earnings Estimate, Next Four Quarters:	$ 1.07	$ 1.15
Earnings Growth Rate (1st five years):	7.0%	15.0%
Earnings Growth Rate (2nd five years):	4.2%	9.0%
Permanent Growth Rate:	3.0%	3.0%
Intrinsic Value:	$ 11.41	$ 20.49
Intrinsic Value PE:	11.41	20.49
Intrinsic Value PEG:	1.63	1.37
Price/Intrinsic Value:	61%	73%

trinsic value, its PE (what I call its *intrinsic value PE*) would equal 13.7, giving it an intrinsic value PEG of 1.96. Buying this stock at a 35 percent discount to its intrinsic value would require a purchase price of $8.91 a share, which produces a PEG of 1.27. By demanding that a firm sell for a PEG of no greater than one, you risk overlooking undervalued businesses and passing up excellent investment opportunities.

If the PEG accurately measured value, then fair value PEs would increase proportionally to increases in earnings growth rates. Thus, a firm growing 20 percent a year should sell for twice the PE of a firm growing 10 percent a year. Table 12.3a shows that is not the case. Company B's growth rate exceeds that of company A by 114 percent, yet its intrinsic value PE is only 80 percent higher. Running the same analysis using various growth rates yields the same results: a firm's intrinsic value PE does not rise in direct proportion to an increase in its earnings growth rate, once again disqualifying the PEG ratio as an accurate tool for comparing the relative valuation of stocks.

INTERNAL RATE OF RETURN

Unfortunately, no short, simple formula takes the place of a sound valuation analysis such as that provided by our discounted cash flow model. Our model also offers another important benefit: you can use your cash flow projections for a business to calculate the expected annual return from investing in it, known as the internal rate of return (IRR).

Unfortunately, there is no formula to compute the IRR. Yes, you read that correctly. There is no formula to compute the IRR—you arrive at it by trial and error. You start by guessing at the answer (say 10 percent). Next, calculate the present value of the projected cash flows using your guess as the discount rate. If the present value comes in lower than the stock price, try again with a lower discount rate, and vice versa. Keep doing this until you find the rate that makes the present value of the cash flows equal the stock's current price.

As you can tell, manually calculating the IRR is simply not feasible—it is much too time-consuming. However, this number can be calculated quickly using a financial calculator or the IRR function on a spreadsheet program.

To illustrate, let's say a stock sells for $36.53 per share. You project the following cash flows for the company:

Year	Projected Earnings	Payout Ratio	Dividends
1	$1.20	10%	$.12
2	$1.44	10%	$.14
3	$1.73	10%	$.17
4	$2.07	10%	$.21
5	$2.49	10%	$.25
6	$2.79	10%	$.28
7	$3.12	10%	$.31
8	$3.50	10%	$.35
9	$3.92	10%	$.39
10	$4.39	10%	$.44

Terminal Value: $75.33

Here are the steps for calculating the firm's IRR using our Texas Instruments BA II Plus financial calculator:

Step	*Keystrokes*
1. Enter the investment amount (investments are negative numbers, inflows are positive)	CF, –36.53, Enter
2. Enter the 1st cash flow received	.12, Enter, down arrow
3. Enter the frequency of the flow (one) *Repeat the last two steps for each cash flow until all are entered* (Remember the last cash flow equals the year 10 dividend plus the terminal value)	1, Enter, down arrow
4. Compute the IRR	IRR, CPT

The calculator quickly computes the correct answer of 8 percent.

Using the IRR function in an electronic spreadsheet is even easier. You can insert the function one time and the program will automatically generate the IRR as soon as you finish inputting your cash flow forecast, allowing you to effortlessly run a multitude of what-if scenarios.

COMPUTING THE IRR IN AN ELECTRONIC SPREADSHEET

To calculate the IRR on an electronic spreadsheet, list the cash flows for each year in a column. Begin with a negative outflow for the initial investment—that is, the stock's price. Just like when you compute the present value of a cash flow stream, you only list the cash flows you would receive—that is, dividends for the first nine years and the dividend and terminal value for the tenth year. Thus, your array of cash flows will take up eleven cells. Show a $0 cash flow for any years the company pays no dividends.

Table 12.4 illustrates using an electronic spreadsheet to calculate the IRR. Once again, we get the answer of 8 percent.

How directly do companies' potential returns correspond to their valuation levels? That is, do two firms that are identically undervalued but growing at different rates offer the same return potential? To find the answer, let's look again at the two businesses we used earlier to illustrate the PEG ratio. Assume both firms pay no dividends over the

TABLE 12.4

Internal Rate of Return

Company X:

Price: $ 36.53

Year	Projected Earnings		Projected Cash Flows		IRR
0			$	(36.53)	8.00%
1	$	1.20	$	0.12	
2	$	1.44	$	0.14	
3	$	1.73	$	0.17	
4	$	2.07	$	0.21	
5	$	2.49	$	0.25	
6	$	2.79	$	0.28	
7	$	3.12	$	0.31	
8	$	3.50	$	0.35	
9	$	3.92	$	0.39	
10	$	4.39	$	75.77	

10-Yr Terminal Value: $ 75.33

Projected Cash Flows:

Year 0:	Initial Investment
Years 1–9:	Annual Dividends
Year 10:	Year 10 Dividend + Terminal Value

next ten years and sell at a 39 percent discount to their intrinsic values, as illustrated in Table 12.5a.

Table 12.5b shows that our model projects both businesses to generate the same 13.47 percent annual return over the next ten years. Running a number of what-if scenarios, varying the earnings growth rates and discount rates, yields the same results: companies with the same valuation levels generate virtually identical IRRs.

What happens when we add dividends to the equation? Tables 12.6a and 12.6b illustrate the same scenario as given previously, only assuming both businesses pay 10 percent of their earnings each year as dividends. We see that the expected IRRs are very similar but differ slightly. Running a number of what-if scenarios, varying the earnings growth rates, discount rates, and dividend payout ratios shows a very strong but not perfect correlation between a stock's valuation level and its expected return over a ten-year period.

So should you prioritize potential investments by their levels of undervaluation or by their expected IRRs? Actually, both methods should yield similar results, but I recommend using stocks' valuation levels for one main reason: the sooner a security reaches its full-value price, the higher the return it will generate. That might easily occur before ten years, in which case your actual annualized return could significantly exceed your projected IRR. Ranking prospective investments by their valuation levels will maximize your opportunities to profit from that occurrence.

THE EXTRA RISK OF HIGH-GROWTH COMPANIES

Investing in rapidly growing businesses can be very rewarding if you buy them at the right prices. However, investing in those firms also presents an extra risk you need to understand and compensate for: missing earnings projections hurts the values of rapidly growing firms more than those of slower-growing companies. To illustrate that point, let's examine two businesses growing at considerably different rates that increase their net incomes slower than investors originally anticipated.

TABLE 12.5A

IRR Illustration

	Company A	Company B
Price:	$ 8.36	$ 15.01
Intrinsic Value:	$ 13.76	$ 24.61
Price/Intrinsic Value:	61%	61%
Dividend Payout Ratio:	0%	0%
Discount Rate:	8%	8%
Prior Year's Earnings:	$ 1.00	$ 1.00
Earnings Estimate, Next Four Quarters:	$ 1.07	$ 1.15
Earnings Growth Rate (1st five years):	7%	15%
Earnings Growth Rate (2nd five years):	4.2%	9.0%
Permanent Growth Rate:	3%	3%

TABLE 12.5B

Internal Rate of Return

Company A

Price: $ 8.36
Dividend Payout Ratio: 0%

Year	Projected Earnings	Projected Cash Flows	IRR
0		$ (8.36)	13.47%
1	$ 1.07	$ —	
2	$ 1.14	$ —	
3	$ 1.23	$ —	
4	$ 1.31	$ —	
5	$ 1.40	$ —	
6	$ 1.46	$ —	
7	$ 1.52	$ —	
8	$ 1.59	$ —	
9	$ 1.65	$ —	
10	$ 1.73	$ 29.58	
10-Yr Terminal Value:		$ 29.58	

Company B

Price: $ 15.01
Dividend Payout Ratio: 0%

Year	Projected Earnings	Projected Cash Flows	IRR
0		$(15.01)	13.47%
1	$ 1.15	$ —	
2	$ 1.32	$ —	
3	$ 1.52	$ —	
4	$ 1.75	$ —	
5	$ 2.01	$ —	
6	$ 2.19	$ —	
7	$ 2.39	$ —	
8	$ 2.60	$ —	
9	$ 2.84	$ —	
10	$ 3.09	$ 53.14	
10-Yr Terminal Value:		$ 53.14	

Projected Cash Flows:

Year 0: Initial Investment
Years 1–9: Annual Dividends
Year 10: Year 10 Dividend + Terminal Value

TABLE 12.6A

IRR Illustration

	Company A	Company B
Price:	$ 8.92	$ 15.81
Intrinsic Value:	$ 14.62	$ 25.92
Price/Intrinsic Value:	61%	61%
Dividend Payout Ratio:	10%	10%
Discount Rate:	8%	8%
Prior Year's Earnings:	$ 1.00	$ 1.00
Earnings Estimate, Next Four Quarters:	$ 1.07	$ 1.15
Earnings Growth Rate (1st five years):	7%	15%
Earnings Growth Rate (2nd five years):	4.2%	9.0%
Permanent Growth Rate:	3%	3%

TABLE 12.6B

Internal Rate of Return

Company A

Price: $ 8.92
Dividend Payout Ratio: 10%

Year	Projected Earnings	Projected Cash Flows	IRR
0		$ (8.92)	13.67%
1	$ 1.07	$ 0.11	
2	$ 1.14	$ 0.11	
3	$ 1.23	$ 0.12	
4	$ 1.31	$ 0.13	
5	$ 1.40	$ 0.14	
6	$ 1.46	$ 0.15	
7	$ 1.52	$ 0.15	
8	$ 1.59	$ 0.16	
9	$ 1.65	$ 0.17	
10	$ 1.72	$ 29.75	
10-Yr Terminal Value:		$ 29.58	

Company B

Price: $ 15.81
Dividend Payout Ratio: 10%

Year	Projected Earnings	Projected Cash Flows	IRR
0		$ (15.81)	13.62%
1	$ 1.15	$ 0.12	
2	$ 1.32	$ 0.13	
3	$ 1.52	$ 0.15	
4	$ 1.75	$ 0.17	
5	$ 2.01	$ 0.20	
6	$ 2.19	$ 0.22	
7	$ 2.39	$ 0.24	
8	$ 2.60	$ 0.26	
9	$ 2.84	$ 0.28	
10	$ 3.09	$ 53.45	
10-Yr Terminal Value:		$ 53.14	

Projected Cash Flows:

Year 0: Initial Investment
Years 1–9: Annual Dividends
Year 10: Year 10 Dividend + Terminal Value

Table 12.7a shows the original valuation analysis for both businesses. Investors expected company A to grow 10 percent annually, yielding a fair value of $17.14, and they projected company B to expand its earnings by 20 percent a year, producing an intrinsic value of $34.88.

Each firm undershot its anticipated growth rate by 20 percent for the first ten years. Table 12.7b shows how the businesses would have originally been valued had their actual future growth rates been known. As the example shows, missing their anticipated growth by the same percent caused company B's value to fall more than company A's. The slower-growing firm's worth dropped by 14 percent, while the value of faster-growing company B fell 24 percent. This illustration partially explains why the stocks of high-growth corporations tend to be more volatile than those of slower-growing firms.

I am not insinuating you should avoid growth companies—far from it! Just make sure you are aware of the extra risk and have adequately compensated for it. Money managers use a variety of methods for doing so. Some managers demand that fast-growing businesses sell at larger discounts to their intrinsic values before investing in them. Others use a bigger discount rate to value high-growth firms. Still other managers handicap the extra risk by limiting firms' long-term growth rates to some maximum level, such as 20 percent, in their valuation calculations. All those techniques serve to increase stocks' risk premiums and expand the managers' margins of safety.

I suggest you give businesses only partial credit for any expected growth over 20 percent when you value them. For instance, suppose analysts project a firm to grow by an average of 32 percent a year for the next five years. One-third of the anticipated growth above 20 percent equals 4 percent. Therefore, value the company using a 24 percent long-term growth rate.

WHAT'S BUILT INTO THE PRICE?

Our valuation model not only can help you determine a firm's intrinsic value, but it can also be used to estimate the future growth rate investors have factored into a company's current price. Simply

TABLE 12.7A

Impact of Missing Growth Projections
Initial Growth Projections

	Company A	Company B
Intrinsic Value:	$ 17.14	$ 34.88
Intrinsic Value PE:	17.14	34.88
Discount Rate:	8.00%	8.00%
Prior Year's Earnings:	$ 1.00	$ 1.00
Consensus Earnings Est., Next Four Quarters:	$ 1.10	$ 1.20
Consensus Earnings Growth Rate (1st five years):	10.00%	20.00%
Earnings Growth Rate (2nd five years):	6.00%	12.00%
Permanent Growth Rate:	3.00%	3.00%

Year	Projected Earnings
1	$ 1.10
2	$ 1.21
3	$ 1.33
4	$ 1.46
5	$ 1.61
6	$ 1.71
7	$ 1.81
8	$ 1.92
9	$ 2.03
10	$ 2.16
11	$ 2.22

10-Yr Terminal Value

Year 11 Dividend	Terminal Value PE	Terminal Value	Discount Factor	Disc Terminal Value
$ 2.22	16.67	$ 37.01	0.4632	$ 17.14

Year	Projected Earnings
1	$ 1.20
2	$ 1.44
3	$ 1.73
4	$ 2.07
5	$ 2.49
6	$ 2.79
7	$ 3.12
8	$ 3.50
9	$ 3.92
10	$ 4.39
11	$ 4.52

10-Yr Terminal Value

Year 11 Dividend	Terminal Value PE	Terminal Value	Discount Factor	Disc Terminal Value
$ 4.52	16.67	$ 75.30	0.4632	$ 34.88

TABLE 12.7B

Impact of Missing Growth Projections
Actual Growth

Company A		Company B	
Intrinsic Value:	$ 14.77	Intrinsic Value:	$ 26.42
Intrinsic Value PE:	14.77	Intrinsic Value PE:	26.42
Discount Rate:	8.00%	Discount Rate:	8.00%
Prior Year's Earnings:	$ 1.00	Prior Year's Earnings:	$ 1.00
Consensus Earnings Est., Next Four Quarters:	$ 1.08	Consensus Earnings Est., Next Four Quarters:	$ 1.16
Consensus Earnings Growth Rate (1st five years):	8.00%	Consensus Earnings Growth Rate (1st five years):	16.00%
Earnings Growth Rate (2nd five years):	4.80%	Earnings Growth Rate (2nd five years):	9.60%
Permanent Growth Rate:	3.00%	Permanent Growth Rate:	3.00%

Year	Projected Earnings		Year	Projected Earnings
1	$ 1.08		1	$ 1.16
2	$ 1.17		2	$ 1.35
3	$ 1.26		3	$ 1.56
4	$ 1.36		4	$ 1.81
5	$ 1.47		5	$ 2.10
6	$ 1.54		6	$ 2.30
7	$ 1.61		7	$ 2.52
8	$ 1.69		8	$ 2.77
9	$ 1.77		9	$ 3.03
10	$ 1.86		10	$ 3.32
11	$ 1.91		11	$ 3.42

10-Yr Terminal Value

Year 11 Dividend	Terminal Value PE	Terminal Value	Discount Factor	Disc Terminal Value
$ 1.91	16.67	$ 31.89	0.4632	$ 14.77

Intrinsic value under projected growth rate =	$ 17.14
Intrinsic value under actual growth rate =	$ 14.77
Difference in value =	14%

10-Yr Terminal Value

Year 11 Dividend	Terminal Value PE	Terminal Value	Discount Factor	Disc Terminal Value
$ 3.42	16.67	$ 57.03	0.4632	$ 26.42

Intrinsic value under projected growth rate =	$ 34.88
Intrinsic value under actual growth rate =	$ 26.42
Difference in value =	24%

Note: This shows the impact of missing earnings projections by 20% on two companies. Note that impact is less on the slower-growing company.

manipulate the earnings growth rate for a business until its intrinsic value matches its current selling price. Then ask yourself: How reasonable is that growth rate? Do you believe the company can sustain that pace for several years?

I use the example of Dell in Table 12.8 to illustrate this use of our valuation model. The company sold for $50 a share at the end of fiscal year 1999, having earned $0.54 per share that year. (That's a PE of almost 93, in case you overlooked it—a sky-high number but par for tech firms at the time.) What kind of earnings expectations had investors factored into Dell's price? By manipulating the growth rate of the firm until its intrinsic value hits about $50, our model shows the computer maker would have had to expand its earnings by an average of 35 percent per year over the next five years to justify its price. That's a lot of computers to sell, especially considering the extra money businesses had already poured into their IT systems in preparation for Y2K. Dell actually averaged slightly under 14 percent annual growth during the following five years.

That type of analysis represents a different approach to valuing businesses and is especially helpful when you are having a hard time estimating the future growth rate of a firm. Instead of trying to nail down the company's intrinsic value, determine if the growth built into the company's price is sensible.

SUMMARY

The following summarizes the topics covered in this chapter:

- While most investors use the price-to-earnings ratio (PE) on a regular basis to value businesses, that figure communicates almost no meaningful data by itself. To appreciate the information that a firm's PE ratio provides, you must understand how the company's growth rate and market interest rates influence it. The faster a company is growing, the higher the PE at which it should sell. Conversely, higher market interest rates should produce lower PEs.
- Investors commonly use the PEG ratio, computed by dividing a firm's PE by its earnings growth rate (G), to compare the valuations

TABLE 12.8

Ten-Year Discounted Cash Flow Valuation Model

Date: Jan 1999
Company: Dell

1. Price:	$ 50.00
2. Intrinsic Value:	$ 49.95
3. Price/Intrinsic Value (#1 / #2):	100%
4. Discount Rate:	8%
5. Prior Year's Earnings:	$ 0.54
6. Earnings Estimate, Next Four Quarters:	$ 0.73
7. Earnings Growth Rate (1st five years):	35%
8. Earnings Growth Rate (2nd five years) (#7 x .6):	21.0%
9. Permanent Growth Rate:	3%

Year	Projected Earnings	Payout Ratio	Dividends	(Table 9-2) Discount Factor	Disc Value Dividend
1	$ 0.73	0%	$ –	0.9259	$ –
2	$ 0.98	0%	$ –	0.8573	$ –
3	$ 1.33	0%	$ –	0.7938	$ –
4	$ 1.79	0%	$ –	0.7350	$ –
5	$ 2.42	0%	$ –	0.6806	$ –
6	$ 2.93	0%	$ –	0.6302	$ –
7	$ 3.55	0%	$ –	0.5835	$ –
8	$ 4.29	0%	$ –	0.5403	$ –
9	$ 5.19	0%	$ –	0.5002	$ –
10	$ 6.28	0%	$ –	0.4632	$ –
					$ –
11	$ 6.47	100%	$ 6.47		

10-Yr Terminal Value:	Year 11 Dividend	Terminal Value PE	Terminal Value	Discount Factor	Disc Terminal Value
	$ 6.47	16.67	$ 107.84	0.4632	$ 49.95

Discounted Value of Dividends:	$ –
Discounted 10-Year Value:	$ 49.95
Intrinsic Value:	$ 49.95

of businesses growing at different rates. However, our model indicates the PEG is a blunt tool lacking the accuracy needed for serious analysis.

- Our valuation model allows you to use your cash flow projections for a business to compute the stock's expected annual return, known as the internal rate of return (IRR).

- Businesses growing at different rates with the same relative valuations should generate identical IRRs if the companies pay no dividends. If those firms pay dividends, a strong but less than perfect correlation exists between stocks' valuations and their expected ten-year returns.

  Ranking companies in order of either their projected IRRs or levels of undervaluation should yield similar results. However, ranking prospective investments by their valuation levels will maximize your opportunities to profit from those stocks reaching fully valued prices before the end of your assumed ten-year holding periods.

- Falling short of their expected earnings growth impacts the values of rapidly growing firms more than those of slower-growing companies. Money managers often compensate for the additional risk in a variety of ways that increase their margins of safety, including demanding larger discounts to intrinsic values when they buy high-growth firms, using higher discount rates when valuing rapidly growing businesses, and limiting the earnings growth rates of firms in their valuation calculations.

- You can use our valuation model to estimate the future growth that investors have built into a stock's price.

CHAPTER 13

Just Do It!

WE'VE COVERED A TREMENDOUS AMOUNT OF TERRITORY. YOU HAVE studied the investment strategies of five of the country's top money managers. I've discussed why you need an investment philosophy, and I've demonstrated how to develop a process for finding investments that meet your criteria. You understand the difference between businesslike investing and speculating, and you have learned a powerful method for valuing companies. Now it's time to put all this knowledge into action!

I will walk you through several stages of the process I developed earlier to illustrate the basics of generating a list of potential investments and analyzing businesses.

RUNNING THE SCREEN PLAY

Let's begin by screening for companies that meet our basic criteria. I set the screen up according to the filters we established in Chapter 8. Keep in mind you will likely need to modify your filters to match the capabilities of your software:

Investment Screen

> *Market capitalization*—$700 million or more
> *Projected earnings growth*—10 percent or higher
> *Five-year historical earnings growth*—8 percent or higher
> *Five-year historical revenue growth*—6 percent or higher

Overall financial strength—B+ or better S&P Earnings and Dividend Ranking[1]
Competent management—ROE at least 14 percent

Running this screen in Thomson Baseline generated a list of 213 companies. Right away we've eliminated thousands of companies that don't stand a chance of meeting our investment criteria, which will save a lot of time for finding businesses we like. We know the firms that remain are projected to grow their earnings by at least 10 percent a year for the next five years, have solid S&P Earnings and Dividend Rankings,[2] and earned a double-digit return on equity last year—quite a fertile hunting ground for finding strong investments! Important items we do not know include their debt and liquidity levels and their relative valuations. Because these firms have relatively strong investment characteristics, many of them, if not the majority, probably sell at prices that reflect their excellent qualities.

You can find the stocks on this list in Appendix 2 at the back of the book.

FOOD, FINANCE, AND CAFFEINE

Let's compare the financial characteristics of three of the firms: Ruby Tuesday, a casual dining restaurant; Paychex, a payroll outsourcing service; and Starbucks, a coffee shop. Tables 13.1a, 13.1b, and 13.1c show our valuation calculations for the three businesses. Table 13.2 compares several financial traits of the companies.

Ruby Tuesday

Ruby Tuesday sports the lowest PE of the three companies at 16.6. Analysts project it to grow its earnings per share by 18 percent a year on average over the next five years. This is believable because the company has grown its earnings at 22 percent annually over the last five years. At its current price of just over $27 a share, our valuation model shows the stock is selling at a 45 percent discount to its intrinsic value! Its current ratio comes in below our threshold of one, which

TABLE 13.1A

Ten-Year Discounted Cash Flow Valuation Model

Date: 9/17/04

Company: <u>Ruby Tuesday</u>

1. Price:	$ 27.25*
2. Intrinsic Value:	$ 49.89
3. Price/Intrinsic Value (#1 / #2):	55%
4. Discount Rate:	8%
5. Prior Year's Earnings:	$ 1.64*
6. Earnings Estimate, Next Four Quarters:	$ 1.90*
7. Earnings Growth Rate (1st five years):	18%*
8. Earnings Growth Rate (2nd five years) (#7 x .6):	10.8%
9. Permanent Growth Rate:	3%

Year	Projected Earnings	Payout Ratio	Dividends	Discount Factor	Disc Value Dividend
1	$ 1.90	4%	$ 0.08	0.9259	$ 0.07
2	$ 2.24	4%	$ 0.09	0.8573	$ 0.08
3	$ 2.65	4%	$ 0.11	0.7938	$ 0.08
4	$ 3.12	4%	$ 0.12	0.7350	$ 0.09
5	$ 3.68	4%	$ 0.15	0.6806	$ 0.10
6	$ 4.08	4%	$ 0.16	0.6302	$ 0.10
7	$ 4.52	4%	$ 0.18	0.5835	$ 0.11
8	$ 5.01	4%	$ 0.20	0.5403	$ 0.11
9	$ 5.55	4%	$ 0.22	0.5002	$ 0.11
10	$ 6.15	4%	$ 0.25	0.4632	$ 0.11
					$ 0.97
11	$ 6.34	100%	$ 6.34		

10-Yr Terminal Value:	Year 11 Dividend	Terminal Value PE	Terminal Value	Discount Factor	Disc Terminal Value
	$ 6.34	16.67	$ 105.62	0.4632	$ 48.92

Discounted Value of Dividends:	$ 0.97
Discounted 10-Year Value:	$ 48.92
Intrinsic Value:	$ 49.89

*Source: Thomson Financial

TABLE 13.1B

Ten-Year Discounted Cash Flow Valuation Model

Date: 9/17/04

Company: Paychex

1. Price:	$ 31.41*
2. Intrinsic Value:	$ 31.01
3. Price/Intrinsic Value (#1 / #2):	101%
4. Discount Rate:	8%
5. Prior Year's Earnings:	$ 0.83*
6. Earnings Estimate, Next Four Quarters:	$ 0.94*
7. Earnings Growth Rate (1st five years):	18%*
8. Earnings Growth Rate (2nd five years) (#7 x .6):	10.8%
9. Permanent Growth Rate:	3%

Year	Projected Earnings	Payout Ratio	Dividends	Discount Factor	Disc Value Dividend
1	$ 0.94	57%	$ 0.54	0.9259	$ 0.50
2	$ 1.11	57%	$ 0.63	0.8573	$ 0.54
3	$ 1.31	57%	$ 0.75	0.7938	$ 0.59
4	$ 1.54	57%	$ 0.88	0.7350	$ 0.65
5	$ 1.82	57%	$ 1.04	0.6806	$ 0.71
6	$ 2.02	57%	$ 1.15	0.6302	$ 0.73
7	$ 2.24	57%	$ 1.28	0.5835	$ 0.74
8	$ 2.48	57%	$ 1.41	0.5403	$ 0.76
9	$ 2.75	57%	$ 1.57	0.5002	$ 0.78
10	$ 3.04	57%	$ 1.73	0.4632	$ 0.80
					$ 6.80
11	$ 3.13	100%	$ 3.13		

10-Yr Terminal Value:	Year 11 Dividend	Terminal Value PE	Terminal Value	Discount Factor	Disc Terminal Value
	$ 3.13	16.67	$ 52.25	0.4632	$ 24.20

Discounted Value of Dividends:	$ 6.80
Discounted 10-Year Value:	$ 24.20
Intrinsic Value:	$ 31.01

*Source: Thomson Financial.

TABLE 13.1C

Ten-Year Discounted Cash Flow Valuation Model

Date: 9/17/04

Company: <u>Starbucks</u>

1. Price:	$ 46.05*
2. Intrinsic Value:	$ 31.68
3. Price/Intrinsic Value (#1 / #2):	145%
4. Discount Rate:	8%
5. Prior Year's Earnings:	$ 0.87*
6. Earnings Estimate, Next Four Quarters:	$ 1.09*
7. Earnings Growth Rate (1st five years):	20%*
8. Earnings Growth Rate (2nd five years) (#7 x .6):	12.0%
9. Permanent Growth Rate:	3%

Year	Projected Earnings	Payout Ratio	Dividends	Discount Factor	Disc Value Dividend
1	$ 1.09	0%	$ –	0.9259	$ –
2	$ 1.31	0%	$ –	0.8573	$ –
3	$ 1.57	0%	$ –	0.7938	$ –
4	$ 1.88	0%	$ –	0.7350	$ –
5	$ 2.26	0%	$ –	0.6806	$ –
6	$ 2.53	0%	$ –	0.6302	$ –
7	$ 2.84	0%	$ –	0.5835	$ –
8	$ 3.18	0%	$ –	0.5403	$ –
9	$ 3.56	0%	$ –	0.5002	$ –
10	$ 3.98	0%	$ –	0.4632	$ –
					$ –
11	$ 4.10	100%	$ 4.10		

10-Yr Terminal Value:	Year 11 Dividend	Terminal Value PE	Terminal Value	Discount Factor	Disc Terminal Value
	$ 4.10	16.67	$ 68.39	0.4632	$ 31.68

Discounted Value of Dividends:	$ –
Discounted 10-Year Value:	<u>$ 31.68</u>
Intrinsic Value:	$ 31.68

*Source: Thomson Financial.

TABLE 13.2			
Company Comparison			
	Ruby Tuesday	Paychex	Starbucks
PE*	16.6	37.8	52.9
5-Year Hist. EPS Growth Rate*	22%	13%	25%
5-Year Projected Growth*	18%	18%	20%
Price*	$ 27.25	$ 31.41	$ 46.05
Intrinsic Value	$ 49.89	$ 31.01	$ 31.68
Price/Int Value	55%	101%	145%
Current Ratio*	0.66	1.21	1.91
Debt/Equity*	0.32	0	0
ROE*	23%	28%	16%
S&P Earnings and Dividend Ranking*,3	B+	A+	B+
Market Capitalization ($MIL)*	$ 1,815	$ 11,692	$ 18,089
IRR	14.80%	7.85%	4.85%

*Source: Thomson Financial

is a little weak. However, it has a low debt/equity ratio and a very strong ROE. This appears to be a situation where strengths in other areas offset the low liquidity level. Based on just this analysis, the stock seems to meet our financial requirements.

Paychex

Paychex has a PE that is over twice that of Ruby Tuesday, yet analysts project it to grow at only the same pace as the restaurant chain. That alone indicates Ruby Tuesday is priced more favorably and might offer better long-term appreciation potential. Running Paychex's numbers through our valuation model indicates the payroll processing firm sells for about its fair value. Its current ratio meets our criteria, it has virtually no long-term debt on its balance sheet, and S&P has assigned it an earnings and dividend ranking of A+. The company also returned an impressive 28 percent on its equity last year. Once again, the business appears to meet our financial criteria, but its price fully reflects its excellent prospects and strong balance sheet. In accordance with our philosophy, we would place this stock on a watch list and wait until it sells at a bigger discount to its intrinsic value before we buy it.

Starbucks

Starbucks possesses the highest PE of the three stocks—over fifty! Analysts project the popular coffee shop to grow its earnings at an average annual rate of 20 percent for the next five years, which is slightly higher than our other two companies. With faster anticipated growth, a higher PE is justified. But how much higher? Our valuation model can help answer that question. Our model shows a fair market value for Starbucks of slightly under $32 a share compared to its price of $46.05, indicating the stock is overvalued by 34 percent. This overvaluation results in a low projected IRR of only 4.85 percent. The business has the highest current ratio of any of the firms and virtually no long-term debt, and its ROE is slightly over our desired 15 percent. However, the company's high valuation would cause us to put the stock on our watch list and wait for a better entry point to buy it.

OF THE THREE COMPANIES, ALL SEEM TO MEET OUR FINANCIAL REQUIRE-ments based on our summary analysis. However, only Ruby Tuesday would qualify as a current buy from a valuation perspective.

ONE FINAL NOTE

Hopefully you have learned a lot about investing from reading this book. As you put your newfound knowledge into action, I want to encourage you to do one more thing—have fun and enjoy yourself! Investing should not be just another activity that adds to your stress level. On the contrary, you should take a lot of pleasure in what you learn and the skills you develop.

Investing is about a lot more than just making money. It's about growing and personal development. Because the market presents new challenges and opportunities every day, investing both tests your character and builds it. Investing forces you to make meaningful decisions about the future with real money at stake based on a limited set of facts. The confidence you develop will impact other areas of your life in a positive way.

The journey and what you learn from it is as important as the destination. Like dance, art, and music, investing is a form of self-expression—your style should reflect your personality.

Almost everybody engages in some favorite activities that offer them a break from the daily routines of life. It just happens that this particular activity has the potential to generate significant financial rewards! Accept up front that you will make some mistakes that cost you money. Learn from those mistakes and become a better investor. You will also get some things right that pay substantial rewards for your efforts, and you'll have good reason to feel great about yourself when that happens. Why? Because you took the time to improve yourself as a person and you'll have tangible evidence it worked!

AUTHOR'S NOTE

Feel free to contact me at my website, www.scottkays.com, to share your experiences with me. I'd love to hear about your successes as well as your mistakes and what you learned from them.

My company, Kays Financial Advisory Corporation (KFAC), sends out frequent financial commentaries via e-mail at no charge. These informative reports and analyses cover the economy, financial markets, tax changes, and the like, and are designed to keep subscribers abreast of our current thinking on a broad array of issues that affect their financial well-being. To subscribe to this complimentary service, visit www.scottkays.com, or call our offices at (770) 951-9001.

APPENDIX 1

Investment Resources

A NUMBER OF DATA SOURCES PROVIDE THE INFORMATION YOU NEED TO analyze companies' investment potential. If you are willing to shell out a little money, some fee services provide extensive capabilities, including recent company news, robust stock screeners, analysts' comments and projections, and financial data. Many of these vendors offer print and electronic versions of their services. Large public libraries often carry the print editions of at least one of these services.

Some Web sites provide their data free of charge or offer a premium membership with more extensive services for a modest fee. Financial Web sites vary significantly in the quality and quantity of information they provide. One site may offer an excellent news service but a weak stock screener, while another may offer copious amounts of financial data on businesses but no current news.

Discount brokerage firms represent a third option for online stock research. Several firms offer excellent investment resources, but they typically reserve those services for their customers.

FEE SERVICES

- *Value Line Investment Survey*: Investors have relied on this excellent service for many years. It provides investors with a wealth of information on approximately 1,700 stocks and offers the ability to screen for a number of characteristics. Value Line's independent research staff also comments on these companies, providing analysis, well-respected timeliness and safety rankings, and forecasts. See www.valueline.com or call (800) 634-3583.

- *Standard & Poor's Outlook*: An advisory service for individual investors that gives unbiased research and analysis on stocks, the market, and the economy. Published forty-eight times a year, the *Outlook* also offers an online delivery option. Go to www.spout lookonline.com or call (800) 852-1641 for details. The *S&P Stock Guide* is another resource for raw data and rankings on stocks. Call (800) 852-1641 and select option #5.
- *Morningstar StockInvestor*: A monthly newsletter delivered via mail or electronically. It features two portfolios for different investment styles with stock analysis on what to buy or sell. Call (866) 608-9570. You will also find excellent information on www.morningstar.com, including a stock screener. This Web site offers the option to upgrade to a premium service that provides more information and its Premium Stock Screener for a very reasonable fee.
- *American Association of Individual Investors (AAII)*: Equips investors with education and tools helpful in managing their finances. AAII offers stock screens representing different investment philosophies, but you can apply your own criteria as well. Go to www.aaii.com or call (800) 428-2244.
- *National Association of Investors Corporation (NAIC)*: This organization is more than a service provider—it is a community of investors over 300,000 strong. NAIC offers a number of products and services to aid investors, including participation in local investment clubs. Go to www.better-investing.org or call 877-275-6242.

WEB SITES

These sites offer an abundance of information at no cost, including news, analysts' comments and forecasts, and stock screeners.

- *Yahoo Finance*: Go to http://finance.yahoo.com or simply www.yahoo.com and select the "Finance" option.
- *MSN Money*: www.moneycentral.msn.com.
- *CBS MarketWatch*: www.cbsmarketwatch.com.

DISCOUNT BROKERAGE FIRMS

- *Charles Schwab*: www.schwab.com.
- *TD Waterhouse*: www.waterhouse.com.
- *Fidelity*: www.fidelity.com.

Stock Investment Screen

COMPANY NAME	Ticker*	PE*	Projected Grth Rate*	S&P Rank†	ROE*	Mkt Cap (mil)*	PEG
ABERCROMBIE & FITCH	ANF	15.0	15.0%	B+	24.6%	3169.000	1.00
ACE	ACE	8.3	13.0%	B+	15.8%	11374.000	0.64
AFFILIATED COMP SVCS	ACS	21.0	20.0%	B+	14.2%	7479.000	1.05
AFLAC	AFL	19.0	15.0%	A	15.5%	20334.000	1.27
ALABAMA NAT'L BANC	ALAB	18.5	11.0%	A	15.9%	1014.000	1.68
ALBERTO-CULVER	ACV	23.4	12.0%	A+	16.2%	4285.000	1.95
ALLIANT TECHSYSTEMS	ATK	15.4	10.0%	B+	25.3%	2134.000	1.54
AMBAC FIN'L GRP	ABK	13.1	14.0%	A+	15.3%	8512.000	0.94
AMER INT'L GROUP	AIG	16.8	15.0%	A+	15.6%	186410.000	1.12
APACHE	APA	11.6	12.0%	B+	20.1%	15253.000	0.97
APOLLO GROUP	APOL	45.8	25.0%	B+	29.7%	15294.000	1.83
APPLEBEE'S INT'L	APPB	19.7	15.0%	A+	22.9%	2073.000	1.31
ARTHUR J. GALLAGHER	AJG	16.5	12.0%	A+	27.9%	2924.000	1.38
BALL	BLL	15.5	16.0%	B+	34.9%	4123.000	0.97
BANKNORTH GROUP	BNK	15.1	10.0%	A	14.4%	5820.000	1.51
BARD (C.R.)	BCR	26.1	14.0%	B+	20.7%	5946.000	1.86
BAXTER INT'L	BAX	17.8	10.0%	B+	34.5%	19644.000	1.78
BB&T	BBT	14.6	10.0%	A−	16.9%	22488.000	1.46
BEAZER HOMES USA	BZH	6.9	15.0%	B+	20.2%	1429.000	0.46
BECTON DICKINSON	BDX	20.6	11.0%	A	21.2%	12917.000	1.87
BED BATH & BEYOND	BBBY	27.9	20.0%	A−	23.1%	11644.000	1.40
BEMIS	BMS	16.6	10.0%	A	15.0%	2821.000	1.66
BERRY PETROLEUM	BRY	15.9	10.0%	B+	23.2%	737.000	1.59
BIOMET	BMET	34.4	15.0%	A−	24.8%	11647.000	2.29
BLOCK (H & R)	HRB	13.2	12.0%	A−	40.6%	8388.000	1.10

(Continued)

261

COMPANY NAME	Ticker*	PE*	Projected Grth Rate*	S&P Rank†	ROE*	Mkt Cap (mil)*	PEG
BRINKER INT'L	EAT	14.2	15.0%	B+	19.2%	2963.000	0.95
BROWN & BROWN	BRO	26.2	15.0%	A+	23.7%	3131.000	1.75
CAPITAL ONE FIN'L	COF	12.5	15.0%	A+	22.3%	17411.000	0.83
CARDINAL HEALTH	CAH	13.6	15.0%	A+	20.2%	20551.000	0.91
CATHAY GENERAL BANC	CATY	23.8	14.0%	A+	16.1%	1840.000	1.70
CDW	CDWC	24.1	17.0%	B+	20.0%	5003.000	1.42
CENTEX	CTX	7.9	15.0%	A+	26.1%	6220.000	0.53
CH ROBINSON WORLDWDE	CHRW	32.3	15.0%	B+	23.0%	3832.000	2.15
CHELSEA PROPERTY GRP	CPG	17.7	10.0%	A–	32.5%	2991.000	1.77
CHICO'S FAS	CHS	27.4	25.0%	B+	31.1%	3375.000	1.10
CHURCH & DWIGHT	CHD	20.7	13.0%	A	20.4%	1885.000	1.59
CINTAS	CTAS	25.7	15.0%	A+	15.8%	7161.000	1.71
CITIGROUP	C	12.4	12.0%	A+	20.8%	243991.000	1.03
CITY NAT'L	CYN	17.3	12.0%	A	16.2%	3325.000	1.44
CLAIRE'S STORES	CLE	17.5	17.0%	A–	23.2%	2473.000	1.03
CLARCOR	CLC	19.5	12.0%	A	15.9%	1180.000	1.63
COMMERCE BANCORP NJ	CBH	19.1	18.0%	A+	19.5%	4340.000	1.06
COMPASS BANCSHARES	CBSS	16.2	10.0%	A+	17.6%	5533.000	1.62
CONSTELLATION BRANDS	STZ	14.8	12.0%	B+	14.2%	3947.000	1.23
COPART	CPRT	21.8	15.0%	B+	14.2%	1684.000	1.45
COUNTRYWIDE FIN'L	CFC	7.5	12.0%	A	35.8%	21188.000	0.63
CVB FIN'L	CVBF	20.0	13.0%	A	20.4%	1131.000	1.54
DANAHER	DHR	27.1	15.0%	A	16.4%	16113.000	1.81
DARDEN RESTAURANTS	DRI	14.1	12.0%	A–	19.8%	3410.000	1.18
DELL	DELL	31.2	17.0%	B+	49.1%	89717.000	1.84
DENTSPLY INT'L	XRAY	22.6	15.0%	A–	16.4%	4136.000	1.51
DIAGNOSTIC PRODUCTS	DP	20.0	18.0%	A–	15.5%	1241.000	1.11

DOLLAR GENERAL	DG	21.3	15.0%	A+	21.3%	6657.000	1.42
DOLLAR TREE STORES	DLTR	17.5	17.0%	B+	18.0%	3117.000	1.03
DONALDSON	DCI	24.8	13.0%	A+	20.4%	2531.000	1.91
DORAL FIN'L	DRL	12.7	20.0%	A+	34.4%	4528.000	0.64
DOREL INDUSTRIES	DIIB	11.7	14.0%	B+	16.5%	905.000	0.84
ECOLAB	ECL	27.0	12.0%	A	22.1%	7919.000	2.25
ELECTRONIC ARTS	ERTS	26.2	18.0%	B+	23.9%	14584.000	1.46
ENGINEERED SUPPORT	EASI	19.0	16.0%	A	26.7%	1240.000	1.19
ERIE INDEMNITY	ERIE	17.6	12.0%	A-	16.0%	3218.000	1.47
EVEREST RE GROUP	RE	7.4	14.0%	A-	17.5%	4163.000	0.53
EXPEDITORS INT'L WA	EXPD	39.9	15.0%	A+	20.6%	5288.000	2.66
EXPRESS SCRIPTS	ESRX	18.2	20.0%	B+	22.2%	4974.000	0.91
FACTSET RESEARCH SYS	FDS	27.9	15.0%	A-	28.6%	1389.000	1.86
FAMILY DOLLAR STORES	FDO	17.9	15.0%	A+	20.1%	4751.000	1.19
FANNIE MAE	FNM	10.1	12.0%	A+	41.2%	74078.000	0.84
FIDELITY NAT'L FIN'L	FNF	7.4	12.0%	A-	23.5%	6533.000	0.62
FIFTH THIRD BANCORP	FITB	16.1	13.0%	A+	20.7%	28143.000	1.24
FIRST AMER	FAF	6.5	12.0%	B+	20.7%	2654.000	0.54
FIRST BANCORP	FBP	18.8	12.0%	A	19.6%	1978.000	1.57
FIRST DATA	FDC	21.7	15.0%	A-	24.2%	38345.000	1.45
FIRST HEALTH GROUP	FHCC	11.4	11.0%	B+	32.0%	1511.000	1.04
FIRST HORIZON NAT'L	FHN	12.1	10.0%	A+	24.6%	5532.000	1.21
FISERV	FISV	20.2	17.0%	B+	15.6%	7022.000	1.19
FLAGSTAR BANCORP	FBC	7.0	10.0%	B+	31.4%	1360.000	0.70
FLORIDA ROCK	FRK	19.8	15.0%	A	16.9%	2018.000	1.32
FOREST LABORATORIES	FRX	21.4	21.0%	B+	25.3%	16403.000	1.02
FORWARD AIR	FWRD	28.2	13.0%	B+	19.6%	812.000	2.17

(Continued)

COMPANY NAME	Ticker*	PE*	Projected Grth Rate*	S&P Rank†	ROE*	Mkt Cap (mil)*	PEG
FOSSIL	FOSL	27.2	21.0%	B+	18.1%	2018.000	1.30
FREDDIE MAC	FRE	10.0	12.0%	A+	24.9%	46740.000	0.83
GANNETT	GCI	18.7	10.0%	A	15.7%	23595.000	1.87
GENERAL DYNAMICS	GD	17.9	12.0%	B+	18.4%	19557.000	1.49
GENERAL MILLS	GIS	16.4	10.0%	A-	22.9%	17676.000	1.64
GENTEX	GNTX	24.3	17.0%	B+	16.3%	2725.000	1.43
GLACIER BANCORP	GBCI	18.4	11.0%	A+	17.0%	735.000	1.67
GOLDEN WEST FIN'L	GDW	15.1	12.0%	A+	19.5%	17562.000	1.26
HARLEY-DAVIDSON	HDI	22.0	15.0%	A+	29.4%	17691.000	1.47
HARMAN INT'L IND	HAR	45.1	25.0%	B+	19.7%	6787.000	1.80
HCC INSURANCE HLDGS	HCC	11.6	14.0%	B+	16.1%	1949.000	0.83
HEALTH MGMT ASSOC	HMA	15.3	15.0%	B+	18.2%	4847.000	1.02
HEARTLAND EXPRESS	HTLD	24.3	15.0%	B+	17.2%	1372.000	1.62
HELEN OF TROY	HELE	13.6	12.0%	B+	18.9%	864.000	1.13
HENRY (JACK) & ASSOC	JKHY	28.6	18.0%	A+	15.1%	1748.000	1.59
HIBERNIA	HIB	14.2	10.0%	A-	16.2%	4105.000	1.42
HILB ROGAL & HOBBS	HRH	15.5	12.0%	A	21.2%	1310.000	1.29
HOME DEPOT	HD	18.3	13.0%	A+	21.1%	86021.000	1.41
HORTON (D.R.)	DHI	9.1	15.0%	A	26.1%	7667.000	0.61
HOT TOPIC	HOTT	18.0	20.0%	B+	24.5%	817.000	0.90
HOVNANIAN ENTP	HOV	8.7	26.0%	B+	31.9%	2464.000	0.33
INDYMAC BANCORP	NDE	11.0	20.0%	B+	18.8%	2160.000	0.55
INT'L BANCSHARES	IBOC	14.7	10.0%	A	19.2%	1749.000	1.47
INT'L GAME TECH	IGT	25.0	15.0%	B+	24.5%	11253.000	1.67
INT'L SPEEDWAY	ISCA	23.1	12.0%	B+	16.5%	2688.000	1.93
INVESTORS FIN'L SVCS	IFIN	24.6	25.0%	A-	23.3%	3117.000	0.98
ITT EDUCATIONAL SVCS	ESI	23.7	20.0%	B+	52.5%	1678.000	1.19

JACOBS ENGINEERING	JEC	16.9	15.0%	B+	14.7%	2193.000	1.13
JOHNSON & JOHNSON	JNJ	20.0	13.0%	A+	31.7%	172535.000	1.54
JOHNSON CONTROLS	JCI	14.0	14.0%	A+	16.8%	10628.000	1.00
KB HOME	KBH	7.8	12.0%	A–	29.5%	3582.000	0.65
KNIGHT TRANSPORTATN	KNGT	29.9	18.0%	B+	16.4%	1177.000	1.66
KOHL'S	KSS	26.7	20.0%	B+	15.2%	16872.000	1.34
KRONOS	KRON	35.6	18.0%	B+	17.3%	1393.000	1.98
K-SWISS	KSWS	13.1	13.0%	B+	30.8%	719.000	1.01
LEGG MASON	LM	19.0	15.0%	A	19.5%	5517.000	1.27
LENNAR CL A	LEN	9.6	14.0%	A–	25.9%	7411.000	0.69
LINCARE HLDGS	LNCR	12.1	19.0%	B+	26.9%	2987.000	0.64
LIZ CLAIBORNE	LIZ	14.6	11.0%	A	19.2%	4252.000	1.33
LOWE'S COMPANIES	LOW	21.1	18.0%	A+	19.9%	41825.000	1.17
M.D.C. HLDGS	MDC	8.6	16.0%	A+	26.4%	2291.000	0.54
MARSHALL & ILSLEY	MI	16.0	10.0%	A	17.0%	9039.000	1.60
MATTHEWS INT'L	MATW	22.9	14.0%	A	19.2%	1159.000	1.64
MBNA	KRB	12.5	13.0%	A+	23.1%	31328.000	0.96
MEDTRONIC	MDT	29.2	16.0%	A–	23.4%	60271.000	1.83
MENTOR	MNT	27.7	13.0%	B+	19.6%	1403.000	2.13
MERCURY GENERAL	MCY	12.1	10.0%	B+	18.8%	2866.000	1.21
MICROSOFT	MSFT	21.6	12.0%	B+	20.0%	294263.000	1.80
MILLS	MLS	13.6	10.0%	A	32.3%	2741.000	1.36
MINE SAFETY APPLIANC	MSA	26.7	16.0%	A–	18.2%	1566.000	1.67
MOHAWK INDUSTRIES	MHK	15.6	20.0%	B+	15.1%	5361.000	0.78
MYLAN LABORATORIES	MYL	17.8	15.0%	A–	18.3%	5221.000	1.19
NIKE INC 'B'	NKE	21.9	13.0%	A	21.1%	20327.000	1.68
NORTH FORK BANCORP	NFB	16.4	10.0%	A–	23.8%	7559.000	1.64
NUVEEN INVESTMENT	JNC	18.4	11.0%	A+	31.9%	2784.000	1.67

(Continued)

COMPANY NAME	Ticker*	PE*	Projected Grth Rate*	S&P Rank†	ROE*	Mkt Cap (mil)*	PEG
NVR	NVR	9.9	12.0%	B+	66.6%	3508.000	0.83
NY COMMUNITY BANCORP	NYB	11.8	10.0%	A–	22.5%	5795.000	1.18
OLD DOMINION FREIGHT	ODFL	21.0	17.0%	B+	14.7%	714.000	1.24
OMNICARE	OCR	12.8	15.0%	A–	14.3%	3074.000	0.85
OMNICOM GROUP	OMC	18.6	11.0%	A+	21.1%	13059.000	1.69
O'REILLY AUTOMOTIVE	ORLY	19.9	18.0%	B+	14.3%	2236.000	1.11
OSHKOSH TRUCK	OSK	18.7	15.0%	B+	19.8%	2006.000	1.25
OUTBACK STEAKHOUSE	OSI	17.2	15.0%	B+	16.0%	2985.000	1.15
OWENS & MINOR	OMI	17.5	15.0%	B+	15.9%	1001.000	1.17
PACIFIC CAP BANCORP	PCBC	16.2	11.0%	A–	20.2%	1376.000	1.47
PACIFIC SUNWEAR CALF	PSUN	18.4	20.0%	B+	23.9%	1667.000	0.92
PATTERSON COMPANIES	PDCO	32.1	20.0%	B+	21.0%	5107.000	1.61
PAYCHEX	PAYX	37.8	18.0%	A+	27.5%	11692.000	2.10
PFIZER	PFE	16.0	12.0%	A	22.2%	242498.000	1.33
PIER 1 IMPORTS	PIR	16.4	14.0%	A–	15.4%	1659.000	1.17
POGO PRODUCING	PPP	10.8	11.0%	B+	18.6%	2880.000	0.98
POPULAR	BPOP	14.7	11.0%	A+	18.1%	6935.000	1.34
PROGRESSIVE	PGR	12.4	10.0%	B+	29.2%	18345.000	1.24
PULTE HOMES	PHM	10.9	15.0%	A	21.3%	7876.000	0.73
QLOGIC	QLGC	20.4	12.0%	B+	16.8%	2811.000	1.70
QUIKSILVER	ZQK	20.7	20.0%	B+	15.8%	1467.000	1.04
R & G FIN'L	RGF	14.7	16.0%	A	25.3%	1960.000	0.92
REGIS	RGS	18.5	14.0%	A–	16.2%	1875.000	1.32
RENAISSANCE LEARNING	RLRN	24.8	16.0%	B+	28.9%	711.000	1.55
RENAISSANCERE HLDG	RNR	6.9	10.0%	A–	25.8%	3685.000	0.69
RENT-A-CENTER	RCII	10.4	13.0%	B+	23.5%	2039.000	0.80
RESMED	RMD	29.4	18.0%	B+	17.0%	1621.000	1.63

ROSS STORES	ROST	16.6	15.0%	A+	30.3%	3527.000	1.11
RUBY TUESDAY	RI	16.6	18.0%	B+	23.2%	1815.000	0.92
RYLAND GROUP	RYL	8.4	11.0%	B+	32.1%	2213.000	0.76
SCANSOURCE	SCSC	26.5	20.0%	B+	18.5%	828.000	1.33
SCP POOL	POOL	24.9	15.0%	B+	29.8%	1488.000	1.66
SEI INVESTMENTS	SEIC	24.1	15.0%	A	44.1%	3619.000	1.61
SHELL TRANSPORT ADR	SC	13.3	14.0%	B+	20.4%	72329.000	0.95
SHUFFLE MASTER	SHFL	42.3	28.0%	B+	75.2%	821.000	1.51
SIMPSON MFG	SSD	21.2	16.0%	B+	17.7%	1485.000	1.33
SLM	SLM	19.2	15.0%	A−	37.9%	18080.000	1.28
SONIC	SONC	24.6	18.0%	B+	20.4%	1406.000	1.37
SOUTH FIN'L GRP	TSFG	15.3	12.0%	A−	16.1%	2047.000	1.28
SOUTHTRUST	SOTR	19.0	11.0%	A+	16.2%	13795.000	1.73
STAPLES	SPLS	23.9	16.0%	B+	18.1%	14743.000	1.49
STARBUCKS	SBUX	52.9	20.0%	B+	15.6%	18089.000	2.65
STATE AUTO FIN'L	STFC	12.7	12.0%	A	17.0%	1187.000	1.06
STATE STREET	STT	16.5	14.0%	A	16.6%	15110.000	1.18
STRYKER	SYK	36.2	20.0%	B+	24.2%	18761.000	1.81
SUNGARD DATA SYSTEMS	SDS	18.3	14.0%	B+	14.4%	7076.000	1.31
SYNOVUS FIN'L	SNV	19.4	13.0%	A+	17.8%	7985.000	1.49
SYSCO	SYY	22.8	15.0%	A+	37.3%	19950.000	1.52
TARGET	TGT	20.9	15.0%	A+	17.7%	41425.000	1.39
TECHNE	TECH	31.1	12.0%	B+	20.2%	1673.000	2.59
TEXAS REGNAL BNC 'A'	TRBS	21.0	12.0%	A	15.1%	1505.000	1.75
THOR INDUSTRIES	THO	16.5	15.0%	A−	22.1%	1588.000	1.10
TJX COMPANIES	TJX	16.0	15.0%	A	48.0%	11116.000	1.07
TOLL BROTHERS	TOL	11.4	15.0%	B+	20.2%	3477.000	0.76
TORCHMARK	TMK	12.8	10.0%	A	14.3%	5789.000	1.28

(Continued)

COMPANY NAME	Ticker*	PE*	Projected Grth Rate*	S&P Rank†	ROE*	Mkt Cap (mil)*	PEG
TOTAL SYSTEM SVCS	TSS	34.7	13.0%	A+	19.9%	4982.000	2.67
TRACTOR SUPPLY	TSCO	25.4	20.0%	B+	19.5%	1503.000	1.27
TRANSATLANTIC HLDGS	TRH	11.3	10.0%	A−	14.2%	3722.000	1.13
TRIAD GUARANTY	TGIC	15.9	12.0%	B+	14.2%	834.000	1.33
UNITED NAT FOODS	UNFI	33.5	20.0%	B+	14.6%	1020.000	1.68
UNITED TECHNOLOGIES	UTX	18.1	10.0%	A+	24.4%	48759.000	1.81
UNITEDHEALTH GROUP	UNH	20.5	17.0%	A	38.6%	46588.000	1.21
UNIVERSAL HLTH SVCS	UHS	14.9	15.0%	B+	15.8%	2533.000	0.99
URBAN OUTFITTERS	URBN	41.2	25.0%	B+	23.5%	2831.000	1.65
VALSPAR CORP (THE)	VAL	17.7	12.0%	A−	15.3%	2465.000	1.48
VARIAN MEDICAL SYS	VAR	31.8	20.0%	B+	26.1%	4857.000	1.59
W HLDG	WHI	16.3	16.0%	A	15.9%	2034.000	1.02
WALGREEN	WAG	29.4	15.0%	A+	17.2%	37919.000	1.96
WAL-MART STORES	WMT	23.9	14.0%	A+	22.1%	226318.000	1.71
WASHINGTON POST	WPO	29.4	15.0%	B+	14.4%	8787.000	1.96
WEBSTER FIN'L	WBS	13.8	10.0%	A	15.0%	2649.000	1.38
WELLPOINT HLTH NTWK	WLP	14.9	15.0%	B+	20.5%	16223.000	0.99
WELLS FARGO	WFC	15.2	12.0%	A	19.6%	99954.000	1.27
WENDY'S INT'L	WEN	16.3	13.0%	A−	15.0%	4106.000	1.25
WESTCORP	WES	13.2	15.0%	B+	18.3%	2273.000	0.88
WILLIAMS-SONOMA	WSM	24.9	18.0%	B+	21.7%	4220.000	1.38
WINNEBAGO	WGO	18.1	15.0%	B+	33.8%	1186.000	1.21
WRIGLEY (WM) JR	WWY	30.0	11.0%	A+	26.1%	14163.000	2.73
ZIONS BANCORPORATION	ZION	14.2	12.0%	A	15.0%	5468.000	1.18

*Source: Thomson Financial.
†S&P Rank = S&P Earnings and Dividend Ranking; © 2005 The McGraw-Hill Companies, Inc. All rights reserved.

NOTES

Chapter 2: Andy Stephens

1. Morningstar Principia, data as of 12/31/2003. © [2004] Morningstar, Inc. All Rights Reserved. The information contained herein: (1) is proprietary to Morningstar and/or its content providers; (2) may not be copied or distributed; and (3) is not warranted to be accurate, complete, or timely. Neither Morningstar nor its content providers are responsible for any damages or losses arising from any use of this information. Past performance is no guarantee of future results.

2. Author's calculations based on Morningstar Principia, data as of 12/31/2002. © [2004] Morningstar, Inc. All Rights Reserved. The information contained herein: (1) is proprietary to Morningstar and/or its content providers; (2) may not be copied or distributed; and (3) is not warranted to be accurate, complete, or timely. Neither Morningstar nor its content providers are responsible for any damages or losses arising from any use of this information. Past performance is no guarantee of future results.

Chapter 3: Bill Nygren

1. Morningstar Principia, data as of 12/31/2003. © [2004] Morningstar, Inc. All Rights Reserved. The information contained herein: (1) is proprietary to Morningstar and/or its content providers; (2) may not be copied or distributed; and (3) is not warranted to be accurate, complete, or timely. Neither Morningstar nor its content providers are responsible for any damages or losses arising from any use of this information. Past performance is no guarantee of future results.

2. From www.morningstar.com data as of 12/31/2003. © [2004] Morningstar, Inc. All Rights Reserved. The information contained herein: (1) is proprietary to Morningstar and/or its content providers; (2) may not be copied or distributed; and (3) is not warranted to be accurate, complete, or timely. Neither Morningstar nor its content providers are responsible for any damages or losses arising from any use of this information. Past performance is no guarantee of future results.

3. Author's calculations based on Morningstar Principia, data as of 12/31/2002. © [2004] Morningstar, Inc. All Rights Reserved. The information contained herein: (1) is proprietary to Morningstar and/or its content providers; (2) may not be copied or distributed; and (3) is not warranted to be accurate, complete, or timely. Neither Morningstar nor its content providers are responsible for any damages or losses arising from any use of this information. Past performance is no guarantee of future results.

Chapter 4: Christopher Davis

1. From www.davisfunds.com.
2. Author's calculations based on Morningstar Principia, data as of 12/31/2002. © [2004] Morningstar, Inc. All Rights Reserved. The information contained herein: (1) is proprietary to Morningstar and/or its content providers; (2) may not be copied or distributed; and (3) is not warranted to be accurate, complete, or timely. Neither Morningstar nor its content providers are responsible for any damages or losses arising from any use of this information. Past performance is no guarantee of future results.
3. Morningstar Principia, data as of 12/31/2003. © [2004] Morningstar, Inc. All Rights Reserved. The information contained herein: (1) is proprietary to Morningstar and/or its content providers; (2) may not be copied or distributed; and (3) is not warranted to be accurate, complete, or timely. Neither Morningstar nor its content providers are responsible for any damages or losses arising from any use of this information. Past performance is no guarantee of future results.
4. From www.morningstar.com, data as of 12/31/2003. © [2004] Morningstar, Inc. All Rights Reserved. The information contained herein: (1) is proprietary to Morningstar and/or its content providers; (2) may not be copied or distributed; and (3) is not warranted to be accurate, complete, or timely. Neither Morningstar nor its content providers are responsible for any damages or losses arising from any use of this information. Past performance is no guarantee of future results.
5. Benjamin Graham, *The Intelligent Investor* (New York: Harper and Row, 1973), 61.
6. Ibid., 3.

Chapter 5: Bill Fries

1. From www.morningstar.com, data as of 12/31/2003. © [2004] Morningstar, Inc. All Rights Reserved. The information contained herein: (1) is proprietary to Morningstar and/or its content providers; (2) may not be copied or distributed; and (3) is not warranted to be accurate, complete, or timely. Neither Morningstar nor its content providers are responsible for any damages or losses arising from any use of this information. Past performance is no guarantee of future results.
2. Morningstar Principia, data as of 12/31/2003. © [2004] Morningstar, Inc. All Rights Reserved. The information contained herein: (1) is proprietary to Morningstar and/or its content providers; (2) may not be copied or distributed; and (3) is not warranted to be accurate, complete, or timely. Neither Morningstar nor its content providers are responsible for any damages or losses arising from any use of this information. Past performance is no guarantee of future results.

Chapter 6: John Calamos, Sr.

1. Morningstar Principia, data as of 12/31/2003. © [2004] Morningstar, Inc. All Rights Reserved. The information contained herein: (1) is proprietary to Morningstar and/or its content providers; (2) may not be copied or distributed; and (3) is not warranted to be accurate, complete, or timely. Neither Morningstar nor its content providers are responsible for any damages or losses arising from any use of this information. Past performance is no guarantee of future results.
2. Author's calculations based on Morningstar Principia, data as of 12/31/2002. © [2004] Morningstar, Inc. All Rights Reserved. The information contained herein: (1) is proprietary to Morningstar and/or its content providers; (2) may not be copied or distributed; and (3) is not warranted to be accurate, complete, or timely. Neither Morningstar nor its content providers are responsible for any damages or losses arising from any use of this information. Past performance is no guarantee of future results.
3. From www.morningstar.com, data as of 12/31/2002. © [2004] Morningstar, Inc. All Rights Reserved. The information contained herein: (1) is proprietary to Morningstar and/or its content providers; (2) may not be copied or distributed; and (3) is not warranted to be accurate, complete, or timely. Neither Morningstar nor its content providers are responsible

for any damages or losses arising from any use of this information. Past performance is no guarantee of future results.

Chapter 7: Five Common Principles of the Professionals

1. Benjamin Graham, *The Intelligent Investor* (New York: Harper and Row, 1973), 1.
2. Ibid., 286.
3. Source: Thomson Financial.

Chapter 8: The Artist Meets the Technician

1. © 2005 The McGraw-Hill Companies, Inc. All rights reserved.
2. The Value Line Investment Survey, www.valueline.com or (800) 634-3583.
3. The Value Line Investment Survey, www.valueline.com or (800) 634-3583.
4. © 2005 The McGraw-Hill Companies, Inc. All rights reserved.

Chapter 9: Finding the Blue Light Specials

1. Benjamin Graham, *The Intelligent Investor* (New York: Harper and Row, 1973), 40.

Chapter 13: Just Do It!

1. © 2005 The McGraw-Hill Companies, Inc. All rights reserved.
2. © 2005 The McGraw-Hill Companies, Inc. All rights reserved.
3. © 2005 The McGraw-Hill Companies, Inc. All rights reserved.

ABOUT THE AUTHOR

Publications and Teaching

Mr. Kays authored *Achieving Your Financial Potential*, published by Doubleday (hardback in 1999, soft cover in 2000). *Achieving Your Financial Potential* was chosen by Crossings Book Club as its Book-of-the-Month in March 1999. Approximately forty-three thousand copies of this book are in print. Mr. Kays was also a contributing author to *How to Manage One Million Dollars or Less* (Gainesville: Bridge-Logos Publishers, 2000).

In addition to authoring a book, Scott has written numerous financial articles for *New Man, Single-Parent Family*, and *Marriage Partnership* magazines. An accomplished public speaker, Mr. Kays has given financial talks for numerous corporations, including IBM, AT&T, BellSouth, Cox Enterprises, and Allied Holdings, and government organizations, including the National Guard, the Centers for Disease Control, and the Drug Enforcement Agency. In all, thousands of individuals have participated in these presentations.

Media Exposure

Mr. Kays has been quoted financially in numerous major newspapers and magazines, including the *New York Times, Washington Post, Investor's Business Daily, Child, Smart Money, Bottom Line–Personal, Journal of Financial Planning, Financial Planning, Registered Investment Adviser, Atlanta Business Chronicle, Atlanta Journal and Constitution*, and the *Ft. Worth Star*.

Scott has also been a guest expert on national television shows, including appearances on *CNNfn* and *Kiplinger Consumer News*. He cohosted *Money Talks*, a weekly two-hour financial radio talk show aired on WGST, the second largest talk-radio station in Atlanta.

Education

Mr. Kays graduated with a BS in industrial management from the Georgia Institute of Technology in 1980 with a 4.0 GPA. In 1986, he graduated from the College for Financial Planning in Denver and obtained the CERTIFIED FINANCIAL Planner™ certification.

Business Experience

Scott worked for Lockheed Martin as a financial analyst from 1980 to 1986. In 1985 (while still employed at Lockheed Martin), he founded Kays Financial Advisory Corporation, an Atlanta-based wealth management firm. Today, KFAC manages approximately $100 million for about 320 clients and requires a $300,000 minimum account size. His firm utilizes both individual securities and mutual funds to implement its investment strategies.

Memberships

Mr. Kays holds memberships in several academic honorary societies, including MENSA, the national high IQ society; Gamma Beta Phi National Honorary Fraternity; and Beta Gamma Sigma National Honorary Fraternity. He is also a member of the Financial Planning Association, the national trade organization for financial planners, and is a former member of the board of directors for the Georgia chapter.

Honors

Mr. Kays has been named in *Cambridge Who's Who Registry of Business Leaders* and *Marquis Who's Who in Finance and Industry*.

INDEX

CPSIA information can be obtained at www.ICGtesting.com
Printed in the USA
LVOW08*2025290316

481302LV00005B/37/P